THE ESSENTIAL GUIDE TO
DOING RESEARCH

THE ESSENTIAL GUIDE TO DOING RESEARCH

ZINA O'LEARY

SAGE Publications
London ● Thousand Oaks ● New Delhi

SAGE Publications Ltd
1 Oliver's Yard
55 City Road
London EC1Y 1SP

SAGE Publications Inc
2455 Teller Road
Thousand Oaks, California 91320

SAGE Publications India Pvt Ltd
B-42, Panchsheel Enclave
Post Box 4109
New Delhi 110 017

British Library Cataloguing in Publication data

A catalogue record for this book is available from the British Library

ISBN 0 7619 4198 3
ISBN 0 7619 4199 1 (pbk)

Library of Congress Control Number 203112195

Typeset by C&M Digitals (P) Ltd., Chennai, India
Printed in Great Britain by The Cromwell Press Ltd, Trowbridge, Wiltshire

Summary of Contents

Contents

7   METHODOLOGICAL DESIGN   85

8   EXPLORING POPULATIONS   102

12   DATA MANAGEMENT AND ANALYSIS   184

13   THE CHALLENGE OF WRITING-UP   205

Acknowledgements

I really love teaching. For me there is nothing more satisfying than helping students understand complex or confusing concepts. Now when you are in the classroom you have the option of working students through ideas in any number of ways until you sense they've 'gotten it'. But when you're writing a text it's a lot more difficult. You only have one chance to explain things as clearly and logically as possible – and the only way to know if you are doing this well is to get feedback during the writing process.

I am therefore grateful to both students and colleagues who have so generously given their time to comment on various chapters of this work. My thanks go to Angela Sidoti, Daniel Davidson, Catherine Holmes, Bob Ryan, and Sid Parissi who offered rich feedback from a student perspective that helped me write effectively for my audience. To my colleagues Bob Hodge, Roger Packham, Gary Wallace, Vladimir Dimitrov, Rosemary Nicholson, and Peter Stephenson – thank you for adding your expertise to this work. A huge note of thanks must also go to Brent Powis who read just about every draft of every chapter and refused to shy away from providing the type of feedback that helps you and your work reach its potential.

I'd also like to thank the team at Sage Publications particularly Michael Carmichael, Patrick Brindle, and Vanessa Harwood who helped take my ideas from conception to final production. Their professionalism and dedication has made for a truly rewarding journey.

Finally, as in all soppy acknowledgements I'd like to thank my daughters Scout and Dakota, who energize me, ground me, and remind me that there is indeed a world outside of academia!

| companion | Go to www.sagepub.co.uk/resources/oleary.htm for |
| website | additional teaching and learning materials |

<table>
<tr><td>

1

</td><td>

Research as a Creative and Strategic Thinking Process

</td></tr>
</table>

'How do creativity and strategic thinking fit into "analytic" research?'

Chapter Preview

- Exploring 'Research'
- The 'Construct' of Research
- Working Through the Complexity
- Putting It All Together

EXPLORING 'RESEARCH'

The *Oxford English Dictionary* (2002) defines research as, 'the systematic study of materials and sources in order to establish facts and reach new conclusions'. Now this may sound straightforward (and is often presented that way), but in practice research is often an open-ended process that is likely to generate as many questions as it does answers.

So how does the inexperienced researcher get a handle on the process? Well it is my contention, and in fact the premise of this book, that just being able to make sense of, or even being a scholar of, methods is not enough to 'do' research. The methods of research, particularly in the social and applied sciences, have evolved to become highly complex and diverse, and having some basic knowledge is certainly a necessity. This knowledge, however, is not in itself sufficient to begin designing and carrying out a study. Without a doubt, you must creatively and strategically 'think' your way through the process. Research needs to be considered both a 'thinking game' and a 'whole-brain' activity.

Research as a 'thinking person's game'

Contrary to many research methods texts that offer 'recipes' for research, I do not believe that the competent researcher can rely on any defined set of rules for selecting, designing, and carrying out research. Good research is a thinking person's game. It is a creative and strategic process that involves constantly assessing, reassessing, and making decisions about the best possible means for obtaining trustworthy information, carrying out appropriate analysis, and drawing credible conclusions.

Now there are many researchers out there who rely on, and even come to 'believe' in, particular methodological approaches. Janesick actually coined the term 'methodolatry' – a combination of method and idolatry that she defines as a 'preoccupation with selecting and defending methods to the exclusion of the actual substance of the story being told'; she describes methodolatry as a '... slavish attachment and devotion to methods' (1998: 48).

As a budding researcher, it is important to remember that particular research strategies are good or bad to the exact degree that they fit with the questions at hand. The perspectives you will adopt and the methods you will use need to be as fluid, flexible, and eclectic as is necessary to answer the questions posed.

Research as a 'whole-brain' endeavour

'Logical', 'analytic', 'systematic', 'formal', 'factual', 'linear', these are words we tend to associate with research, while 'organized', 'disciplined', and even 'pedantic' are words we associate with researchers. These are also the words that psychologists use to describe left-brain thinking. In fact as shown in Table 1.1, many of the descriptors for the left-brain double as adjectives for research itself.

TABLE 1.1   LEFT- AND RIGHT-BRAIN ATTRIBUTES

Left hemisphere		Right hemisphere	
Analytic	Formal	Intuitive	Informal
Logical	Linear	Spontaneous	Holistic
Temporal	Verbal	A temporal	Non-verbal
Sequential	Factual	Random	Imaginative
Orderly	Concrete	Diffuse	Metaphoric
Systematic		Causal	

(Adapted from Cherry et al. 1993)

But what about the creative or the right side of the brain? Words such as 'intuitive', 'spontaneous', 'random', 'informal', and 'holistic' are rarely associated with 'rigorous' research. Well in my mind, this is like trying to understand a two-sided world using only one-sided skills and thought processes. As Albert Einstein once said: 'The intuitive mind is a sacred gift and the rational mind is a faithful servant. We have created a society that honors the servant and has forgotten the gift' (Einstein 1931, p. 97). Research needs to be seen as a process equally reliant on both the creative right as well as the strategic and logical left.

The creative right-brain
The right-brain explores the possibilities of situations and thrives on creativity. Its primary functions are synthesis, seeing relationships, and providing an overview. Now given the criteria of 'originality' in research and the unexpected complexities that invariably arise throughout the process, the right-brain would be as essential researching as the left. As researchers, a lack of creativity will see us finding exactly what we expect to find. Without the ability to 'think outside the square', we will always dwell within it.

While creative, right-brained thinking may not be credited as endemic to rigorous research, it can often be found as an unarticulated part of the process. For example, Kekule, the chemist who discovered the 'benzene ring', described the moment when he came to question the presumption that all molecules were based on two-ended strings of atoms, as one of profound creativity and vision:

> I turned my chair to the fire and dozed. Again the atoms were gamboling before my eyes. ... I could distinguish larger structures, of manifold conformation; long rows, sometimes more closely fitted together; all twining and twisting in snakelike motion. But look! What was that? One of the snakes had seized hold of its own tail, and the form whirled mockingly before my eyes. (in Findlay 1965)

Like Kekule, those most closely associated with creative genius speak of inspiration as a space between the rational and irrational; a place where the known and the unknown converge and the conventional and the innovative meet. Box 1.1 lists some of the traits/skills that are important for creativity. Some are traits you may already possess; others are skills that can be acquired and developed.

Box 1.1   Working Creatively

The thinking processes of the 'creative' often involve:

- **Fluency and flexibility** – can think somewhat effortlessly, can easily abandon old ways of thinking and adopt new ones
- **Originality** – can come up with ideas that are outside common logic
- **Remote associations** – can form associations between elements that most would not see as linked together
- **Redefinitions** – can use familiar objects in new ways
- **Sensitivity to problems** – can perceive difficulties or deficiencies in bio-physical, social or environmental institutions
- **Acceptance of ambiguity** – can accept some uncertainty in conclusions
- **Divergence** – can engage in open-ended thinking, where there is not a single right answer

---

The logical left-brain

Stressing the importance of creativity is not meant to imply that there isn't a place for the logic and strategy of the left-brain. In fact, if good research is dependent on thinking outside the 'square', then it is equally dependent on the ability of the researcher to find focus and structure. Research is an activity that needs to be attacked, while not necessarily in a prescribed fashion, then certainly in a logical one.

Unfortunately, there are many creative and brilliant people whose potential to contribute to a body of knowledge is never met. More than one research student with incredible insight and creative 'potential' has abandoned the research endeavour because they could not manage their way through the process. As shown in Box 1.2, while it may be advisable to openly explore a topic, a story line must eventually be scripted, followed, and told.

Box 1.2   The Case of the Perpetual 'Mapper'

I have a linear mind. It is logical and structured and thinks in terms of lists and dot points. I can think from start to finish, but it takes a conscious effort to explore connections between various issues. I was therefore quite intrigued to take on a research student whose notes were always jotted down in bubbles, doodles, and interconnecting linkages with no obvious linear structure. I worked closely with this perpetual 'mindmapper' and found that the student was quite exceptional at building theory and finding possibilities. He seemed unlimited in his ability to find remote associations and engage in insightful analysis that was not always self-evident.

The student was committed to this non-linear approach and had great success in building richness and depth. When it was time to begin the writing of the final document, however, the process became more difficult – so we discussed the need for a more linear approach. I explained that even for a perpetual mindmapper, a thesis needs to have a structure; a structure that invariably includes both chapters and pages presented in a numerical order. It is after all, a linear document.

The challenge for the 'linear thinker' is to consciously look for interconnections and possibilities, while the challenge for the 'mindmapper' is to be able to construct and tell their story in a logical and structured fashion.

I think the best researchers are those who manage to be creative in thinking, yet logical in structure. They manage to:

- be original, innovative, and imaginative ... yet know where they want to go
- think outside the square ... yet stay squarely on target
- use their intuition ... but are able to share the logic of that intuition
- are fluid and flexible ... yet deliberate and methodical
- are inspired, imaginative, and ingenious ... in the development of methods that are realistic, practical, and doable.

THE 'CONSTRUCT' OF RESEARCH

Thirty or forty years ago, defining the construct of research would have been a breeze. I could have defined it as 'the production of knowledge through rigorous scientific investigation'. Researching was simply a scientific enterprise that followed the rules of scientific method. Sure, the object of scientific inquiry might differ, i.e. chemistry, biology, physics, the social, etc., but research was united by common objectives, logic, presuppositions, and general methodological approaches. Social science fell under the scientific paradigm of the day (positivism) and worked within its assumptions. Enter the later half of the twentieth century, however, and many positivist assumptions, and therefore research assumptions, began to be questioned, critiqued, and even denigrated.

Positivism

For positivists, the goal of research is describing what we experience through observation and measurement in order to predict and control the forces that surround us. The social is seen as an object that can be studied 'scientifically'. Put simply, positivism assumes that social phenomena can be approached with scientific method and makes a number of assumptions about the world and the nature of research.

The world
Positivists believe that the world is a fixed entity whose mysteries are not beyond human comprehension. They believe that the world is: *knowable* – what we do not know will be uncovered in the future as technology improves and science evolves; *predictable* – there are laws, theories, and maxims that regulate the world, for example the theory of relativity and the law of gravity; and *singular* in truth and reality – there is a truth out there that is applicable to all.

The nature of research
For positivists, social research is a purely scientific endeavour that needs to follow set rules and procedures. It is *empirical* – involves exploration of those things that can be seen, felt, heard, tasted, and smelled as the grounds for all scientific knowledge; and it is often *reductionist* – involves the study of discrete parts of a system, rather than the system itself or its interconnectivity.

The researcher
Positivists believe that research is a specialist activity that needs to be undertaken by trained and qualified 'scientists'. Researchers should be: *experts* – generally scientists who have appropriate experience and qualifications; and always *objective* – a researcher's personal biases have no part in the research endeavour. The purpose of research is to produce knowledge not contingent on the researcher's beliefs, desires, or biases.

The methods
For positivists, methods are defined sets of procedures that need to be carried out with exacting detail. The methodologies are usually: *deductive* – researchers test a theory and look for confirmation through observations; *hypothesis-driven* – researchers propose a tentative statement that they attempt to prove/disprove; *reliable* – researchers use methods that will give the same results under repeated trials; and *reproducible* – methodological procedures can be repeated by other scientists who will glean similar findings.

The findings

Positivists generally want their findings to have broad applicability to the whole of a population. Findings are generally: *quantitative* – represented through numerical data; *statistically significant* – results are shown to be true beyond mere chance; and *generalizable* – findings are applicable to a population beyond a sample.

The times they are a changing

Enter the 1960s and things get much more complex. I saw a cartoon recently that showed two scientists staring at a blackboard full of formula. One says to the other 'You know what's really depressing? Knowing that everything we prove now will be disproved in a few years.'

There are probably a lot of scientists who don't find that joke particularly funny. It is, however, a joke that we now have a place for in a society that is increasingly sceptical of positivist assumptions. For example, is the world really knowable and predictable? Physicists now recognize the role of chaos and complexity in a universe that we may never 'capture'. And what about the nature of truth in the social world? Whose truth is it anyway? There are many 'post-positivists' who are looking at possibilities for the construction of knowledge beyond positivist assumptions, and in doing so are questioning the very heart of the scientific endeavour.

While there is much debate over the nature of post-positivists, anti-positivists, and many other postmodern 'ists', I have chosen to use the term 'post-positivist' to simply refer to the diverse range of philosophers, scientists, researchers, and others who are calling the assumptions of positivism into question.

The world

Post-positivists believe that the world may not be 'knowable'. They see the world as infinitely complex and open to interpretation. Post-positivists see the world as: *ambiguous* – science may help us to someday explain what we do not know, but there are many things that we have gotten wrong in the past and many things that we may never be able to understand in all their complexity; *variable* – the world is not fixed, 'truth' can depend on the limits of our ability to define shifting phenomena; and *multiple* in its realities – what might be 'truth' for one person or cultural group may not be 'truth' for another.

The nature of research

For post-positivists, reflexive research demands that understandings of the scientific endeavour begin to shift. While research can be based on the senses, it can also be: *intuitive* – hunches, metaphorical understandings, and the creative are all legitimized as appropriate ways of knowing and exploring the world; and *holistic* – research needs to explore systems because the whole is often seen as more than the sum of the parts.

The researcher

Post-positivists believe that the traditional gap between the researcher and the researched is one that can (and should) be diminished. Post-positivists researchers can act in ways that are: *participatory and collaborative* – rather than research focusing

TABLE 1.2   THE ASSUMPTIONS

from *Positivist*		to *Post-positivist*
The world		
Knowable	⇦ --------------------------------------- ⇨	Ambiguous
Predictable	⇦ --------------------------------------- ⇨	Variable
Single truth	⇦ --------------------------------------- ⇨	Multiple reality
The nature of research		
Empirical	⇦ --------------------------------------- ⇨	Intuitive
Reductionist	⇦ --------------------------------------- ⇨	Holistic
The researcher		
Objective	⇦ --------------------------------------- ⇨	Subjective
Removed expert	⇦ --------------------------------------- ⇨	Participatory & collaborative
Methodology		
Deductive	⇦ --------------------------------------- ⇨	Inductive
Hypothesis-driven	⇦ --------------------------------------- ⇨	Exploratory
Reliable	⇦ --------------------------------------- ⇨	Dependable
Reproducible	⇦ --------------------------------------- ⇨	Auditable
Findings		
Quantitative	⇦ --------------------------------------- ⇨	Qualitative
Statistically significant	⇦ --------------------------------------- ⇨	Valuable
Generalizable	⇦ --------------------------------------- ⇨	Idiographic or transferable

solely *on* a particular group, post–positivist researchers can also work both *for* and *with* participants; and *subjective* – researchers acknowledge being value-bound. They admit to biases that can affect their studies. The question for post-positivist researchers is how to recognize and manage, and in some situations, even–value and use subjectivities endemic to the research process.

The methods
For post-positivists, methods often reject or expand upon the rules of scientific method. Methods are often: *inductive* – the process moves from specific observations to broader generalizations and theories; *dependable* – while reliability in method may not be possible, post-positivists attempt to use systematic and rigorous approaches to research; and *auditable* – the context-specific nature of researching may not lend itself to reproducibility, but research should be verifiable through full and transparent explication of method.

The findings
Post-positivists recognize the uniqueness of situations and/or cultural groups, but can still seek broader value in their findings. They seek findings that are: *idiographic* – (unique) may not be able to be generalized, yet have their own intrinsic worth – or are *transferable* – the lessons learned from one context are applicable to other contexts; *valuable* – post-positivist researchers are often interested in both the

production of social knowledge and contributions to change; and *qualitative* – findings are often represented through imagery and words.

The position of the creative and strategic researcher

Many researchers feel a need to position themselves as a particular type of researcher, and identify themselves with a defined way of knowing. The question to consider is whether there can be value in accepting various assumptions that lie at divergent points across Table 1.2. Can divergent, disparate, and distinct understandings of the world, and in particular research, simultaneously exist? For the researcher who approaches research as a 'thinking game', the answer is yes. As highlighted by the example in Box 1.3, there is no need to be pigeonholed. Each research situation and research question is unique, and assumptions can be as varied as the situations. The trick is to understand what assumptions you are working under and how they might affect your study.

Box 1.3 Positivist Assumptions and Banana Consumption!

I once had a student who wanted to explore whether recycled 'grey' water could be used to irrigate bananas. She did this in two phases. The first phase involved the formulation of a hypothesis that stated there would be no bio-physical differences between bananas irrigated with town water and those irrigated with recycled grey water. For this phase of the study she (quite appropriately) accepted the positivist assumptions, and conducted her research according to the 'rules' of scientific method – she was the consummate lab-based objective scientist.

Her second phase explored whether consumers would buy bananas irrigated with recycled water regardless of 'no difference' in quality. For this phase of the study, the student thoughtfully explored her assumptions and realized that in relation to this particular question, she found herself moving into 'post-positivist' territory. She struggled with her own subjectivity and realized that 'truth' and 'reality' can be two different things (many consumers who believed findings of 'no difference' claimed that they would still be hesitant to purchase the bananas). There was no defined set of rules to best answer this question, but her willingness to 'think' her way through the process and be flexible in her approach allowed her to draw conclusions that were seen as both credible and valuable.

WORKING THROUGH THE COMPLEXITY

Given the diversity of assumptions that are represented by positivist and post-positivist perspectives, the plethora of approaches that have emerged for engaging in research may not be too surprising. In the past few decades, the number (and complexity) of research methods has increased dramatically, particularly in the social/applied sciences. Let's see … there are quantitative and qualitative approaches.

There is empiricism, positivism, social constructivism, and interpretivism. Don't forget grounded theory, ethnography, critical ethnography, radical ethnography, and auto ethnography. What about conversation analysis, document analysis, univariate analysis, and multivariate analysis? Oh yeah I almost forgot … hermeneutics, unobtrusive methods ethnomethodology and phenomenology. Then there's surveying, interviewing … ARGHHHH!!!! No more. I'm confused …

It really is a bewildering tangle of methods, and the challenge for any research student is to be able to make some sense of it all. Unfortunately, this is something that can be quite difficult. Research methods/approaches are often lumped together and not organized in a logical fashion. For example, some methods texts tend to treat things like positivism, interviewing, and ethnography in a parallel fashion without a logical schema to understand how it fits together. But this is essential. In order to make your way through the tangle of 'methods' you need a framework for organizing the various aspects of research.

One way to construct such a framework is to consider the diverse range of methods listed above as 'answers' to particular research questions. Once you know the question, the methods simply fall into place. Table 1.3 offers a set of questions for wading through methods. Understanding the relationship between these questions and various aspects of method can help you make sense of, and navigate your way through, a highly complex field.

PUTTING IT ALL TOGETHER

 Paradigms, perspective, methodologies, methods, rules, procedures … How does the reflexive researcher (one with the ability to think both creatively and strategically about and within the research process) go about putting all the pieces of the research jigsaw together? Well for a start, there needs to be recognition that there is no 'best type' of research. There are only good questions matched with appropriate procedures of inquiry, and this is always driven by the researcher, not the method. It is up to the researcher to thoughtfully put together the pieces of the jigsaw in order to form a meaningful picture of the world being explored.

The goal of this book is to act as a guide for bringing the picture into focus with clarity and authenticity. In doing so, it explores: the groundwork necessary for getting started; how to define a topic/question; central considerations in 'reflexive' research; how to work with the literature; how to adopt, adapt and create designs, methodologies, and methods; and finally how to communicate findings.

Laying the groundwork

Chapter 1 has highlighted the need for creative and strategic thinking in the research process, and introduced you to the paradigms, perspectives, and methods that make up 'research'. Having some understanding of the discipline can go a long way in helping to ground your own research approach.

TABLE 1.3   WADING THROUGH METHOD

How do I understand the world?	This is the land of *isms*. It is the set of assumptions that define an intellectual understanding of how the world operates and how knowledge is produced, i.e.:

- **Positivism** – the view that all true knowledge is scientific, and can be pursued by scientific method
- **Empiricism** – belief that all concepts are derived from sense-experience
- **Interpretivism** – acknowledges and explores the cultural and historical interpretations of the social world
- **Constructivism** – claims that meaning does not exist in its own right; rather it is constructed by human beings as they interact and engage in interpretation
- **Subjectivism** – emphasizes the subjective elements in experience and accepts that personal experiences are the foundation for factual knowledge.

What methodological approach will best answer my questions?	This is the strategy or set of procedures used to gather and analyze data. It is often paradigm and discipline driven, and covers a diverse range of approaches. Some of the more common methodological approaches used in the social and applied sciences are:

- **Scientific method** – methodological procedure that consists of: developing a theory that is consistent with observations; using the theory to make predictions (hypothesis) and to test those predictions (see Chapters 8 &12)
- **Ethnography** – exploration of cultural groups in a bid to understand, describe, and interpret a way of life from the point of view of its participants (see Chapters 9 & 10)
- **Phenomenology** – description of a 'phenomenon' as it presents itself in direct awareness. Phenomenology disregards historical or social contexts (see Chapter 9)
- **Ethnomethodology** – study of the methods that individuals use to make sense of their social world and accomplish their daily actions (see Chapter 9)
- **Action research** – a research strategy that pursues action and knowledge in an integrated fashion through a cyclical and participatory means (see Chapter 10).

What are the methods or techniques that I will use to collect my data?	These methods (which are discussed in detail in Chapter 11) get down to the nitty gritty of data collection and can be used in conjunction with any of the methodological approaches discussed above.

- **Interviewing** – asking questions and listening to individuals in order to obtain information or opinions
- **Surveying** – questioning or canvassing a wide array of people in order to obtain information or opinions
- **Document analysis** – exploring written documents for content and/or themes
- **Observation** – can be 'removed' or 'participant' and involves the recognition and recording of facts, situations, occurrences, and empathetic understanding.

(Continued)

TABLE 1.3 CONTINUED

What type of data will I be collecting?	There is a plethora of literature on quantitative and qualitative methods, but in actuality, quantitative and qualitative refers to types of data – not method. There are plenty of methods – in fact, all of those listed above that can collect data of both a quantitative and qualitative nature (see Chapter 7).
	• **Quantitative data** – numerical data; can be naturally occurring numbers, i.e. age/income, or data that is numerically coded, i.e. female = 1, male = 2 • **Qualitative data** – data collected as words and/or images' not numerically coded for analysis.
How will I analyze my data?	As discussed in Chapter 12, quantitative and qualitative data demand distinct treatment with quantitative data analyzed statistically and qualitative data analyzed thematically.
	• **Statistical analysis** – can be descriptive (to summarize the data), or inferential (to draw conclusions that extend beyond the immediate data) • **Thematic analysis** – can include analysis of words, concepts, literary devices, and/or non-verbal cues. Includes content, discourse, narrative, and conversation analysis; semiotics; hermeneutics; and grounded theory techniques.

Chapter 2 acknowledges that undertaking research can be both a difficult and alienating activity, and attempts to offer strategies for staying on top of the process. It covers: what you need to know to start your research journey; how to best navigate the research process; and how to stay on track.

Defining your question

Chapter 3 discusses the art and science of knowing what you want to know. It takes you through the process of defining research questions so that they can guide your 'methods'. Now this may sound like common sense ... questions direct methods ... but with so many competing paradigms and perspectives, it can be hard to remember. It's just too easy to fall into the trap of selecting a familiar method rather than approaching method as a critical thinking exercise aimed at answering particular research questions. It is amazing how much simpler it is to adopt, adapt, or create appropriate methodological approaches when you are absolutely clear about what you want to know.

Researching reflexively

Reflexivity in research refers to the ability of the researcher to stand outside the research process and critically reflect on that process. Research as a 'reflexive' thinking process involves constant consideration of the researcher, the researched, and the integrity of the process.

Chapter 4 explores relationships of power and the ethical dilemmas that can arise from the distinction between the researcher and researched. The chapter discusses worldviews and highlights the importance of understanding dominant and alternate 'realities'. It asks how researchers can best negotiate their role in order to protect the integrity of the research process.

Chapter 5 discusses the criteria and indicators of good research that are used to assess the credibility of a process aimed at creating new knowledge. The goal of research is to make a contribution to a field, a contribution that may influence policy and practice or will become the basis for other people's learning. There is therefore a huge responsibility to 'get it right', to make it credible, and to approach it with rigour and integrity. This chapter looks at the underlying criteria for credibility and offers indicators that are appropriate to various research approaches.

Exploring the literature

I often tell students that before they begin 'doing' research, they need to convince me of three things: (1) that the questions they wish to answer are worthy of research; (2) that they are the right person for the job (they know their stuff); and (3) their methodological approach is the best 'doable' way of getting the answers to the questions they pose. And to do this, they need to read. They need to show me that they have thoroughly engaged with both the general and scientific literature in their area.

Working with literature, however, is a big challenge for any student researcher. Knowing what to read, how to find it, how to put boundaries on it, how to manage it, how to organize it, how to annotate it, and how to construct arguments with it, means that new researchers need a tremendous amount of guidance in negotiating the process. The goal of Chapter 6 is to help students work with literature.

Exploring design, methodologies, and methods

Conducting research is more than simply adopting and carrying out particular methodologies and methods. It is about thinking your way through the process. Yes, you need to be familiar with methodologies and methods, but you also need to be able to reflexively consider their appropriateness to the task at hand.

Chapter 7 highlights the importance of thinking your way through methodological design. It covers the possibilities for moving from questions to answers; prerequisites for good methodological design; how to work through the nitty gritty of design; as well as some thoughts on the qualitative/quantitative divide.

Of course being able to best think your way through methodological design is highly dependent on your knowledge base. The variety of research paradigms and perspectives that have constructed research offer quite a few well-defined options for exploring the social world. Chapter 8 addresses the methodological approaches commonly used in exploring and representing populations, while Chapter 9 tackles methodologies that can help researchers delve into the complexities of a particular case, culture or phenomenon. Methodological approaches that legitimize change as a goal of the research process are explored in Chapter 10.

Chapter 11 covers methods of data collection and highlights the rigour needed to achieve credibility in any and all approaches. This chapter discusses issues of access before tackling the complexities, basics, and procedures of surveying, interviewing, observation, and document analysis.

Communicating through research

Too many students think that once their data is collected, they are pretty much finished. They just need to run some analysis and write up. Well, your research relies on your ability to not only analyze and write-up, but on your ability to think your way though the process of analysis and communicate your finding with an audience.

Chapter 12 emphasizes the importance of keeping a sense of the overall project as you work through statistical and/or thematic analysis. It stresses the importance of grounding your analysis in the questions, aims, and objectives of your research project so that significant, credible, and valuable storylines can emerge.

Finally, Chapter 13 discusses writing as a process, or even a mode of analysis, rather than just a product. The chapter stresses the importance of seeing the write-up as a 'conversation' that needs to be mindful of its audience, have a logical structure, and communicate a clear storyline. The chapter concludes by offering a number of suggestions for preparing your work for submission and highlights the importance of dissemination.

CHAPTER SUMMARY

- Creative and strategic thinking should be seen as central to the research process. Research can be thought of as a 'thinking game' and a 'whole-brain' activity that often demands that researchers think outside any set of prescriptive 'rules'. It demands creativity that is effectively balanced with focus and structure.
- Scientific research was born of 'positivism' and adopted the assumptions of that paradigm. These assumptions include: a knowable and predictable world; empirical and reductionist research; objective and expert researchers; hypothesis-driven methods; and statistically significant, quantitative findings.
- Over the past decades, the assumptions of positivism have been brought into question. Post-positivist researchers acknowledge: a world that is ambiguous and variable; research that can be intuitive and holistic; researchers that can be subjective and collaborative; methods that can be inductive and exploratory; and findings that can be idiographic and qualitative.
- Rather than positioning the researcher according to paradigmatic assumptions, the reflexive researcher can consider whether it is possible to explore the assumptions of various paradigms as they relate to particular research questions.

- A potential strategy for wading through methods is to ask a series of questions that can help organize the methods landscape. These include questions related to: worldviews; methodological approaches; methods of data collection; data types; and data analysis.
- Getting your head around the pieces of the research jigsaw can be confusing. The major pieces of the puzzle include: laying the groundwork; defining your question; researching reflexively; working with literature; understanding design, methodologies, and methods; and communicating your findings.

Managing the Process

'Where do I begin and will I be able to do it?'

Chapter Preview

- **The Research Journey**
- **Navigating the Process**
- **Staying on Course**

THE RESEARCH JOURNEY

Researching is a process that demands planning, forethought, commitment, and persistence. In fact, research is more of a journey than a task; and like any journey, it needs to be managed, navigated, and negotiated from early conception to final destination. Now it's not unusual for students to question their ability to successfully navigate this journey. After all, researching is a skill that is just being developed, so the thought of embarkation can be quite daunting. Students can be unsure of how to start (some jump in without a strategic plan, while some wallow too long in the planning stages). Others tend to make a good start, but get lost or lose motivation along the way.

As you work your way through the process, it is worth keeping in mind that as a student researcher, your journey to produce knowledge will also be a learning journey about both research itself and your ability to manage intricacies and complexity. The goal of this chapter is to help you manage this research/learning journey by familiarizing you with the ins and outs of undertaking research. It covers what you need to know to get underway, strategies for best navigating the process, and how to stay on track. It begins, however, by asking you to reflect on your own approach to knowledge. Knowing how your mind best works can be central to successfully managing the journey to come.

Exploring your own approach to knowledge

We spend a lot more time in formal education learning about the world than we spend explicitly learning about ourselves. We learn how to do things and we learn about things, but rarely are we given the opportunity to reflect on how we best learn those things. While your education to date may have seen you without too many options for directing the nature of your own learning, your research journey will allow you the opportunity to design your study in accordance with how you best approach knowledge.

There are a number of defined 'learning styles' that can help you understand how you best process, assimilate, and produce knowledge, and knowing your style can go a long way in helping you plan your research. Some of the more common learning styles are summarized below, but if you want to find out more, have a look on the internet. Not only can you find more information, you can also take part in online quizzes that assess your own learning style.

Brain-hemisphere dominance

While very few people fall at the extremes, understanding brain-hemisphere dominance (as discussed in Chapter 1) can explain an individual's preference for various ways of learning, knowing, and researching.

Left-brain: Analytic, organized, and logical – can struggle with randomness and spontaneity. In research, those with left-brain dominance can have difficulty 'thinking outside the square'.

Right-brain: Intuitive, holistic, and imaginative – can struggle with structure and order. In research, those with left-brain dominance can struggle in defining their methods, finishing, and writing-up.

VAK

The VAK learning style looks at the basics of sensory preference and explores an individual's predilections for gathering information and data though various senses.

Visual learners: Tend to gather data through 'sight'. They often think in pictures, learn best from visual displays, and take detailed notes in order to absorb information. In research, they often enjoy observation.

Auditory learners: Tend to gather data through 'hearing'. They learn best through verbal input and often interpret the underlying meanings of speech by listening to tone, pitch, speed, and other nuances. Auditory learners often benefit from listening, talking, and reading aloud, and in research, they are likely to make good interviewers.

Kinesthetic learners: Tend to learn through moving, doing, and touching and enjoy a hands-on approach to exploring the world around them. Kinesthetic researchers may find it hard to sit and read, but often enjoy data collection and find satisfaction from engaging in action research.

Kolb learning styles

Kolb saw learning as a cycle of concrete experiences, reflective observations, abstract conceptualization, and active experimentation. The learning styles he proposes are based on the premise that individuals may prefer one or more stages of the cycle and consequently neglect others (Kolb 1984).

Assimilator (or Theorist): Tend to use abstract conceptualization and reflective observation. Assimilators enjoy creating theoretical models and are interested in abstract concepts. Their interests don't usually extend to working with others or to the practical application of knowledge.

Converger (or Pragmatist): Tend to use abstract conceptualization and active experimentation. Convergers generally enjoy the practical application of ideas and tend to approach work with objectivity. They prefer to deal with things rather than people and often specialize in the physical sciences.

Accommodator (or Activist): Tend to use concrete experience and active experimentation. Accommodators enjoy 'doing' and can adapt readily to new circumstances. They tend to solve problems intuitively and rely on others for information.

Divergers (or Reflectors): Tend to use reflective observation and concrete experience and enjoy thinking about a topic. Divergers generally have excellent imaginations and are often interested in the lives and emotions of others. They often have broad cultural interests and tend to specialize in the arts.

Surface, deep, and strategic learning

According to Marton and Säljö (1976) learning can be driven by: (1) a desire to acquire facts, or (2) a desire to have a deep and integrated understanding of an issue or phenomenon. A third more strategic motivation is the desire to pass, get good grades, finish the degree, etc. (Wisker 2001).

Surface learners: Interested in 'facts', they often rely on memory and do not enjoy conceptualization, theorizing, or making connections. In research, they may be more comfortable dealing with statistical tests rather than theory building.

Deep learners: Enjoy the search for meaning. They are often good at linking learning to experience and have an ability to integrate new knowledge with prior studies. In research, they generally look at problem situations holistically and can be eclectic in their methodologies.

Strategic learners: Pursue learning in order to achieve defined goals. I think there's probably a bit of strategist in us all. If there wasn't, it would be awfully hard to get through formal schooling. The independent and rigorous nature of research, however, can often leave the strategist with a crisis of motivation. The trick for the strategist is to make sure research questions can engage a real and sustainable interest.

As you reflect on the learning styles presented above, it is worth remembering that most individuals do not fall neatly inside any one categorization. Many will find themselves with characteristics that span the descriptors and see themselves as individuals capable of approaching knowledge in diverse ways. But even if you find yourself relating very strongly to a particular categorization, it does not mean that you need to develop research skills that fall within your comfort zone. Some may do this, but others may actively seek to develop new skills that will add richness and depth to their current abilities.

NAVIGATING THE PROCESS

Research is a process that simultaneously demands imagination, creativity, discipline, and structure, and needs to be navigated strategically from start to finish. So in addition to knowing your own approach to knowledge, it is well worth considering a number of practicalities related to the process. In order for students to navigate a path through the research process, they need to: familiarize themselves with their institution/programme's resources and requirements; get appropriately set-up; negotiate the advisory process; and manage their workload.

Knowing your institution

Moving strategically through the research process demands that you become familiar with the requirements and resources of your university. If you don't, you are likely to waste precious time by: (1) undertaking and producing research that falls outside set guidelines; and/or (2) not taking advantage of the full gamut of available resources.

Research requirements

One of the greatest frustrations for students and lecturers alike is when good work does not meet set requirements. The best way to ensure that all university protocols are met is to find out what they are early on and to remain cognizant of them throughout the research project. Common research requirements include:

- *Meeting deadlines* – late submissions might not be accepted, or may be subject to penalties. It is well worth knowing your deadlines and familiarizing yourself with policies for late submission and extensions.
- *Staying within word limits* – word limits vary with level of study, discipline, and university. But whatever the limit is, it is generally expected that it will take close to this to produce a quality research paper/thesis. As a lecturer, seeing a very 'thin' paper is almost (but not quite) as disappointing as seeing one you will have to get home with a trolley. Try not to go too far under or over the prescribed word count. Some lecturers/institutions can be quite strict with works that fall outside set limits.
- *Gaining ethics approval* – this is essential for most research that involves human (or animal) participants and is discussed fully in Chapter 4. Each university

will have its own requirements, committees, and deadlines for gaining such approval.

- *Progress reports/seminars* – for longer projects, universities often require reports to be submitted by students, supervisors, or both, on an annual or biannual basis. Students might also be expected to present in regularly scheduled seminars.

- *An examination process* – this too varies by level of study and university. Some research write-ups will be given a grade or level, while others are simply deemed satisfactory/unsatisfactory. For higher degrees, the examination process often involves external examiners that the student may or may not have a say in. It may also involve an oral defence of the work. It is highly advisable to discuss the issue of examination/examiners with your supervisor quite early in the process. There can be great benefit in knowing what to expect.

- *Originality and avoidance of plagiarism* – virtually all universities have clear policies on originality and plagiarism. Familiarizing yourself with what constitutes plagiarism can help you avoid some deadly grey areas.

Resources

Many students do not ask … therefore they do not receive. Finding out what your university/programme offers research students should be high on the list of initial priorities. As highlighted in Box 2.1, nothing is more frustrating than finding out about an excellent service or facility just a bit too late.

Box 2.1 Damn! I Wish I Knew that Six Months Ago

SCENARIO 1
'$1300! You got $1300 for your field trip? How in the world did you get that?"
'All research students are entitled to $1300 a year to help cover costs; you just have to put in a form.'
'You're kidding me. How come I wasn't told?'

SCENARIO 2
'Hey, how did you get an access number for the photocopier?'
'Debbie in main office, the school provides them for all Masters and PhD students.'
'Aw, that's just great; do you know how much I have spent on photocopying over the past six months!?!'

SCENARIO 3
'So where are you headed?'
'Can you believe I have to go halfway across town to Nelson Library to pick up a book? They don't have it on this campus.'
'Oh … Why didn't you do an inter-campus loan on the internet? They send it right to you.'
'You are joking … since when?'

Some of the resources you may want to check on are:

☑ *Accommodation* – Is dedicated or shared office space available?

☑ *Equipment* – Will you have access to software, telephone, computer, and/or photocopier?

☑ *Funds* – Is there any money available to help with costs such as university fees, books, photocopying, postage, consumables (paper, ink cartridges, cassette tapes), travel costs (site visits, conference attendance), and equipment (tape recorder, transcription machine, pc, laptop, software, etc.)?

☑ *Library facilities* – What databases are available? Is there a system of inter-library loans? Will you have internet access?

☑ *Methods assistance* – Is there any assistance available for questionnaire design, transcription, data entry? Is statistics advice available?

☑ *Writing assistance* – Are there workshops that can help you put together a proposal, or structure a final draft? Is there anyone to help with editing?

Getting set up

Researching is an activity that requires more independence and autonomy than general learning, and requires that researchers spend a fair amount of time reading or working at a computer. Getting set up therefore requires: access to a quiet place to work; a good reliable computer; and proficiency in the use of that computer.

- *The study/office* – having a comfortable place to lock yourself away is essential. Researching can be an alienating activity and creating or finding a space where you can work comfortably is well worth the effort.
- *The computer* – most students find an up-to-date word processing program and internet access essential to researching. You may also need to run statistical and/or qualitative data management programs that can be demanding on the system. It is well worth investing in a system that can not only meet your current needs, but can meet needs that might arise with use as the research process gets underway.
- *Proficiency* – when I went to school, there was no need to learn to type unless you wanted to become a secretary. In today's computer age, however, being able to fly across the keyboard is a skill I wish I had from the start. If you plan to undertake research and you are yet to master the art of touch typing and word processing, the time you take to learn the skills is time you will get back in spades.

Getting the right advice

Student research is generally undertaken with the guidance and support of a mentor or supervisor, and for many this is a new experience. You are well advised to do all you can do to ensure good communication. Open communication and clear expectations can really facilitate the research journey.

Good communication

The relationship that you will develop with your supervisor is likely to be more intimate than any previously experienced with an academic, and that can be quite intimating because the student/supervisor relationship is one of very unequal power. On one side is the professor and expert, on the other is student and novice. Now the goal of the relationship might be mentorship and mutual respect but, as highlighted in Box 2.2, it is a relationship that can quite easily leave students feeling patronized or even intimidated.

Box 2.2 The Power of the Red Pen – Kate's Story

When I switched universities, I was assigned to a supervisor who had just received her PhD and had sociological interest similar to my own. We met a few times, and I can't say it went well. While her PhD was in an area similar to mine, our approaches seemed worlds apart and I got the distinct feeling that she thought my approach was not just different, but wrong. So it was with much trepidation that I handed her an early chapter of my thesis, and I awaited the feedback with great apprehension.

I got the chapter back a few weeks later and it was even worse than I thought. The paper was literally covered in red ink. Angry, vile, 'I have power over you', 'you are wrong', red ink. Well I went from feeling apprehensive to angry. There was no need to exercise that type of power trip on me. I did not need hyper-critical judgement, what I needed was support, guidance, advice, and perspective. In the end, what I needed was a new supervisor.

This does not mean that you and your supervisor need to be on the same 'wave length'. As highlighted in the following thesis acknowledgement, a lot can be learned from a supervisor whose style pushes your boundaries.

'My thanks to Dr. Sherman who was a great supervisor for the way my mind works. And my thanks to Dr. Hakim who was an equally great supervisor for the way it doesn't'.

Perhaps the easiest way to ensure a positive supervisor/student relationship is to agree to open communication. If you can develop a healthy rapport with your supervisor, you will make the journey that much easier.

Expectations

If you are new to supervisory relationships, you may not be aware of just how varied the expectations within them can be. Some relationships are based on student autonomy and independence, while other relationships are much more collaborative and dependent. The only way to know where you stand is to work on open communication that includes negotiation of both student and supervisor expectations.

Keep in mind that if you don't do this early, you may be setting yourself up for a tremendous amount of frustration and angst. Box 2.3 highlights some of the expectations you may want to openly negotiate with your supervisor.

Box 2.3 Negotiating Expectations

Expectations that need to be clarified in student/supervisor relationships include:

AUTONOMY

- Who is responsible for orienting the student to university resources/ requirements?
- Who sets the timelines?
- How much advice/direction can/will the supervisor provide on the selection of topic, question, methodological, and theoretical frameworks?
- Will the student be expected to submit all drafts for review/comment?
- Do all new directions need to be cleared with the supervisor?
- Will writing/editing assistance be provided by the supervisor?
- Who makes the final decision on acceptability?

THE PROGRAMME

- How regularly will you meet?
- What is the expected turnaround time for getting and responding to feedback?
- Are seminar presentations required?

THE NATURE OF THE RELATIONSHIP

- Will the relationship be purely professional or professional/personal?
- Will emotional support be provided?
- Is open and frank discussion on progress expected?

Managing the workload

One word that I stress in all student research projects, regardless of level or discipline, is 'doability'. Is it doable? Now assessing doability involves more than just looking at the quality of the research design. It also involves looking at the full gamut of pressures and responsibilities that you as an individual need to manage. Realistically assessing and managing your workload is essential to success.

Timelines/time management

Unmanaged time has a funny way of slipping away from you, so while there are no set rules for time management there is mandate that you attempt it. Whether you are a night owl, an early bird, someone who can multi-task, someone who can

	Jan	Feb	Mar	April	May	June	July	Aug	Sept	Oct	Nov	Dec
Groundwork	xx	xx										
Literature review		xx	xx	xx	xx	xx						
Defining methods			xx	xx								
Data collection					xx	xx	xx					
Progress seminar						12th						
Data analysis							xx	xx	xx			
Write first draft		xx	xx	xx	xx	xx	xx	xx				
Write second draft								xx	xx	xx		
Final seminar											27th	
Write final draft										xx	xx	xx
Thesis Due												15th

FIGURE 2.1 GANTT CHART

only tackle one task at a time, someone who enjoys spontaneity, or someone who feels anxious without a defined schedule, having a work plan is essential in managing what is likely to end up a very complex and, at times, seemingly unending task.

One time management strategy is to develop and use a Gantt chart. As shown in Figure 2.1, a Gantt chart can be used to map out a project from start to finish. Now keep in mind that researching is often a fluid and flexible exercise likely to incorporate the unexpected, and your chart will invariably need to shift in order to reflect the dynamic nature of research. However, having a document that can be negotiated and modified is more likely to keep you true to deadlines than not having one at all.

Working with discipline vs inspiration

For some, discipline comes naturally. These amazing individuals are able to get up at a pre-defined time, work diligently to a plan, and take only minimal food and toilet breaks. AND they manage to do this five days a week. For most ordinary humans, however, the procrastination skills we have developed over many years of formal schooling are much too sophisticated to see us succumb to that level of discipline. Instead, we wait for inspiration. Which is fine if inspiration strikes with enough frequency and regularity … but if it doesn't? Well then, you may have to trick yourself into some sort of pseudo-inspirational state. Some things you might want to try are:

- *Working on/reading over your research journal* – an invaluable tool for any researcher is a good journal that can capture creative inspiration and help you manage the process. Your journal might include observations, notes on method and theory, lists of relevant contacts, notes/reminders to yourself, and any other ideas, doodles, concept maps etc. that come to mind. Adding to your journal, or simply reading it over, may get the creative juices flowing.
- *Forcing yourself to get on the computer* – often doing some menial task can be a catalyst for going on to do richer work. Try starting with relatively mindless

editorial work, data cleaning, referencing, and then try to move to whatever you are procrastinating over. If you don't approach the computer at all, then nothing gets done. But if you sit down to a task, not only is the task accomplished, but the real work might get going as well.

- *Writing a letter to a real or fictional friend* – if you are feeling stuck, try writing an informal letter that tells 'whoever' what you are trying to do. Freeing yourself from academic writing can often help liberate ideas.
- *Go for a walk* – sometimes a good head-clearing walk can be a trigger for a flood of fresh ideas. Having a small tape recorder handy (which if kept by the bed can also capture early morning inspiration) can capture those thoughts you are bound to forget.

STAYING ON COURSE

I don't think I've been involved in the supervision of one student who has not agonized over the research journey. For most, their research project is likely to be the biggest academic project ever undertaken. Knowing a field, being responsible for the production of 'new knowledge', designing method, collecting and analyzing data, and writing it all up can be an intimidating challenge – particularly for those whose roles and responsibilities in the real world extend beyond those of student. But rest assured, feelings of frustration, confusion, and even incompetence, are both common and surmountable. Being able to find a balance and deal with a crisis are part and parcel of researching.

Finding a balance

Student, employee, parent, child, partner … no student is a student alone. We all have a variety of roles to play. Yet sometimes those around us, and even ourselves, forget that we need to manage and balance all of these simultaneously – even if they are sometimes incompatible. Balance is essential. No one can reach or work to their potential if they are neglecting important areas of their life.

So how do you find balance when you know you need to focus on your studies, yet you are feeling pressure at work, and you realize that you must reprioritize family? Well, whether it be at work, home, or university, being honest and open about your needs is a good start. That, combined with the ability to say 'no', can go a long way in feeling on top of it all.

- *At work* – try taking the time to discuss the demands of study with your managers. Hopefully they will be supportive. If not, at least you know where you stand. If your research is work-related, it may be possible to negotiate time and resources for your project, particularly if you explain the significance and potential benefits of your research to the workplace.
- *At home* – having support of family is essential, not only for the practical support that can come from assistance with domestic duties, children care, etc., but also for the emotional support that can be quite crucial during the process.

Unfortunately, some partners can be threatened by, or envious of, your achievements. Working through this dilemma, or again at least knowing where you stand, can put you in a stronger position of power.

- *At university* – I think the best advice is to be professional, but put your concerns on the table for legitimization. Being open and honest with your supervisor is crucial to your ability to set realistic and, most importantly, achievable goals.

Box 2.4 No Time for Guilt! – Dakota's Story

I spent much of my time doing my Masters degree thinking about what I wasn't doing. When I was studying, I often wasted hours and hours daydreaming about being with friends, family, going out. … I was quite good at making myself miserable and unproductive. When I was with friends and family, things weren't necessarily better. I spent a fair portion of that time feeling guilty about the work I knew was waiting for me.

I decided to start my PhD when my youngest daughter turned one … so I knew I had to get my act together. I now had two small children at home, and I could not afford to waste so much time agonizing over what I thought I should be doing. So I made a conscious decision to 'give up guilt'. I put the kids in high-quality part-time day care, and simply let it go. And you know what? It worked. When the kids were in care I simply focused on my work and did not allow myself the luxury of worrying about them. When I was with the family, however, I was really with the family. I was fully there and simply enjoyed. … In the end, I finished my thesis in good time. I have come to realize that there is simply no productivity in angst and guilt.

Dealing with 'crisis'

> 'Next week there can't be any crisis. My schedule is already full.'
>
> –Henry Kissinger

It would be unusual to undertake a major research project without it intersecting with some sort of 'crisis'. If you are finding it all too much, are starting to doubt yourself, or doubt what you are doing, it is important to know that you are not alone. Knowing what to expect, knowing how others cope, and developing and using a support system can help you get through inevitable rough patches.

Crisis of motivation

It can be awfully hard to stay motivated for an extended period of time. What starts as an exciting and interesting project can quickly end up being one you just want to finish. In fact, a colleague of mine recently told me that he regularly advises his students to only research the things they are *not* interested in, because if they are really interested in it, they will be sick to death of it before they finish. Now I'm not sure if I agree with that advice, but it does highlight how universal the problem is.

Developing a supportive research culture can go a long way in keeping up motivation. Whether it be an attentive/sympathetic ear at home, interested work colleagues, a peer support network, or even a relevant internet chat group, engaging with others can help keep your interest up. It might also be worth reminding yourself to 'enjoy the process' and that 'the end will indeed come'.

Crisis of confidence

There are a lot of people who start their 'research' careers at the end of very successful 'learning' careers. These are people who are used to competence and success. Well, research students generally set their own agenda, work independently, and attempt to work to their potential; and herein lies the problem. Working to your potential pushes at your own personal limits, often in ways prior learning has not. Feeling like an impostor, thinking that it is beyond your intellectual capabilities, and believing that your work is not good enough are, believe it or not, fears widely shared.

Getting a more objective sense of how you are going can help put things in perspective. If you talk to your supervisor and your peers, you will often find that others have more faith in you than you have in yourself. I often tell students who are facing a crisis of confidence to remember that 'the first is generally the worst'. You are in the midst of a learning process; your skills and confidence will grow with time.

Lacking direction

Research often starts with broad-ranging exploration that can take you down many tangents. The up-side is that this exploration will undeniably increase your learning and often lead to new insights. The down-side, however, is that you risk feeling lost. It is pretty easy to get yourself off course and feel like you have no idea where you are going.

Finding direction can come from reflecting on what it is that you really want to know, having open and candid discussions with your supervisor, and in the end remembering that the answers may not simply appear. You may need to make some hard decisions about the direction you will take.

Feeling disorganized

It's too easy to say 'you need to be organized'. You probably knew that before you got yourself in a mess. The need for self-discipline may be obvious, but the ability to exercise it is much harder. If physical disorganization is your downfall, taking a week or two off from 'doing' research and just cleaning up and organizing is time well spent. If, however, the disorganization is in the mind and you feel as though you can't even think straight, you can (1) try the above – an organized desk and office can pave the way for an organized mind, or (2) get away from it all. Sometimes a good weekend away is all you need to refresh the mental batteries.

Personal crisis

I think it was John Lennon who said 'life is what happens while you are making other plans'. It would be nice if the world stopped while you got on with your research, but that is simply not going to happen. Whether it be difficulties with finances, partners, parents, children, in fact any of life's less wonderful surprises, the research process necessarily coincides with life's inevitable ups and downs.

Reach out to your support network and speak openly with your supervisor. My experience is that people are generally supportive. Perhaps most important of all, don't put too much pressure on yourself. Get support and then make a guilt-free decision to press on, take it slower, or have a hiatus until the crisis subsides.

CHAPTER SUMMARY

- Research is a process that needs to be actively managed. Being strategic in your preliminary planning, being organized and prepared, and creating the mental space necessary for research is an important part of the process.
- We all have preferences for how we approach knowledge. Familiarity with your own learning styles can help facilitate the development and implementation of your research plan.
- In order to produce research that falls within university guidelines, you will need to familiarize yourself with your institution's requirements. Similarly, taking advantage of all possible resources involves knowing what they are.
- Navigating a path through the research process should begin by making sure you have access to an adequate workspace and computer system/programs.
- Supervisory relationships can be difficult to negotiate. Working towards good communication with clear expectations, as well as striving for a sense of comfort in power relations, can help ensure a positive and productive relationship.
- Researching can present real challenges in terms of workloads and timelines. Using Gantt charts and working with both discipline and inspiration can help you manage the process.
- Most students carry the burden of having a variety of roles. Finding balance is essential to personal well-being and hence success in all endeavours, including research.
- The research process is rarely an easy and straightforward journey. It often involves crises of confidence and motivation, and coincides with life's ups and downs. Knowing that you are not alone and that there is support can help get you through.

3 | Developing Your Research Question

'I know the general area ... but I'm not quite sure of my research question.'

Chapter Preview

- **The Importance of Good Questions**
- **Defining Your Topic**
- **From Interesting Topics to Researchable Questions**
- **Characteristics of Good Questions**

THE IMPORTANCE OF GOOD QUESTIONS

Perhaps the first major hurdle in any research project is developing the research question; and this is generally easier said than done. Some students aren't sure of their topic, while others know their topic, but aren't sure of the aspects they want to explore. Others come in with their ideas pretty much narrowed down. Very few, however, can articulate their ideas into well-formed research questions.

But this is crucial, because it is the research question that gives focus, sets boundaries, and provides direction. Knowing what you want to know, and being able to articulate it as a well-formed question allows you to assess whether the question is appropriate for research. If it passes this test, the research question can then be used as the project's blueprint.

Now this may sound like research questions are reductionist devices that take all exploration, creativity, and fluidity out of the research process. Not at all. Research questions themselves can be designed so that they are open and exploratory. As well, research questions can, and often do, change, shift, and evolve during the early stages of a project. Not only is this fine, it is appropriate as your engagement in the literature evolves both your knowledge and thinking. Yes, research questions define an investigation and provide direction, but it is up to the researcher to define and redefine questions so that they can most appropriately accomplish these tasks.

Defining the investigation

A well-articulated research question can provide you (and your eventual audience) with a tremendous amount of information about your project. A well-defined research question will:

- *Define the topic* – whether your focus is on youth suicide, environmental degradation, secularization, etc.
- *Define the nature of the research endeavour* – whether your aim is to discover, explore, explain, describe, or compare.
- *Define the questions you are interested in* – whether you are interested in what, where, how, when, why.
- *Indicate whether you foresee a relationship between concepts you are exploring* – whether you are looking for impacts, increases, decreases, relationships, correlations, causes etc.

Boundaries

In investigating a topic, you are likely to find yourself facing interesting tangents, and a well-defined question can help you set boundaries on your research. When faced with an interesting tangent, ask yourself: 'What does this have to do with my question?'

I'd suggest that there are three potential answers:

1. 'Actually nothing … I will have to leave it. I suppose I can always pick this up in my next project.'
2. 'Actually it is quite relevant … if you think about it, it really does relate to my…' (this can be very exciting and add new dimensions to your work).
3. 'Well nothing really, but I actually think this is at the heart of what I want to know. Perhaps I need to rethink my question.'

Providing direction

As well as defining the investigation and setting boundaries, research questions act as a blueprint for the project. They point to the theory you need to explore; the literature you need to review; the data you need to gather; and in particular, the methods you need to call on.

In fact, I would say that it is nearly impossible to define a clear methodology for an ill-defined research question. Now I know that sounds like common sense, but it has to be one of the most common research *faux pas* I see from students. Students often ask me to have a look at their methods to see if they are on the right track. When I say, 'Sure, what are you researching?', some waffle on for 20 minutes, yet bring me no closer to the heart of their research. And this is because they are yet to articulate their question in their own heads, let alone share it with someone else. If you do not know what you want to know, you will not be in a position to know how to find it out.

DEFINING YOUR TOPIC

All this talk about the importance of research questions is fine, but what if you're not even sure of your topic area and you have no idea what interests to pursue? Well, you're probably not alone. Yes, there are plenty of students who are quite clear about what they want to research, but there are also a lot who really struggle with the idea of generating a research topic. In fact, many feel that coming up with something worthy of research is beyond them.

So how do you decide on a topic that can lead to a potential research question? Well, you work on generating ideas by honing in on your curiosity, using your creativity, and exploring your options with an eye towards practicalities.

The importance of curiosity

'Discovery consists in seeing what everyone else has seen,
and thinking what no one else has thought.'

–Albert Szent-Gvorgi

When asked 'What do you plan to research?' students often struggle for an answer. But if you chat with them about the types of things they tend to think about or what raises their curiosity, they generally have no problem running off a list of potential 'research' ideas.

Ideas for research are generated any time curiosity or passion is aroused. Everyday we are surrounded by events, situations, and interactions that make us wonder, stop and think, or bring emotions of joy, frustration, relief, or anger bubbling to the surface. This is the rich and fertile ground from which research ideas are born. Think about what stirs you up, what you argue about with your friends, family, and peers, and what issues are topical in the world, at home, or in your workplace. You will soon find that research topics abound. If you can learn to catch yourself thinking, 'Gee I wonder…', you will have an unending supply of ideas.

The role of creativity

Is there a role for creativity in the development of research ideas? In a word, yes. Creative inspiration has surely been responsible for as many advances in science as the tendency to follow the rules. If you are stuck for ideas you can try creating a concept map, playing with metaphor, or drawing inspiration from poetry and song.

Concept mapping
We often fall into the trap of thinking in a linear fashion, particularly when it comes to research. One creative, 'right-brain' skill you can call on in the development of your research question is concept mapping. Mapping allows you the freedom to think laterally as well as linearly. It uses free association to allow the mind to jump from one idea to another, thereby enhancing creative processes. Concept mapping can facilitate brainstorming, drawing out connections, and building themes; and can also be successful in overcoming writer's block. Figure 3.1 shows a simple concept map used to draw out potential research topics.

Metaphor
The use of metaphor can allow us to think and express with creativity. For example, how do you describe the research process? Is doing research similar to choreographing a dance, completing a puzzle, navigating the sea, following a path, or

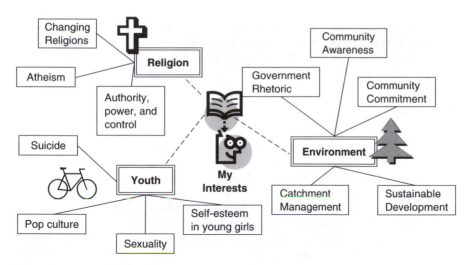

FIGURE 3.1   CONCEPT MAP OF POTENTIAL RESEARCH TOPICS

embarking on a journey? Each metaphor suggests a somewhat different orientation to the task. In developing topics for research, metaphors have the ability to capture and articulate ideas in ways that go beyond the potential of conventional language.

One metaphor for God that stuck in my mind came from a student who argued that God was simply Santa for adults. They both know when you've been naughty or nice, they both have wondrous powers, and, for both, existence relies on 'faith'. The main difference is that Santa's wrath is a lump of coal and God's is eternal damnation!

Poetry and song

I cannot think of any aspect of the human condition that has not been profoundly captured in poetry and song. The desire to understand our world is as much the fodder of the arts, as it is research. While many research ideas will come from academic literature, do not discount the creative arts. As highlighted in Box 3.1, thinking about the poems and songs that have had meaning for you, or exploring the themes in your own creative writing, can be a fountain of research inspiration.

Box 3.1   Coming up with Ideas – Dennis' Story

If you ask most people how they came up with their topics, they talk about intense personal experiences, things related to their work, or issues connected to theory. Sometimes I feel a bit foolish saying my research was inspired by a song. I have been a Billy Joel fan for as long as I can remember, and I love the song 'James'. I find the lyrics profound. Billy Joel's 'hypothesis', so to speak, is that it is hard to find internal contentment if you are 'carrying the weight of family pride'.

> For my thesis, I decided to research the same. Using a sample of 200 full-time white-collar employees aged 25–45, I am exploring relationships between 'the weight of family pride', success, and internal contentment.

Practicalities

As limiting as it may seem, curiosity, creativity, and even passion need to be checked by practicalities. Sometimes open choice of topic is restricted. Research students are well advised to consider, discuss, and negotiate:

- ☑ *Appropriateness* – there are many students who come up with ideas that are not relevant to the degree they are undertaking. I once had an Industrial Design student undertake a research project in extraterrestrial abduction (which I think was based on rich personal experience...). As a topic, maybe there was some potential, but the requirements of the subject clearly stated that research needed to be related to developing professional practice, and I'm not sure what the career options are in AA (alien abduction, of course). Now granted this may be an extreme example, but there are plenty of research students who, after a period of time, feel that they are not in the right department. Fitting in and finding a cohort you can relate to can be crucial to success.
- ☑ *Supervision* – not many students manage to readily negotiate a major research project without a great deal of supervisory support. Finding out whether appropriate supervision for your topic is available before you lock yourself into a project is well advised.
- ☑ *Funding body/employer requirements* – if a funding body or employer has sponsored you to conduct research in a particular area, you may not be able to shift topics. Even within a defined project, however, there can be scope to concentrate on particular aspects or bring a fresh perspective to an issue. Open negotiation and even a 'sales pitch' covering the relevance and potential benefits of your proposed research can give you more creative potential.

FROM INTERESTING TOPICS TO RESEARCHABLE QUESTIONS

If a topic defines the general area you are examining, then the research question defines what aspects of that topic you plan to investigate. Going from a topic of interest to a well-defined research question, however, is no easy task. As shown in Figure 3.2, you need to move from a topic to an issue, narrow it all down to a manageable scope, and finally generate researchable questions.

Finding an angle

Moving from broad topical interests to questions that can be answered through the research process often involves finding an 'angle'. In looking for an angle you may want to consider:

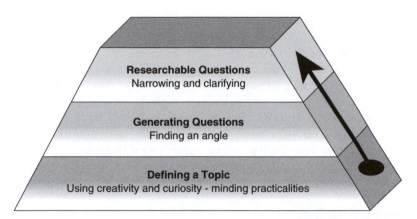

FIGURE 3.2   FROM TOPICS TO RESEARCHABLE QUESTIONS

- *Personal experiences* – sometimes our own experiences of a particular phenomenon, event, or cultural group can give 'insights' worth exploring. For example, you may have an interest in the topic of racial discrimination because, as an Asian student in a primarily white school, you felt that those who verbally attacked you did not appreciate the pain, fear, and anger that resulted from such abuse. A question you now want to explore is: 'How is the practice of racial slurs defended in the school yard?'
- *Theory* – theoretical inspiration is most likely to happen when you find yourself relating theory to a real-world situation; the theory resonates and you think 'aha' maybe that's why a particular situation is the way it is, or perhaps that is why they do what they do. A student of mine had such a moment when he read a work by Althusser that highlights the role of institutions such as the family, schools, and the Church, in embedding Government ideology into individual consciousness. The student began to view the role of the Church in a new light and decided to investigate if and how the Irish Catholic Church operates as an arm of the Government in the socialization of its citizens.
- *An observation* – it can be quite hard to see what surrounds us everyday, so viewing the world through fresh eyes can provide powerful research insights. This happened to a student of mine who was on his 'daily' train, when he suddenly became fascinated by the unwritten rules of personal space. He found himself intrigued by the rules that governed who sat where, how close they sat, who moved away from whom, and under what circumstances. He watched with fascination as people jockeyed for seats as the number of carriage occupants changed with each stop, and decided that he wanted to study the rules that govern such behaviour.
- *Contemporary/timely issues* – sometimes an old topic can take on fresh life. A topic might suddenly become an agenda at the workplace, or may even become the focus of global attention. The Western world's interest, fascination, and judgement of Islamic faith is a case in point. 'Angles' become easy to find

and questions such as: How is the media covering the topic?; What is the policy, practice, and rhetoric of government?; What impact is this having on school yard racism? become quite easy to generate.

*   *Gaps in the literature* – the importance of reading for research (covered in Chapter 6) cannot be overemphasized. When you are conversant with topical literature, it can be quite easy to find an angle. You can explore whether an important aspect of an issue has been ignored; whether there are assumptions underpinning a body of work that need to be re-examined; or whether further questions have been posed by researchers at the end of their papers. If you can identify the gaps and holes in the literature, you can quite readily generate relevant questions.

Narrowing and clarifying

Having an angle is not the end of the task. Once you have an angle, you need to work on narrowing and clarifying in order to generate that 'researchable' question. Now expansive questions can be the focus of good research, but ambiguity can often arise when questions are broad and unwieldy. Being bounded and precise makes the research task easier to accomplish. If you are worried about being too limited, keep in mind that each question can be likened to a window that can be used to explore rich theory and depth in understanding. 'Focused' is not a synonym for 'superficial'.

The concept map revisited

Just as a concept map can be used to brainstorm research topics, it can also be used for question clarification. The map shown in Figure 3.3 explores 'why young girls have a poor self image'. The student has mapped out some major influences – peers, parents, and the media – and has begun to think about causes of the 'problem'. This leads to some interesting ideas that may all be researchable. The student then takes this further by asking two things: (1) what aspects am I most interested in; and (2) do I have any insights that I might be able to add. From this, the student has two 'aha' moments and research questions begin to come into focus. The first looks at the role of media as a whole and asks: 'What do young girls consider normal in terms of body image?' The second comes from an interesting reflection on the compliments parents give to daughters, and how often they relate to how 'pretty they are'. The student begins to wonder whether parents are subconsciously teaching their daughters that worth is determined by external beauty.

The need to define and redefine

Students often think that once they have developed their research question, the job is done. The question is clear, the terms are well defined and unambiguous; and the student feels ready to get going. Now while, yes, developing a clear question is essential for direction setting, it is important to remember that the research journey is rarely linear. Research is a process that generates as many questions as it answers. It takes you in unexpected directions and is determined to undermine your best laid plans. The best advice – set a course, but be ready for the detours.

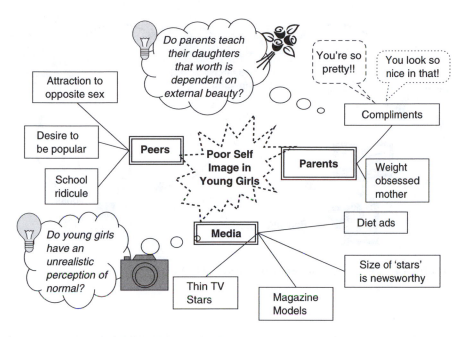

FIGURE 3.3 MAPPING YOUR QUESTIONS

Fixed or fluid?

In order to do research you need to do the following:

1. Define your research question so that you can identify the body of literature you need to become conversant with and eventually review.
2. Extensively read and review a body of literature so that you are in a position to form appropriate, researchable questions.

What comes first, the chicken or the egg? In the case of reading and question setting, one need not precede the other; rather, they should be intertwined. Research generally starts with an idea – the idea may come from life experience, or it may come from reading. The idea should then lead to more reading, this reading should lead to the development of a potentially researchable question, the potential question should lead to more specific reading, and the specific reading should modify the question. As shown in Figure 3.4, forming a question is an iterative process, one that needs to be informed by reading at all stages.

A similar situation can occur when you begin to explore your methodology. Delving into 'how' your research might unfold can peak your interest in aspects of your topic not reflected in your currently defined question. Yet without that defined question, you might not have gone as far in exploring potential methods.

In fact, as you get going with your research, you may come across any number of factors that can lead you to: query your aims and objectives; see you modify your

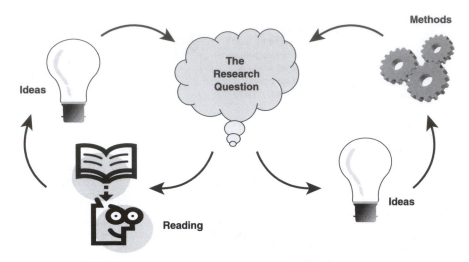

FIGURE 3.4   CYCLES OF RESEARCH QUESTION DEVELOPMENT

question; add questions; or even find new questions. The trick is figuring out what are 'tangents' you should let go, and what are evolutionary developments and necessary refinements that should be endemic to the process. Discussing the issues with your supervisor can provide you invaluable support in making such determinations.

Do I need a hypothesis?

This must be one of the most common questions asked by students, and there seems to be two clearly defined paradigmatic schools of thought driving the answers. Positivists (see Chapter 1) believe that the hypothesis is the cornerstone of scientific method and that it is an absolutely necessary component of the research process. Post–positivists, however, often view the hypothesis as a reduc-tionist device designed to constrain social research and take all life force from it.

Unfortunately, this tendency for dichotomization offers little assistance to students struggling to figure out if a hypothesis should drive their research. To answer this question, students need to know two things: (1) how 'hypothesis' is defined and; (2) whether what they want to know is appropriate to the task.

Hypothesis defined

Hypothesis: Logical conjecture (hunch or educated guess) about the nature of relationships between two or more variables expressed in the form of a testable statement.

In other words, a hypothesis takes your research question a step further by offer-ing a clear and concise statement of what you think you will find in relation to your variables, and what you are going to test. It is a tentative proposition that is subject to verification through subsequent investigation.

For example, let's say you're interested in research on divorce. Your research question is 'what factors contribute to a couple's decision to divorce?' Your hunch is that it has a lot to do with money – financial problems lead to divorce. Here you have all the factors needed for a hypothesis: logical conjecture (your hunch); variables (divorce and financial problems); and a relationship that can be tested (leads to). It is therefore a perfect question for a hypothesis – maybe something like 'financial problems increase the likelihood of divorce'.

Take another example from the concept map in Figure 3.3, which asks 'Do young girls have an unnatural perception of normal (body image)?' If your answer is 'yes – I think so', and you think you can give a reason, then you can write a hypothesis. In this case, you may think that young girls have an unnatural perception of normal body size because of the propensity of the media to use models, actors etc. who have a body-mass index well below average. Your hypothesis might be: 'A proliferation of thin female models and actors in the media gives young girls an unrealistic perception of normal body size.' Perception (variable) depends (relationship) on the size of models/actors in media (variable).

If you have a clearly defined research question – and you've got variables to explore – and you have a hunch about the relationship between those variables that can be tested, then a hypothesis is quite easy to formulate.

Appropriateness

Not all research questions can be easily 'converted' into a hypothesis, nor should they. The definition of a hypothesis limits its applicability for many types of research, and many research questions.

A hypothesis may *not* be appropriate if:

- *You do not have a hunch or educated guess about a particular situation* – For example, you may want to study alcoholism in the South Pacific, but you do not feel you are in a position to hypothesize because you are without an appropriate cultural context for educated guessing.
- *You do not have a set of defined variables* – Your research may be explorative in a bid to name the contributing factors to a particular situation. In the case of alcoholism in the Pacific Islands, your research aim may be to identify the factors or variables involved.
- *Your question centres on phenomenological description* (see Chapter 9) – For example, you may be interested in the question, 'What is the experience of drinking like for Pacific Islanders?' A relationship between variables does not really come into play.
- *Your question centres on an ethnographic study of a cultural group* (see Chapter 9) – For example, you might want to ask, 'What is the cultural response to a defined problem of alcoholism in a South Pacific village?' In this situation, force fitting a hypothesis can limit the potential for rich description.
- *Your aim is to engage in, and research, the process of collaborative change* (see Chapter 10) – In 'action research', methodology is both collaborative and emergent, making predetermined hypotheses impractical to use.

Whether a hypothesis is appropriate for your question depends on the nature of your inquiry. Again, the hypothesis is designed to express 'relationships between variables'. If your question boils down to this, a hypothesis can clarify your study to an extent even beyond a well-defined research question. If your question, however, does not explore 'relationships between variables', generating a hypothesis is likely to be an exercise in confusion.

CHARACTERISTICS OF GOOD QUESTIONS

Once you come up with a research question, you will want to know if it is worthy of research. Try running through the questions discussed below and summarized in Box 3.2. If you find yourself struggling to answer yes, it may indicate a need to rethink your questions.

☑ *Is the question right for you?*

They say you need to set a realistic research plan that includes assessing your level of commitment and the hours you will need to dedicate to the task ... then double it. Research often goes that way. You need to consider whether your question has the potential to hold your interest for the duration. As discussed in Chapter 2, it's very easy to lose motivation, and you are likely to need a genuine interest to stay on track.

There is, however, a flip side. Questions that can truly sustain your interest are usually the ones that best bring out your biases and subjectivities. As discussed in Chapter 4, these subjectivities and biases need to be carefully explored and managed in ways that will ensure the integrity of the research process. You may want to give careful consideration to:

- Researching questions where you know you have an axe to grind. Deep-seated prejudices do not generally lend themselves to credible research.
- Researching issues that are too close to home, i.e. domestic violence or sexual abuse. While researching such issues can be healing and cathartic, mixing personal and professional motivations in an intense fashion can be potentially detrimental to both agendas.

☑ *Is the question right for the field?*

The role of research is to do one or more of the following: advance knowledge in a particular area/field; improve professional practice; impact policy; or aid individuals. Research questions need to be significant − not only to you, but to a wider academic or professional audience as well.

Imagine that you want to undertake a particular project and you are applying for competitive funds to cover the cost of your research. Before you can convince a funding body that you are competent to do the research and that your approach is likely to give meaningful and credible results, you need to convince them that the topic itself is worthy of funding. You need to be able to articulate:

- Why the knowledge is important.
- What is the societal significance.
- How the findings will lead to societal advances.
- What improvements to professional practice and or policy may come from your research.

An early task in the research process is to be able to clearly articulate a rationale for your study that outlines the significance of the project. Your question needs to be informed by the literature and be important to your 'audience'.

☑ *Is the question well articulated?*

Research questions not only indicate the theory and literature you will need to explore and review, they also point to the data you will need to gather, and the methods you will use to collect and analyze this data. This makes clear articulation of research questions particularly important. Terms need to be unambiguous and clearly defined.

Take the question: 'Is pornography a problem?' As a question for general debate, it is probably fine. As a research question, however, it needs a fair bit of clarification. How are you defining pornography? What boundaries are you putting on the term? How are you defining problem? Social, moral, religious, economic, legal, all of the above? And who are you speaking for? A problem for whom? The more clarity in the question, the more work the question can do, making the direction of the study that much more defined.

Another point to consider is whether your question rests on unfounded assumptions. Take the question: 'How can women in Fijian villages overthrow the patriarchal structures that oppress them?' There are a few assumptions here that need to be checked:

1. That there are patriarchal structures. This information might exist and be found in literature. Assuming this is true…
2. That these patriarchal structures are indeed oppressive to the women concerned.
3. That there is a desire on the part of Fijian women to change these patriarchal structures.
4. That 'overthrowing' is the only option mentioned for change. It is a loaded term that alludes to strong personal subjectivities.

☑ *Is the question doable?*

Perhaps the main criterion of any good research question is that you will be able to undertake the research necessary to answer the question. Now that may sound incredibly obvious, but there are many questions that cannot be answered through the research process. Take for example the question: 'Does a difficult labour impact on a newborn's ability to love its mother?' Not researchable. For one, how do you define love? And even if you could define it, you would need to find a way to measure a newborn's ability to love. And even if you could do that, you are left with the dilemma of correlating that ability to love to a difficult labour. Interesting question, but not researchable.

Other questions might be researchable in theory, but not in practice. Student research projects are often constrained by:

- a lack of time
- a lack of funds
- a lack of expertise
- a lack of access and
- a lack of ethical clearance

Making sure your question is feasible and that it can lead to a completed project is worth doing early. Nothing is worse than realizing your project is not 'doable' after investing a large amount of time and energy.

☑ Does the question get the tick of approval from those in the know?

When it comes to articulating the final question it makes a tremendous amount of sense to ask the advice of those who know and do research. Most supervisors have a wealth of research and supervisory experience, and generally know what questions are 'researchable' and what questions will leave you with a massive headache. Run your question past lecturers in the field, your supervisor, and any 'experts' you may know.

Box 3.2   The Good Question Checklist

IS THE QUESTION RIGHT FOR ME?

- Will the question hold my interest?
- Can I manage any potential biases/subjectivities I may have?

IS THE QUESTION RIGHT FOR THE FIELD?

- Will the findings be considered significant?
- Will it make a contribution?

IS THE QUESTION WELL ARTICULATED?

- Are the terms well defined?
- Are there any unchecked assumptions?

IS THE QUESTION DOABLE?

- Can information be collected in an attempt to answer the question?
- Do I have the skills and expertise necessary to access this information? If not, can the skills be developed?

- Will I be able to get it all done within my time constraints?
- Are costs likely to exceed my budget?
- Are their any potential ethics problems?

DOES THE QUESTION GET THE TICK OF APPROVAL FROM THOSE IN THE KNOW?

- Does my supervisor think I am on the right track?
- Do 'experts' in the field think my question is relevant/important/doable?

CHAPTER SUMMARY

- Developing a well-articulated research question is an important part of the process because it defines the project, sets boundaries, and gives direction.
- The ability to generate topics for research can be a real challenge. If you can learn to hone in on your passions, use your curiosity, look for inspiration from the creative arts, and develop 'right-brained' skills like concept mapping, your ability to generate ideas will undoubtedly grow.
- Research directions are not always at the full discretion of the researcher. Practicalities include: appropriateness of the topic; your ability to get supervisory support; and funding opportunities and commitments.
- Moving from ideas to researchable question can be daunting. Using insights derived from personal experience, theory, observations, contemporary issues, and engagement with the literature can give you an 'angle' for your research.
- Narrowing, clarifying, and even redefining your questions is essential to the research process. Forming the right 'questions' should be seen as an iterative process that is informed by reading and doing at all stages.
- Hypotheses are designed to express relationships between variables. If this is the nature of your question, a hypothesis can add to your research. If your question is more descriptive or explorative, generating a hypothesis may not be appropriate.
- Good research questions need to be: right for you; right for the field; well articulated; doable; and get the tick of approval from those in the know.

4	**Exploring Power and Ethics in Research**

'What responsibilities do I have as a researcher?'

Chapter Preview

- Power, Politics, and Research
- Attributes and Attitudes
- Navigating Worldviews
- Ethical Responsibilities

POWER, POLITICS, AND RESEARCH

'No science is immune to the infection of politics and the corruption of power.'

–Jacob Bronowski

Research as a purely objective activity removed from all aspects of politics and power is a myth no longer accepted in the research world. As early as the turn of the twentieth century, Max Weber recognized that 'the existence of a scientific problem coincides personally with ... specifically oriented motives and values' ([1904] 1949). It is now recognized that research, and therefore researchers, are responsible for shaping the character of knowledge; and responsibilities associated with this knowledge production have led to a growing recognition and acceptance of the need for ethical and political awareness to be a mainstream consideration in the research process. Power, politics, and ethics must now be actively managed by the researcher.

Negotiating power

When I began 'doing' research, I don't think I felt necessarily powerful or privileged. I was just a student, just as I had always been. And even if I'd thought of myself as powerful, I don't think I would have made the connection between my position of power and my ability to conduct credible research. I was enrolled in a sociology department where the only students discussing issues like power and privilege were either the 'feminists' or 'theorists'. I was interested in 'science' not 'politics'. For me, power was not a consideration.

But of course it should have been, because I did have power – and I was exercising it. It was power derived from being well-educated and middle-class, power derived from being in a position to conduct research, power that comes from being in a position of control and authority, but it was power that I did not recognize, and therefore was in no position to manage.

This chapter stresses the need for all researchers, regardless of paradigmatic positioning, to recognize the political nature of research and to manage the position of power afforded the researcher. Researchers need to recognize that power can influence the research process, and that with power comes responsibility. Both the integrity of the knowledge produced and the well-being of the researched are dependent on the ethical negotiation of power and power relationships.

As will be discussed in this chapter, the negotiation of power involves accepting responsibility to:

- ☑ **Recognize and appreciate your own reality as a researcher. Awareness of your own basic attributes, ideological assumptions, position of power, and subjectivities is fundamental to the process. Your worldview and your position of power within a culture or subculture must be acknowledged.**
- ☑ **Be cognizant of how your worldview, assumptions, and position can unwittingly influence the research process. Knowing that how others see you and how you see the world can shape your research puts you in a position to protect the integrity of the process.**
- ☑ **Act ethically. Research should be conducted in a manner that balances the biases and subjectivities of the researcher, and protects the dignity and welfare of the researched.**

ATTRIBUTES AND ATTITUDES

In terms of objectivity, perhaps the best researchers would be entities that stand outside all aspects of humanity. They would not be identifiable by gender, class, or race; they would be fluent in all languages and dialects; and would be unaffected by history, politics, and any/all aspects of socialization. These 'super researchers' would be detached, unbiased, and unprejudiced. Sounds good, unless you stop to consider that they would also be unsympathetic, unempathetic, and without an ability to relate to what or whom they are studying. And besides, it is simply impossible. We are all products of the social forces that surround us. We carry with us the biases and prejudices of both our attributes and our socialization.

Recognizing the importance of 'self'

It would be nice to think that basic sociological constructs such as gender, age, ethnicity, religion, social class, etc., no longer caused or created prejudice. But it does. Your attributes affect both how others see you, and how you see the world. And as inequitable as it might be, certain traits are associated with power and privilege, while others are not. This fact is self-evident to anyone who has been the

TABLE 4.1 POWER, PRIVILEGE, AND SELF

Power and privilege	Disadvantage and marginalization
White	Person of colour
From a developed country	From a developing country
Christian	Muslim, Hindu, Buddhist
Post-graduate qualifications	Secondary education or less
Middle class	Working class
Midlife	Young/old
Male	Female
English as first language	No English skills

victim of discrimination. But for those whose attributes place them in the dominant position (see Table 4.1), potential power can go unrecognized. For years, anthropologists conducted research without this reflexive awareness of self, and for years, their findings were imprinted with the biases and assumptions of white, patriarchal, Western society. Recognizing the power and privilege associated with your own attributes, set within your research context, is the first step in the negotiation of power.

Now there is no doubt that the research process can be significantly impacted by the identity and reality of the researcher; and credibility and integrity is reliant upon reflexive awareness of how your attributes might affect the process. You have a gender, you come from a particular place, you have the characteristics of a certain race or races, you speak a particular language(s), and have an individual 'presence'. Others, including research participants, will naturally respond to these attributes.

Gender

Are you simply a 'researcher' or are you man/woman doing research? When you are conducting research, people will likely respond to you as a 'gendered' individual and, without even realizing it, you will most likely respond as a 'gendered' self. As highlighted in Box 4.1, the power of our sexuality is often underplayed and unseen. Yet, the rapport and trust you will build with respondents, the slant on stories you will hear, and the memories you will extract can be very dependent on gender.

Box 4.1 Gender, Sexuality, and Roller Coasters – Anne's Story

There was supposed to be a group of us going to the amusement park from graduate school, but it ended up just being John, his male partner, and me. Being the 'third wheel' to an in-love couple is bad enough, but to be the third wheel to a gay couple was really strange. All the little acts of chivalry that I never really noticed before were suddenly conspicuous by their absence. No one offered to pay for anything, no one let me go first, no one tried to win me anything. I even had to ride the roller coaster by myself. Two men together in the front carriage, me by myself behind them. You couldn't help but stop and

---

reflect on that. In fact, until that day, I had no idea how much I related to men as a 'woman'. I was shocked by the realization that my interactions with men were so coloured by my sexuality.

I reflected on this experience in relation to my own research, and realized just how important the role of gender and sexuality might be, particularly when collecting data. I realized that if I wanted to really understand what I was studying, my own practice as a researcher needed to take into account who I was.

Age

The answer to a question can often depend on who is doing the asking. Take for example the question, 'How was your weekend?' The answer you give your grandmother is probably quite different from the one you give your friends. Feeling comfortable with someone and being able to relate to them can often be age-dependent. Age can also be a factor in respondents wanting to impress a researcher, or in agreeing to do something they are not quite comfortable with. Ensuring the integrity of the research process necessarily involves consideration of the impacts of the researcher's age on both the respondent's welfare and on the data generated.

Ethnicity

There is little doubt that the ethnic and cultural background of the researcher can influence the research process. There is, however, tremendous debate about what is appropriate. Should only individuals from within a particular ethnic group study that ethnic group? What is the impact of 'outsiders' researching 'others'? What are the issues in building rapport and trust? What insights can researchers who research their own ethnic group, bring to a study – on the flip side, what biases might shape their findings? Can 'First World' research into the 'Third World' be done in a manner that can ensure that an imbalance of power is not skewing results?

Students often wish that I would give an answer other than 'it depends' to such questions. But it does depend. There are no hard-and-fast rules. In the end, it is up to individual researchers to consider the potential impacts on their research and to manage the process in a way that can best yield trustworthy and credible results – something that cannot happen if researchers are not cognizant of the issues.

Social status

Our position in society can have great bearing on the research process. Researchers are often from the 'right side of town', while the researched may not be. How do you break down potential barriers? How do you build trust and rapport? How do you get people to believe that you are not judging them? The way you dress, even the words you use can either build walls or build bridges. Being aware of your own social status and the social status of the researched puts you in a position to manage any potential power related issue that might influence your research.

Education

Being a student researcher is an interesting crossroad. You are a student – a position of minimal power. Yet you are likely to be better educated than many you will be researching – the power position. In addition, the respect afforded formal schooling can vary tremendously; from admiration, to deference, to scepticism over the value of book learning. It is therefore important for researchers to consider how respondents will relate to them as student researchers – and present themselves appropriately. Field-based researchers, for example, often learn that building trust and rapport grows from their ability to show respect for the researched regardless of any educational differential.

Position of power and privilege within a culture or subculture

An imbalance of power can be a common difficulty for researchers working within a culture where they are cast as a 'scientist' or 'expert'. Gary Larson once did a cartoon showing 'natives' in a hut frantically hiding their stereos and TVs while yelling out 'Anthropologists!' He very insightfully illustrates how deference to the expert changes the researched. The dilemma for many doing cross-cultural studies is knowing how you can conduct 'authentic' research when you are immersed in a culture where your position of power and privilege finds those you are researching acting in ways that may not be 'natural'.

NAVIGATING WORLDVIEWS

We make sense of the world through the rules we are given to interpret it. But because we are immersed in these rules and surrounded by them, they can be very hard to see. For example, those born into a religious faith don't often remember when they first heard about God; he simply is. Our sense of patriotism, our understandings of family, our belief in justice and equity – our morals and most core beliefs – are established within us before we have the ability to recognize or reflect on them as constructs. These beliefs are embedded within us. They are a part of how we understand and make sense of the world … and how we might research it. Working towards credible research therefore demands reflexive awareness of our worldviews and a conscious effort for us to take them into account as we enter into the research journey.

Western worldview

We are the products of a particular time and place in history. Our understandings of the world and the actions of those within it are generally seen through a 'Modern Western' worldview. But truth, morality, beauty, even what is seen as 'correct', varies widely across cultures. Sometime it takes immersion in a 'foreign' culture for us to see the constructed nature of our own. Table 4.2 offers a few alternatives for common Western beliefs that help expose our unchecked assumption about the nature of reality.

TABLE 4.2 DECONSTRUCTING A FEW ASSUMPTIONS OF THE WEST

Common Western conceptions	An alternate view
History is what happened in the past.	History is what someone consciously decided to record about the past.
Divorce is a major societal problem.	Divorce is the answer to the rampant societal problem of bad marriages, and maybe the outdated construct of marriage itself.
If we do not take care of this Earth, we will destroy it.	The world will survive; the only thing we will destroy is its capacity to support human life.
Dog is man's best friend.	In the Islamic faith, dogs are seen as unclean. Angels will not enter a house where a dog is fed.
The internet now connects the whole world.	Almost half the world's population (2.7 of 6.2 billion people) do not have electricity. Less than 1% own a computer.

Seeing the world through coloured glasses

Without an appreciation of how attributes, positions of power and privilege, and worldviews conspire to create subjectivities, researchers can easily fall into the trap of judging the reality of others in relation to their own reality. Suspending judgement is crucial, yet it can be quite a challenge when you are faced with realities, belief systems, and worldviews so different from your own. I recently saw an insightful t–shirt that said, 'reality' is the only word in the English language that should always be in quotation marks. Realities vary, and researchers need to accept the potential for realities they may not understand.

The challenge for lab–based scientists is to put aside any preconceived notions about what is under the microscope and be perfectly objective. Complexity of subjectivities is generally minimal and manageable, because what is being researched is generally outside the self. The challenge for social science researchers is much more difficult because it is society itself that is under the microscope, and researchers are necessarily a product of society. Social science researchers need to recognize how their attributes and ideological assumptions embed bias and subjectivity into identity. Researchers are value–bound – and given that social science research involves analysis set within particular value systems, the ability to be objective is problematic, if not impossible.

All aspects of the research process need to be considered in light of the assumptions and biases of the researcher. Without recognition of the impact of one's own ideological positioning, ensuring unbiased research is nonsensical. Researchers need to be aware that a lack of reflexivity will find research tainted with a variety of unrecognized preconceptions.

The tendency to be 'self'-centric

Feminists have long critiqued the social sciences for their tendency to analyze and interpret the world from a privileged, white, male perspective. If who we are colours what we see and how we interpret it, then the need to hear, see, and appreciate multiple perspectives or realities is essential to rigorous research. For example, imagine the difficulty in trying to analyze the reluctance of black inner-city youth to enter paid employment if you as a researcher have no appreciation of a 'culture of poverty'; a cultural reality likely to be far removed from your own middle-class existence. Suspending judgements based on your own worldview becomes essential, yet if the researcher is unreflexive of his or her own positioning, it is virtually impossible.

A different type of example comes from a student of mine in Hong Kong who decided to investigate workers' complaints about the comfort of their new 'ergonomic' desks. He contacted the 'international' company and was told that the desk design was based on research into the most comfortable dimensions for average office workers. It turned out, however, that 'average' referred to US males who are much larger than Asian males, let alone Asian females. The possibilities of 'others' must not have entered this 'international' company's research design, even though they market extensively throughout Asia.

Insensitivity to race, class, culture, and gender

Insensitivity often arises from the tendency for researchers to be self-centric, and refers to the practice of ignoring race, sex, class, gender etc., as possible variables in a study. Researchers need to be cognizant of the need to allow for alternate realities based on the unique attributes of the researched. For example, a study of the fear of walking alone at night would be less meaningful without gender as one significant variable.

Only hearing the dominant voice(s)

The tendency to hear and represent only the dominant occurs when researchers study individuals of only one race, class, gender, etc. (often the characteristics or comfort zone of the researcher) but then present the findings as though they are applicable to a larger population. For example, surveying only residential university students, and then talking about university students in general. Or presenting the concerns of a multicultural community assessed through a survey of residents, without taking into consideration the exclusion of those who cannot speak English. Attempting to empower traditionally marginalized voices is essential in responsible research. Indigenous peoples, minorities, children, women, gays, and lesbians are often not heard, yet their voices are essential to any rich social fabric being explored. Given that research findings are often taken as 'truth', it is essential that all perspectives are considered as we attempt to speak of or for a society or culture. (Box 4.2).

Box 4.2   The People in my Shire – Keith's story

I was conducting some research with a local council and had already interviewed the mayor and a few of the local councillors about the community, when I attended my first council meeting. The meeting was a real eye opener. The ethnic background for the region I was studying was about 45% Anglo,

25% Asian, 20% Indian, and 10% Greek, with at least seven different religions. Yet, when I walked into the meeting I was asked to give my 'Christian' name, and the meeting started with a prayer from the Protestant minister. At that stage, I took a good look around and realized that ALL of the councillors looked to be of Anglo descent. In fact, almost everyone present at the meeting was Anglo.

I then thought of all the times the mayor and councillors had spoken of their 'community'. I was left wondering what their 'community' was. Was their frame of reference the range of constituents in their jurisdiction, or was their frame of reference individuals with the same demographic background as themselves – in other words 'community' as the white Christians who came to the council meetings. From that point on I was committed to ensuring that my research reflected the 'real' community, not just those with the ability/propensity to be heard.

Dichotomization and double standards

Dichotomization refers to the tendency to put groups at two separate ends of the spectrum without recognition of overlapping characteristics. This can be seen in our propensity to talk about 'men' and 'women' or 'blacks' and 'whites'. Research that adopts this tendency to dichotomize risks embedding stereotypes and societal assumptions into the research process, limiting possibilities for drawing rich conclusions outside the expected.

Using a double standard refers to analysis of the same behaviours, situations, or characteristics by different criteria, depending on whether respondents are black or white, male or female, rich or poor, etc., For example, studying the increasing tendency of families to put infants in childcare, yet only asking the mother (and not the father) about the decision to work full-time; or exploring motivations for attending university and having different sets of responses for different social classes. In research, there is an essential need to guard against the assumptions and biases inherent within our society.

Disregard for the power of language

Research is coloured by our use of language in a number of ways. First is the subtle yet formidable power of words themselves. The words we use to speak to respondents can be easily misunderstood and misrepresented. Similarly, the words of respondents can be easily misconstrued by the researcher. For example, language that might be 'shocking' for one group, might be quite 'everyday' for another. Analysis of words needs to come from the perspective and reality of the researched, not the researcher.

Working with respondents with whom you do not share a common language presents an added level of difficulty for the researcher. There does not exist a computer program that can accurately translate one language to another; and that is because languages are highly metaphorical, mythical, poetic, and are full of hidden meanings, riddles, and assumptions. Accurate interpretations, let alone the nuances of language and speech, are often lost through interpreters or in the process of translation. The researcher who assumes that English can capture thoughts processed in a different language with any sophistication risks reducing the richness and complexity of a respondent's ideas and views. Researchers working outside their first language need to find ways to confirm that their data's accuracy and richness is not lost in the process of interpretation and translation.

ETHICAL RESPONSIBILITIES

Researchers are unconditionally responsible for the integrity of the research process. The power to produce knowledge requires responsibility for integrity in its production. Similarly, the power relation inherent in researcher–researched interactions requires responsibility to ensure the dignity and well-being of the researched. Ethics is foundational to all research; with power comes responsibility.

Most universities will require you to obtain ethics approval from relevant committee(s) for any study you plan to undertake. This will require you to carefully examine all aspects of your study for ethical implications, and address each aspect in a systematic manner. This is required to ensure the integrity of the knowledge produced and to promote the practice of ethical responsibilities towards participants.

Responsibility for the production of knowledge

Because the aim of research is to produce new knowledge, it is crucial that the task is approached with integrity and rigour. Responsibility for knowledge production requires that researchers attempt to: recognize and balance subjectivities; give accurate research accounts; act within the law; and develop required expertise.

Recognizing, understanding, and balancing subjectivities

As discussed throughout this chapter, researchers need to: recognize their 'reality'; consider how this 'reality' may affect the researched and the research process; and attempt to manage, negotiate and balance their research in a manner that can best ensure the integrity and authenticity of the knowledge produced. Unfortunately, managing the influence of a researcher's reality is not straightforward; there are no hard-and-fast rules that cover all situations. Box 4.3, however, does offer a few strategies that reflexive researchers can call upon in an attempt to balance subjectivities, and conduct responsible research.

> ### Box 4.3   Strategies for Negotiating Researcher Subjectivities
>
> **APPRECIATING ALTERNATE 'REALITIES'**
>
> - Actively explore the personal and societal assumptions that underpin the understandings of the researcher and the researched, and accept that these may be quite distinct.

- Suspend initial judgements. We live in a society where it is common to judge what we do not understand. Yet as researchers, not understanding is precisely why it is important not to judge.
- Check your interpretation of events, situations, and phenomena with 'insiders'. This is particularly relevant in cross-cultural research. Finding out how someone from within a cultural reality understands a situation can help illuminate your own potential biases.

GETTING THE FULL STORY

- Attempt to empower silenced voices – those we seek out and those willing to participate are often those with the strongest voices. Your research design should seek representation from all those you wish your research to speak for or about.
- Seek out and incorporate alternate and pluralistic points of view. In a bid to crystallize our interpretations, the richness and complexity that can come from viewpoints outside the dominant can be lost.

ENSURING THE AUTHENTICITY OF DATA

- Work towards researcher–researched relationships built on trust and mutual respect. Recognizing and appreciating the researched for what they are giving to the research process can go a long way in the researched feeling comfortable enough to expose themselves and provide candid data.
- Triangulating data and findings. This refers to using more than one source of data to confirm the authenticity of each source. For example, exploring the commonalities and divergences in data derived from observations, interviews, and surveys.
- Ask the researched to confirm the accuracy, relevance, and authenticity of interpretations. Researchers can ask respondents to confirm that they have captured the essence of their 'story'.

Accurate reporting

It is the responsibility of the researcher to minimize the possibility that the results they generate are false or misleading. In order to safeguard against 'fraud', researchers are expected to be open and accountable. In fact, some codes of ethics require that researchers keep their raw data for a period of five to seven years. Researchers are also encouraged to admit any shortcomings and outline any limitations within their research process, thereby protecting themselves from accusations of fraud or misrepresentation. Nevertheless, misrepresentation and fraud are thought to be quite rampant, particularly in student research. The price, however, is high. Students shown to be acting fraudulently are often terminated from their degree programmes. Researchers (including students) have been known to:

- blatantly fabricate data or falsify results
- omit cases or fiddle with numbers in order to show 'significance'

- plagiarize passages from articles or books without crediting the original author(s)
- misrepresent authorship by: (1) using a ghost writer; (2) taking full credit for authorship when more than one author was involved; (3) naming a co-author who had no involvement with the study.

Acting within the law

Clearly the laws of society stand in the world of research. If it is illegal for the general public, then it is illegal for a researcher or a research participant. All research must abide by common law.

Researchers also need to consider whether there is an obligation to report any illegal activities they may become aware of in the course of their research. For example, imagine you've come across a case of child abuse where you think there is imminent danger. Do you have an ethical obligation to maintain promised confidentiality; a moral obligation to 'do something'; a legal obligation to go to the police; or all three? The law here is often ambiguous and can vary by both country and case. If your research is likely to contend with illegal activities, getting the advice and approval of an appropriate ethics committee is imperative.

Develop appropriate expertise and experience

Researchers, including student researchers, are responsible for knowing the research landscape before conducting their study. There is an implicit obligation for researchers to know about: their topic; previous research; and commonly used methods, including their shortcomings. Researchers are also expected to have, or be able to draw on, experience in conducting research.

Responsibility for the researched

Responsibility for the dignity, respect, and welfare of respondents, both mentally and physically, is central to research ethics. Respecting the rights of individuals and cultural groups; researching in an equitable fashion; and ensuring that no harm will come to participants are prerequisites for any research study.

Respecting the rights of cultural groups

Certain aspects of research may be deemed culturally inappropriate. In Aboriginal cultures in Australia, for example, it is offensive to look at images of the deceased. A research project that asked this of Aboriginal respondents would not be acceptable. Anthropologists and sociologists generally believe that their first responsibility is to the lives and cultures they are researching. The interests of the researched takes precedence over any other research goals.

Designing and conducting equitable research

Just and equitable research is concerned with the practice of asking only some people to participate in research, while others are immune from such requests. A student of mine came across this principle when he sought permission to interview students who were part of a university entrance programme for the underprivileged. The request to interview this group of students was met by a definitive NO from the programme coordinator. As it turned out, it was the third such request to 'research' that group of students and the coordinator wanted it known that that group of students was at university *to study* not *be studied*.

Ensuring respondents have given informed consent

The concept of informed consent emphasizes the importance of researchers accurately informing respondents/participants of the nature of their research. Participants can only give informed consent if they have a full understanding of their requested involvement in a research project, including time commitment, type of activity, topics that will be covered, and all physical and emotional risks potentially involved. Informed consent implies that participants are:

- *Competent* – they have the intellectual capacity and psychological maturity necessary to understand the nature of the research and their involvement in the study.
- *Autonomous* – they are making self-directed and self-determined choices. Others, such as parents or guardians, cannot make the decision to participate for them.
- *Involved voluntarily* – they must be made aware of the research being conducted. Research 'on them' cannot be conducted without their knowledge and consent.
- *Aware of the right to discontinue* – participants are under no obligation to continue their involvement, and pressure to continue should not be applied.
- *Not deceived* – researchers need to be honest about the nature of their research, about the affiliation or professional standing, and the intended use of their study.
- *Not coerced* – positions of power should not be used to get individuals to participate in a study, as can happen when employers or teachers apply pressure on their charges to engage in research.
- *Not induced* – an offer of money or some other reward that entices individuals to participate in research that they would otherwise avoid is considered inducement. While it may be acceptable to compensate individuals for their time and effort, it should not be to an extent where it compromises a potential participant's judgement.

Ensuring no harm comes to respondents

The concept of harm in social science research generally refers to emotional or psychological harm, rather than physical harm. This can make protection against 'harm' a tricky area. Risks of psychological harm can be hard to identify and difficult to predict. Asking participants to engage in research that sparks resentment, causes fear or anxiety, is demeaning or embarrassing, or causes one to relive unpleasant memories or emotionally trying times, can be unplanned and unintentional – yet easy to do.

You will still find some research texts referring to the concept of 'potential benefits outweighing potential harm', but this needs to be seriously questioned.

Regardless of any potential benefits to society, or even informed consent, risks of any type of harm, including damage to self-esteem or self-respect, should be ethically and/or morally unacceptable. It is also worth remembering how litigious society has become. Even if your conscience or your professional ethics can justify risk, your wallet may not.

Ensuring confidentiality and, if appropriate, anonymity

Confidentiality involves protecting the identity of those providing research data. While researchers are able to identify the data generated by a particular respondent, they agree to not make any such identification public; all identifying data remains solely with the researcher. Protection of confidentiality may involve secure storage of data; restricting access to raw data; obtaining permission for subsequent use of data; publication of research findings in a manner that does not allow for ready identification of subjects; and eventual destruction of raw data.

There are two cases where ensuring confidentiality can become problematic. The first is when it is possible for others to figure out who actual respondents are. Pseudonyms may not be enough to hide identity, particularly when the role the individual plays in a community or organization is made public. If others can figure out who you are speaking about, or who is doing the speaking, the researcher needs to further mask identity or seek approval for disclosure from the respondent. The second case involves research that may uncover illegal activities. In the legal system, researchers are not afforded the same rights as lawyers, doctors, and priests. A researcher's data and files can be subpoenaed by the courts; assurances of confidentiality do not outweigh legal obligation.

Anonymity goes a step beyond confidentiality and refers to protection against identification from even the researcher. Information, data, and responses that are collected anonymously cannot be identified with a particular respondent. A good example of this is 'anonymous' class evaluations where students should feel confident that there is no chance of damning feedback coming back to bite them.

CHAPTER SUMMARY

- There is growing acceptance of the power inherent in creating knowledge. With this acceptance comes acknowledgement of the need for ethical and political awareness to be a mainstream consideration in the research process.
- Negotiating power involves the researchers' need to: recognize their subjectivities; consider how their positioning may impact on the researched and the research process; and attempt to manage their research in a manner that best ensures integrity and authenticity – while ensuring the researcheds' dignity and welfare.
- The 'reality' of researchers including their attributes and worldview can influence the research process. Being cognizant of the researchers' 'reality' is fundamental to the process.

- How researchers are 'seen' can influence the nature of researcher–researched interactions. These interactions are often characterized by an imbalance of power that needs to be negotiated in order to ensure ethical treatment of the respondent and authenticity in data collection.
- How researchers 'see' the world can also influence the research process. Researchers need to guard against research tainted with insensitivity, over generalizations, double standards, and dichotomizations.
- Researchers are ethically responsible for integrity in the production of knowledge, as well as the dignity and welfare of the researched.
- Integrity in the production of knowledge demands that researchers: recognize, understand, and balance their subjectivities; accurately report on their research; act within the law; and develop appropriate expertise and experience.
- Responsibility to the researched demands that researchers: show respect for cultural beliefs; treat respondents in a manner that is just and equitable; get informed consent from all research participants; do no harm through the research process; and protect the confidentiality of the researched.

5

Indicators of Good Research

'How do I know that what I have done will be credible in the research world?'

Chapter Preview

- Frameworks for Credibility
- Managing Subjectivities
- Striving for Methodological Consistency
- Capturing 'Truth'
- Working Towards Applicability
- The Need for Accountability

FRAMEWORKS FOR CREDIBILITY

Credibility: The quality, capability, or power to elicit belief.

For research to have the potential to create new knowledge, it must be seen as credible. In other words, it must have the 'power to elicit belief'. Research that is not seen as credible is unlikely to be accepted as a contribution to a larger body of knowledge. Now outside the research world, credibility can come from that which is believable, convincing, plausible, likely, probable, and realistic. But within the research world, credibility takes on a more specialized meaning and is demonstrated by indicators such as reliability, validity, authenticity, neutrality, auditability, etc. Such indicators point to research that has been approached as disciplined rigorous inquiry and is therefore likely to be accepted as a valued contribution to knowledge.

One of the early challenges for research students is to become conversant with indicators of good research. Not only will you need to work towards such indicators in your own research, your ability to critically engage with relevant literature will be enhanced if you can assess the work of others in accordance with appropriate criteria. Critical awareness and understanding of the appropriate indicators of quality research is necessary groundwork.

Developing an 'appropriate' framework

Knowing what indicators are relevant and appropriate for a particular research project is not without ambiguity. As the assumptions that underpin research expand beyond the realms of positivist knowing (see Chapter 1), debate over how research should be critically evaluated intensifies. For positivists, indicators of good research are premised around a world that can be quantifiably measured through defined rules of inquiry; can be approached with objectivity; and is, in fact, knowable. These assumptions, however, have been called into question by those critiquing the positivist paradigm. It is now recognized that an alternative set of indicators is more appropriate for research premised around a 'post-positivist' world — a world that is recognized as infinitely complex and without a defined 'truth'; recognizes and values subjectivities; and is unlikely to be captured by statistics alone.

The difficulty for many researchers is that the assumptions that underpin their research may not fit neatly into one paradigmatic way of knowing. To pigeonhole themselves and their research into either positivist or post-positivist frameworks limits their ability to think and act reflexively. Designing studies that can cross the constructed boundaries dividing these two camps is difficult when you adopt frameworks derived from within the paradigms.

So rather than be paradigmatically based, this chapter is issue-based in an attempt to raise an awareness of the challenges that need to be met in order to ensure good research. As shown in Table 5.1, the chapter is structured around a set of key questions that researchers can use as a framework for evaluating the credibility of their own work as well as the work of others. It is then up to the researcher to determine the appropriate indicators for each of these questions through an examination of their own worldview and assumptions, the aims and objectives of the research, and the methodological approaches adopted.

MANAGING SUBJECTIVITIES

The question here is not whether researchers are subjective entities, but rather: (1) do researchers recognize their subjective positioning; and (2) do they negotiate and manage their potential biases (for a much fuller discussion of researcher subjectivities please see Chapter 4). In social and applied science research, three indicators are generally used to assess whether the potential for researcher bias has been suitably managed. The most appropriate indicator to use is dependent upon both the assumptions of the researcher and the nature of the research endeavour.

Objectivity

Objectivity has long been a standard benchmark in scientific research and indicates that judgements, findings, and conclusions are completely independent of personal subjectivities. Objectivity implies distance between the researcher and the researched, and suggests that relationships are mediated by protocol, theory, and method. This standard exists in order to prevent personal bias from 'contaminating' results — a goal held by many post-positivist, as well as positivist, researchers.

The real question, then, is whether a subjective individual can conduct objective research. The answer is not without tremendous debate. There are research

TABLE 5.1   INDICATORS OF 'GOOD' RESEARCH BY ISSUES AND PARADIGM

'Positivist' Indicators	'Post-Positivist' Indicators
Have subjectivities been managed?	
Objectivity – conclusions based on observable phenomena; not influenced by emotions, personal prejudices, or subjectivities	*Neutrality* – subjectivities recognized and negotiated in a manner that attempts to avoid biasing results/conclusions
	Subjectivity with transparency – acceptance and disclosure of subjective positioning and how it might impact on the research process, including conclusions drawn
Are methods approached with consistency?	
Reliability – concerned with internal consistency, i.e. whether data/results collected, measured, or generated are the same under repeated trials	*Dependability* – accepts that reliability in studies of the social may not be possible, but attests that methods are systematic, well-documented, and designed to account for research subjectivities
Has 'true essence' been captured?	
Validity – concerned with truth value; i.e. whether conclusions are 'correct'. Also considers whether methods, approaches and techniques actually relate to what is being explored	*Authenticity* – concerned with truth value while recognizing that multiple truths may exist. Also concerned with describing the deep structure of experience/phenomenon in a manner that is 'true' to the experience
Are findings applicable outside the immediate frame of reference?	
Generalizability – whether findings and/or conclusions from a sample, setting, or group are directly applicable to a larger population, a different setting, or to another group	*Transferability* – whether findings and/or conclusions from a sample, setting, or group lead to lessons learned that may be germane to a larger population, a different setting, or to another group
Can the research be verified?	
Reproducibility – concerned with whether results/conclusions would be supported if the same methodology was used in a different study with the same/similar context	*Auditability* – accepts the importance of the research context and therefore seeks full explication of methods to allow others to see how and why the researchers arrived at their conclusions

topics in which curiosity builds a desire for open exploration without preconceived notions. There are also research projects for which the methodological protocols have built-in safeguards designed to preclude any researcher bias. In these cases, researchers may legitimately claim that regardless of who they are, their conduct as a researcher is strictly objective.

Neutrality

Neutrality is very akin to objectivity, but more explicitly recognizes that most researchers have some positioning in relation to their research topics, making objectivity problematic and perhaps unachievable. The desire to keep findings and conclusions free from bias, however, still remains and is addressed through a process of recognizing, naming, and developing strategies for counteracting identified subjectivities. Neutrality demands that researchers reflect on their own subjective positioning and attempt to mediate them in order to be true to the research process. This indicator suggests that the researcher has engaged in reflexive practice that has considered issues of personal positioning.

Subjectivity with transparency

Quite far removed from the 'objective' scientist is the researcher with an agenda; the researcher who wishes to emancipate, liberate, and work towards sometimes radical change. Activist or researcher? The construction of the social sciences may lead you to say 'activist', but a history of research dedicated to liberation and on-the-ground change is quite rich – with Karl Marx easily falling into this domain (Chapter 10 offers a full discussion of the nature of change-based research and its place in social/applied science).

The nature of agenda-based research means that subjectivities take on a key role in the research process, and are managed only to the extent that they are made transparent and do not bias data analysis. The goals, aims, and objectives of this type of research need to articulate both the knowledge that is likely to result from the process, as well as the researcher's agenda for change. Similarly, the background and rationale of the study should clearly show the positioning of the researcher. Others can then be in a position to critically evaluate the nature and credibility of the knowledge produced, given named agendas and subjectivities.

STRIVING FOR METHODOLOGICAL CONSISTENCY

Regardless of paradigm or approach, researching is not a haphazard activity. Rather, it is an activity that needs to be approached with both discipline and rigour. New knowledge and even change can be the result of research; therefore, methods need to be consistent. Two indicators, reliability and dependability, are offered to assess consistency and quality control in method, and can be delineated by the researcher's assumptions regarding the nature of the researched.

Reliability

Reliability is premised on the notion that there is some sense of uniformity or standardization in what is being measured, and that methods need to consistently capture what is being explored. Reliability is thus the extent to which a measure, procedure, or instrument provides the same result on repeated trials. A good example is bathroom scales. If you were to jump on your scales ten times in a row and got the same results each time, the scales would be reliable. The scale could be wrong – it may always be ten pounds heavy or light – but it would be reliable. A more complicated example might be trying to measure self-esteem with a questionnaire. First, you would need to believe that self-esteem could be measured as a consistent construct. Reliability would then mean that results are not dependent on things like who administered the questionnaire, what kind of day respondents were having, or whether or not they took their medication. The indicator of reliability gives an assurance that the tools you are using will generate 'consistent' findings. Again, they may be wrong (see Capturing 'Truth' below), but they are constant.

Dependability

Dependability assumes that what is being studied may not be reliable, consistent, or standard – or that capturing what is seen as standard may not be possible. Are people consistent? It is a lot easier to look for consistency in the laboratory than it is in society. People are complex and multifaceted and at any given time, for any given reason, they may only reveal part of themselves. People provide information about themselves that can shift for any number of reasons. Who does the asking; what mood they are in; and what happened the night before may lead to varied, yet possibly all authentic, presentations of self.

Dependability indicates quality assurance through methodological protocols that are designed and developed in a manner that is consistent, logical, systematic, well-documented, and designed to account for research subjectivities. If your assumptions about the nature of the researched find you questioning whether reliability is even possible, dependability can be a useful alternative indicator.

CAPTURING 'TRUTH'

> 'The truth is out there.' –Fox Mulder
> vs
> 'There are no facts, only interpretations.' –Nietzsche

The indicators you would use to show 'truth' clearly depend on how you define and understand the nature of truth. The indicator of validity would be appropriate if you believe that there is only one truth that can be uncovered and understood, while authenticity is more likely to be appropriate if you believe that there may be more than one version of any event, and that truth is dependent on context.

Regardless of the indicator you see as most appropriate for your study, credibility rests on whether your data has the 'power to elicit belief'; do others believe what you have said. I think the most exciting feedback I ever received came from a well-respected professor who was asked to comment on an early work. His comment: 'Not only is this pretty good, but I think the author may be right!'

Validity

Validity is premised on the assumption that what is being studied can be measured or captured, and seeks to confirm the truth and accuracy of this measured and captured 'data', as well as the truth and accuracy of any findings or conclusions drawn from the data. It indicates that the conclusions you have drawn are trustworthy. There is a clear relationship between the reality that is studied and the reality that is reported, with cohesion between the conceptual frameworks, questions asked, and findings evident. Conclusions need to be justified from what was found, and what was found needs to accurately reflect what was being studied.

For example, for there to be validity in the finding 'gender identification causes girls to relate better to their mothers than do boys', you would have to: (1) show that how you measured 'relate' truly reflected 'relating'; (2) show that you had a sample size large enough and representative enough to make the claim about girls and boys in general; (3) show that it truly is gender identification that is affecting the ability to relate, and not any other factors. In short, validity indicates that your methods warrant your conclusions.

Authenticity

Authenticity is also concerned with truth value, but allows for an expansion of the conventional conception of singular truths. For example, I know that when my parents describe our family, it sounds nothing like the family I lived with for the first 16 years of my life. And I'm sure my siblings would describe a reality distinct from both that of my parents and myself – yet no one is wrong. It is simply a case of multiple realities – all valid, all true – at least from the perspective of those doing the describing. Authenticity indicates that while the links between conceptual frameworks, questions, and findings may not lead to a single valid truth; rigour and reflexive practice has assured that conclusions are justified, credible, and trustworthy.

Box 5.1   Whose Reality Anyway?

I once took a group of humanities students to a local school to look at the layout of the 5th grade classroom. There were 42 10-year-old children sitting down in seven rows of six, all facing forward. The teacher was standing in the middle of the front of the classroom, facing the children. I broke my students up into two groups and asked them to find out why the classroom was set up in this manner.

The eventual responses were quite distinct. The first group attempted to answer the question from the perspective of the teacher. They interviewed her and found that this was the best set-up, and that there is no other logical way the room could be arranged. The students need to face both the teacher and the blackboard. They also found that this set-up minimized the propensity for the children to distract or be distracted by each other, and allowed them to direct their focus on the teacher.

The analysis of the second group was completely different. They answered the question from the perspective of critical literature, and claimed that the structure was typical of how most classrooms are set up, which is a clear mechanism of control. The seating arrangement exists because it facilitates a relationship of power between teacher and student that is all one way. There is no respect for what peers can give to each other. This structure alienates students from each other, making them unable to act as a collective and therefore rendering them powerless. It also limits learning because it tends to facilitate rote memorization, rather than hands-on engagement.

Which group was right? I guess this is the point – it is not a matter of right or wrong. It is simply a matter of reality and perspective; and a cognizance of the realities you are presenting as well as those you are not.

WORKING TOWARDS APPLICABILITY

The credibility of a research project relies in part on the broad applicability of its findings. To have conclusions relevant to only a particular sample or only within a particular research setting severely limits the capacity of the research to represent significant new knowledge. Indicators of applicability show that findings have relevance for a larger sector of society than the sampling or setting itself, thereby showing consequence and worth. The standard indicator of applicability has long been generalizability – whether a sample speaks for a population. The proliferation of smaller-scale studies focusing on the collection and analysis of primarily qualitative data, however, has led to the need for alternative indicators such as transferability – whether lessons learned have relevance to other settings/populations.

Generalizability

Generalizability (also referred to as external validity) indicates that the findings of a sample are directly applicable to a larger population. While findings from the sample may vary to that of the population, findings considered generalizable show statistical probability of being representative. A good example is political polling where less than 1% of a population might be polled in order to estimate voting patterns for the entire population. Speaking for a population, however, is far from straightforward and requires appropriate sampling strategies that ensure both adequate and broad representation (see Chapter 8). This is most likely to be possible for studies whose large sample sizes often limit data to that of a quantitative nature.

Transferability

There are a range of studies that do not have the sample size necessary to ensure generalizability. These may be case studies, action research projects, or studies focused on the collection of qualitative data. Nevertheless, illustrating the significance of findings to larger populations or within other contexts is still often a goal. For research of this nature, transferability can be a useful indicator of applicability. Rather than make 'claims' about populations, transferability highlights that lessons learned are likely to be applicable in alternative settings or across populations. For example, the results of an in-depth case study of university agricultural students in South America may not be generalizable to university agricultural students worldwide, but there are likely to be lessons learned that could illuminate relevant issues within other cultures. The indicator of transferability suggests that researchers have provided a highly detailed description of the research context and methods so that determinations regarding applicability can be made by those reading the research account.

THE NEED FOR ACCOUNTABILITY

'In the spider-web of facts, many a truth is strangled.'

–Paul Eldridge

Indicators for good research are necessary because conducting research is a highly complex process fraught with the potential for error, inaccuracy, and misinterpretation. Without a doubt, it is hard to get it right – and that is not just for the student researcher. As you become more and more familiar with the standards of good research, you will find that it is not too difficult to find fault with, and critique, many of the studies that make up an area of literature. It is therefore expected that researching be a process that is both open and accountable. Others should be able to assess whether the methods and approaches used by researchers logically lead to the conclusions drawn.

Auditability

The indicator of auditability points to full explication of methods so that others can trace the research process and appreciate how and why researchers came up with their data, findings, and conclusions. All research, regardless of paradigm, approach, or methods, should be auditable. It is expected that research be open and transparent. Readers should not be left in the dark in relation to any aspect of the research process. The explication of the process should contain sufficient details of the research context, the researched, and the methods used to collect and analyzes data, so that other researchers can evaluate or audit the original research process. This serves a number of purposes. First, the explication of the research process can be part of the learning for readers – those reviewing literature are often looking for methodological references as well as topical ones. Second, the development of a sound methodological protocol for investigating a particular topic can be a contribution to knowledge in its own right. Finally, full explication of the research process puts others in a position to make determinations about the process's credibility in order to evaluate the trustworthiness of the data and the value of the study.

Reproducibility

Reproducibility is directly concerned with issues of credibility and indicates that the research process can be replicated in order to verify research findings. In other words, conclusions would be supported if the same methodology was used in a different study with the same/similar context. Suppose, for instance, that the findings of a particular study showed a correlation between the use of microwave ovens and the development of warts. The credibility of these findings might be initially doubted. If a variety of researchers, however, found the same results using the same methods, credibility would undoubtedly increase. If a study, when reproduced, leads to similar conclusions, then the research process is seen to be scientifically sound. Reproducibility, however, can only be expected in studies where the influence of context, the subjectivities of the researcher, and any variability within or of the researched is accounted for and controlled.

CHAPTER SUMMARY

- Understanding appropriate credibility indicators is crucial to critically reviewing relevant literature and reflexively designing sound methodologies.
- Traditional indicators of 'good' research emerged from the assumptions of positivism and include: objectivity; reliability; validity; generalizability; and reproducibility. Post-positivist researchers have now complemented these indicators with those more suitable to post-positivist assumptions and include: neutrality or transparent subjectivity; dependability; authenticity; transferability; and auditability.
- Rather than selecting indicators strictly by paradigm, researchers are encouraged to determine appropriate indicators by critically examining their own worldview and assumptions; the aims and objectives of their research; and their methodological approaches.
- In order to manage subjectivities, researchers need to reflect on their own positioning and determine whether they will approach their research with objectivity, neutrality, or with named subjectivities.
- Methods need to be approached with consistency, and can be shown through reliability or dependability. Reliability assumes standardization in the researched and indicates that methods can consistently capture what is being explored. Dependability does not assume standardization or the potential for capturing it, but works towards quality assurance through conscientiously developed methods.
- The indicators used to show 'truth' hinge on the how truth itself is defined. Validity seeks to establish accurate and true findings and assumes that 'truth' is both knowable and measurable. Authenticity is also concerned with truth, but recognizes the potential for multiple and alternate realities.
- Researchers often seek findings that are applicable beyond an immediate frame of reference. Generalizability, whether a sample speaks for the population, is an appropriate indicator of applicability for large-scale studies. Transferability, whether there

are lessons learned that have relevance to other settings/populations, is more appropriate for smaller-scale studies focusing on the collection and analysis of qualitative data.

- Researching is expected to be an open, accountable, and verifiable process. Auditability relates to the full explication of methods so that others can trace/audit the research process and should apply to all types of research. Reproducibility, whether conclusions would be supported if the same methodology was used in a study of the same/similar context, is a more rigorous form of verification that requires that all variations in research context can be controlled.

6

Working with Literature

'What should I be reading, and what do I do with it all?'

Chapter Preview

- The Importance of Working with Literature
- Finding Literature
- Managing the Literature
- Using the Literature
- The Formal 'Literature Review'

THE IMPORTANCE OF WORKING WITH LITERATURE

'I not only use all the brains that I have, but all that I can borrow.'

–Woodrow Wilson

Research may be done alone – but it is never done in isolation. The production of new knowledge is fundamentally dependent on past knowledge. Knowledge builds, and it is virtually impossible for researchers to add to a body of literature, if they are not conversant with it. Put simply, working with literature is an essential part of the research process. It inspires, informs, educates, and enlightens. It generates ideas, helps form significant questions, and is instrumental in the process of research design. It is also central to the process of writing-up; a clear rationale supported by literature is essential, while a well-constructed literature review is an important criterion in establishing researcher credibility.

Unfortunately, working with literature is often seen as an onerous task. The multiple purposes, the volume and variety, the difficulty in finding it and managing it, dealing with the inconsistencies within it the need to formally review it; and perhaps underpinning all of this, your own lack of knowledge, experience, and proficiency can make dealing with the literature quite daunting.

The aim of this chapter is to help you navigate your way through the literature. Once you realize there are people and resources you can call on, skills you can develop, and strategies you can employ, you can begin to see working with the literature as a manageable endeavour. Figure 6.1 outlines the variety of tasks involved in working with literature, and explores some of the steps you can follow to find it, manage it, use it, and review it.

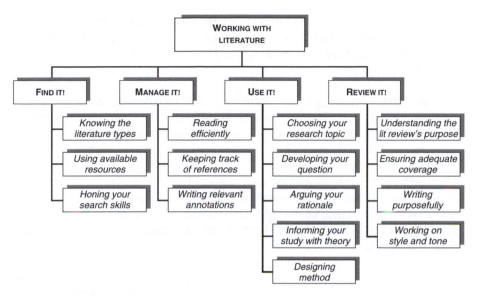

FIGURE 6.1 WORKING WITH LITERATURE

FINDING LITERATURE

You don't have to be a rocket scientist to realize that in order to work with appropriate literature you need to be able to identify it and find it. In order to do this, you need to have an understanding of various literature types; be able to identify and utilize available resources; and develop search skills that allow you to locate a range of sources relevant to your topic/question.

Types of literature

Students often ask what types of literature are appropriate to the research process. The answer is any and all. In addition to contributing to your formal literature review, literature will be used to inform all stages of the research process, including background and context, theoretical and methodological directions, and writing-up. Appropriate literature types thus include:

Discipline-based reference materials: It's easy for those who speak the language of a particular discipline to forget that many of its terms are not a part of everyday speech. If you are relatively new to a particular discipline or paradigm, subject-specific dictionaries and encyclopedias can help you navigate your way through the discipline's central terms, constructs, and theories.

Subject-specific books: Introductory and advanced texts, anthologies, research reports, popular non-fiction, and even fiction works can provide background and context, while seminal or foundational works, often produced as books, can be core to your formal literature review. Books are also likely to inform theory and method. Keep in mind, however, that the lengthy production time for books will mean that contemporary research is unlikely to be found in this format.

Journal articles: These generally form the heart of a formal literature review because: (a) they are often targeted for 'academic' audiences; (b) specificity of content and regularity of production mean that articles are likely to be both relevant and current; and (c) in peer reviewed journals, articles have met benchmarks for credibility.

The array, specialization, and the accessibility of journal titles is ever increasing. When I began researching, getting your hands on a journal not held in your own library was a task to rival climbing Mount Everest. The advent of online journals and computer-based inter-library loan schemes, however, has made access much more possible.

Grey literature: This refers to both published and unpublished materials that do not have an International Standard Book Number (ISBN) or an International Standard Serial Number (ISSN). This includes conference papers, unpublished research theses, newspaper articles, and pamphlets/brochures. Most researchers generally utilize some type of grey literature in the course of their study. Recent theses and conference papers can be a valuable source of contemporary original work, while newspaper articles, pamphlets, and brochures can be used for background and context – or in the process of document analysis (see Chapter 11).

Official publications, statistics, and archives: Such material can be a valuable source of background and contextual information, and often helps shape a study's rationale. This type of literature, however, can also be used as a source of data. Secondary data analysis and document analysis is often drawn from this category of literature.

Writing aids: This includes bibliographic reference works, dictionaries, encyclopedias and thesauruses, almanacs, yearbooks, books of quotes, etc. Such resources can offer significant support during the writing-up process and can be used to: improve the linguistic style of your work; add points of interest to the text; check facts; and reference those facts.

Using your resources

If there was only one piece of advice that I could give in regards to searching for and finding appropriate literature, it would be 'Don't go it alone!' As shown in Figure 6.2, there are excellent resources and experts out there who can give you the advice you need to make a start.

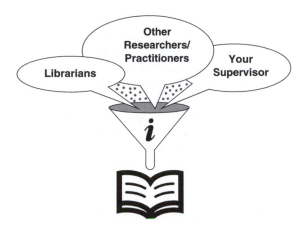

FIGURE 6.2 CALLING ALL EXPERTS

Librarians

In doing my background research for this book, I was dumbfounded at how many methods texts – all published in 1998 or later – referred to card catalogues in their 'literature' sections. I thought card catalogues had gone the way of vinyl records and 8-track tapes. This is antiquated advice, and the amazing rate of advancement in information technology means that if I were to give you specific advice on how to find literature, especially internet resources, it would probably need to be updated before it was even published.

My first-year university students often grumble about the need for library orientations. But things are changing so fast that students and professional researchers alike need to update their skills on a regular basis. See your librarian! Not only are librarians likely to be experts on the latest computer/internet searching facilities, they can often provide you with the training necessary to have you searching for books/articles in libraries all over the world. It is also worth knowing that many librarians are designated to a particular academic area, i.e. social science, environment, humanities, etc. These 'specialists' can introduce you to relevant databases, journals (both hardcopy and electronic), bibliographies, abstracts, reviews, etc., specific to your area.

Supervisors

Talk to your supervisor/lecturers. I still find the knowledge held by some academics to be absolutely amazing. They often know the literature and are able to point you in the right direction, or can at least direct you to someone better acquainted with your topic who can give you the advice you need to make a start. Also see if you can browse through their book shelves. While any one academic's library is unlikely to cover all perspectives or be completely up to date, academics often hold key readings that can kick start your search.

Other researchers/practitioners

Do not reinvent the wheel! There is a good possibility that another researcher has recently sourced and reviewed your area of literature – or an area quite close. I have had any number of students tell me that they are having difficulty finding relevant literature and can only find one of two recent studies that relate to their research question. I ask these students, 'Well, who did these people cite? Who is in their reference list?' One journal article on your topic should lead to several relevant readings. Have a look at Masters and PhD theses as well; these works generally require large literature reviews. If you can find a thesis with a topic related to your own, then you are likely to have a huge head start when it comes to sourcing the literature. Don't forget that you can also turn to practitioners – those who actually work in relevant fields often know the literature. Finally, try attending relevant conferences. It is quite likely that this will lead to a wealth of leads in your literature search.

Honing your search skills

The tools for literature searching are certainly changing at a rate of knots. Card catalogues have been replaced by CD ROM databases, and an amazing amount of research literature is now accessible on the internet using commonly available search engines. Literature far beyond the confines of the local library is now readily available. But commensurate with this explosion in availability, is an increasing need to develop skills for wading through it. Luckily, the skills needed for literature searching are actually becoming part of everyday computer usage. Finding anything on the internet demands an understanding of search engines, key words, and even Boolean operators.

Working with key words

General internet search engines, as well as search engines specific to applicable databases rely on key words to find relevant information. It is therefore essential that you are able to identify your topic, subtopics, main variables, theories, theorist, methods, key concepts, etc., in the form of key words. You will then be able to search for works by both single and combined key words searches.

For example, say you were interested in body piercing, and were particularly interested in teenagers. Your first keywords might be:

- body piercing (earrings, nose rings, etc.)
- teenagers (girls) (boys)

A search using these key words will generate a mass of literature, which can be culled by adding key variables you find particularly relevant or interesting. Say:

- rebellion
- rites of passage

You can further cull through the relevant literature by adding more variables, i.e. family background, or exploring whether a particular theorist comes up in conjunction with this area, for example Foucault.

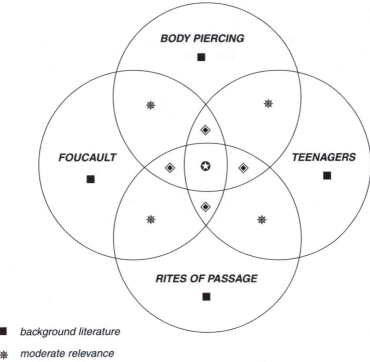

■   *background literature*

✳   *moderate relevance*

◈   *high relevance*

✪   *highest relevance*

FIGURE 6.3   INTERSECTING AREAS OF LITERATURE

Figure 6.3 highlights the relevance of the generated literature based on key concepts and their interrelationships. Keep in mind that some areas of intersection may not yield much literature, but if you keep playing around with ideas, concepts and variables, you are bound to build a solid literature base.

MANAGING THE LITERATURE

Once you find your literature, you will quickly realize that you need to develop a system for managing it. Students are often shocked at just how much literature can be relevant to a research project. If you can quickly and efficiently cull through the materials, keep track of relevant sources, and annotate your references in a manner that captures relevance, you will be that far ahead when it's time to call on these resources.

Efficient and selective reading

It is unlikely that you will be able to read every word of every piece of relevant literature you have located. But if you can quickly and efficiently wade through this literature in order to assess relevance and importance, or in other words 'get the gist', you can save yourself a lot of time and energy.

If you are reading a journal article, the first thing you should look at is the abstract or executive summary. This should give you a good sense of relevance. In a book, peruse the table of contents, the back cover blurb, and the introduction. Also have a look at the conclusion offered at chapter ends, as well as the overall conclusion. Within a few minutes you should be able to assess if a work is likely to be of value to your own research process.

Students often find the use of a simple ranking system, using 'post-it' notes, to be quite effective in keeping track of relevance. For example, if a student is looking at literature related to three distinct concepts I suggest they use three different colour post-its and then rank the overall work, or chapters within a work, with a 1 (minimally relevant), 2 (somewhat relevant), or 3 (highly relevant). It is amazing how much time this can save when you begin a more rigorous review of materials.

Keeping track of references

There is more than one student who has gone on a frantic last-minute hunt for that lost reference. It could be a quote with a missing page number, or a fact with no citation, or that perfect point that needs to go right there, but you just don't know what book it was in. It is essential that each and every one of your sources be incorporated into a management system to prevent it becoming forever lost – just like socks in the laundry.

Keep and file copies of relevant books, articles, etc., and avoid lending out your 'only copies'. It's amazing how many books and articles never get returned, even when the lendee swears they will get it back to you by the end of the week. You also need to keep good references. Now as common as it may be to see bad referencing, I refuse to believe that proper referencing is an intellectually difficult task. A pain in the neck and lower – yes, but it really is not that hard to do right. You just need to be organized and diligent. Find out right from the start what your recommended referencing style is, get a style guide, and as Nike says, 'just do it'. Rigorous referencing and appropriate filing can save you much grief in the future.

You may also want to consider using bibliographic file management software such as *Procite*, *Endnote*, or *Reference Manager*. These programs can automatically format references in any number of styles, i.e. Harvard, author–date, Vancouver, etc., once basic bibliographic details are entered. Just one final point … be sure to back up anything and everything related to your project, including references. If there is one thing you can rely on, it's that computers can't be relied on.

Annotating your references

It is definitely worth developing a systematic approach to note taking that allows for a methodical and organized review of materials from first read. There are an unlimited number of students who peruse/read materials without such a systematic approach who later find that they need to go back and reread the material – often when they are short of time and hard pressed to meet deadlines. Consider compiling an annotated bibliography. This is basically a systematic review and record of all significant literature that you have sourced. It is designed to remind you of the relevance, accuracy, and quality of the sources cited. Now while 'annotating' every single relevant reference may seem like a highly onerous task, you'll be grateful for the annotations when you undertake a formal literature review, or when you need to call on the references while writing-up.

Annotations vary in both content and length depending on the relevance of the reviewed work. But my students generally find that if they take notes on the author and audience; briefly summarize the work; add critical comment; and make notes on relevance (as outlined below and shown in Box 6.1), they minimize the time it takes to incorporate these works into their own.

Author and audience

The ability to retrieve vast amounts of literature has increased the need to assess the quality of that literature. The internet is full of propaganda, uninformed opinion, and less than credible research. A good preliminary check on your references can be done through an examination of the author and the intended audience. Who is doing the writing? What are their qualifications? Are they professionals, politicians, researchers, unknown? And who is the work written for? Is it for an academic audience, general public, constituents, clients? If the answers to these questions leave you feeling less than comfortable with the source, it is probably best to move on to more credible literature.

Summary

I often get asked how long a summary should be. The answer is … it depends. Remember that annotations are notes for your own use. They are not often an end product. You may be able to summarize a less relevant work in a sentence or two, while others will be much more instrumental to your own thinking and researching and require more in-depth coverage. Now you can write annotations in any manner/style with which you feel comfortable; there is no need to be formal in your writing. Doodles, concept maps, quotes, page numbers, etc., are all fair game. The bottom line is that these annotations will be an aid to your researching and writing. Write what you think you will want to know later on, and try to not fall into the trap of trusting your memory. What you think you will remember today is likely to be forgotten, if not tomorrow, then certainly in a few months.

Critical comment

Students generally don't have many problems summarizing information. Where they often struggle, however, is in their ability to be critical. Now I know that the word 'critical' has a tendency to imply negative, but in academic reviewing the word 'critical' means informed and considered evaluation. Nevertheless, students often feel uncomfortable commenting on the work of published authors. But when you decide to engage in research and produce new knowledge, you have decided to enter a domain that demands critical reflection on the literature. You need to be able to ask and answer the question 'What did I really think of that and why?'

You may find that you have a gut reaction to a work; if so, your task is to reflect on and articulate why you had that reaction. If you don't have that gut reaction, you will need to systematically address various components of the work. In reviewing research studies, you may find the criteria of good research, as discussed in Chapter 5, a handy framework for critical evaluation. Consider whether:

- the authors have managed their subjectivities. Is their study approached with objectivity or neutrality, or are subjectivities accepted but made open and transparent?
- methods are approached consistently. Are methods thoughtfully and rigorously developed and applied such that they can be seen to be dependable and/or reliable?
- findings appear to capture 'truth'. Are they valid/authentic?
- findings are applicable outside an immediate frame of reference. Are they generalizable, or, if not, are they transferable?
- the research can be verified. Is methodological detail sufficient to audit the process? Is the study reproducible?

Finally, keep in mind that you can compare and contrast a work – on any number of dimensions – to others in the same area.

Notes on relevance

The citation, author/audience, and summary are all notes about the work itself, while the critical comment is about how you think the work sits in relation to the field. Make the section on relevance your own. This is where you can really make the connection between what others have done and what you want to do. Ask yourself how this work sits in relation to your own. How does the theory or ideology compare? What about the methods? Is there anything in the work that makes a light bulb go on in your head? Is there some flaw in the thinking/methods that makes you want to explore this area/topic/question from a different angle? Is there a quote, passage, or section that really gets to the heart of what you are trying to do or say? Look to be inspired. Look to be surprised. Look to be appalled. Use this section to get the creative juices flowing.

> **'Reading furnishes the mind only with materials of knowledge;**
> **it is thinking that makes what we read ours.'**
>
> –John Locke

USING THE LITERATURE

Ok, so you've found it, perused it, culled it, referenced it, and annotated it. Now what exactly do you do with it? In short ... everything. Research requires

---

Box 6.1   Brief Sample Annotation

O'Leary, Z. (2001) 'Conversations in the Kitchen', in A. Bartlett and G. Mercer (eds), *Postgraduate Research Supervision: Transforming (R)elations*. New York: Peter Lang.	*Citation (Harvard reference)*
The author is a senior lecturer at the University of Western Sydney who has written a chapter in a book targeting postgraduate research students and supervisors.	*Author/Audience*
This is basically an anecdote that discusses, and attempts to normalize, the emotional and intellectual hardships many research students can go through when trying to juggle family obligations and study.	*Summary*
The anecdote is quite short and written in a warm and personal style that makes it very easy to relate to. It is not, however, a research study backed up by any data/rigour and therefore does not allow one to assess the extent of the issues raised to whether the concerns she raises are widespread. That said, it does seem to relate well to the more rigorous research studies conducted by Field and Howard (2002) and Dreicker (2003) on similar issues.	*Critical Comment*
This relates quite well to my chapter on 'coping mechanisms and strategies for managing roles and workloads' and may be good for a quote or two, especially if I feel my text is too dry.	*Relevance*

---

engagement with the literature at each and every stage of the process. As highlighted in Figure 6.4, literature informs the research process by helping you: focus your ideas; develop appropriate questions; argue the societal and scientific relevance of your work; inform your thinking/approach with theory; design suitable methods; and construct and write the formal literature review.

Exploring a topic

Not many students, or researchers for that matter, know all they need to know about a particular research area, and many find that engaging with a wide variety

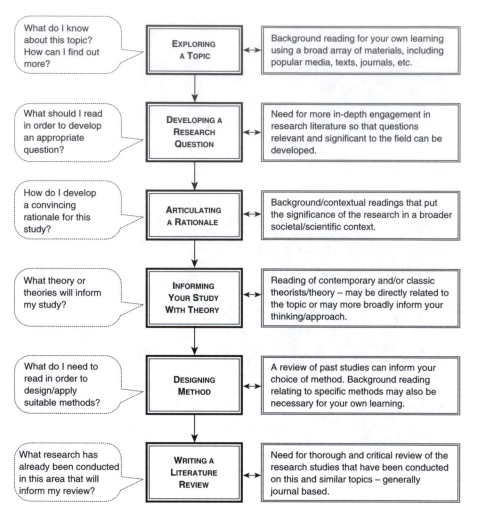

FIGURE 6.4 LITERATURE AND THE RESEARCH PROCESS

of topical literature is a good way to focus in on issues. This can involve reading texts, popular media, as well as research studies that make up the scientific literature in a particular area. Given that a genuine interest in a topic or curiosity about a particular issue drives most research, students usually enjoy delving into readings that develop their own topical knowledge and expertise.

Developing a research question

As discussed in Chapter 3, one of the key places to look for guidance on the development of your research question is in the literature. Popular media that covers current debates, controversy, and disputes around a particular issue can help generate questions of societal significance. Engagement with scientific literature can also be instrumental in the development of questions. Finding 'gaps', exploring questions that have not been adequately addressed, or attempting to ask questions within a new context, are strategies for question development that are dependent on in-depth engagement with research literature.

Articulating a rationale

A well-articulated rationale is part and parcel of any research proposal, and needs to suggest why time and money should be invested in addressing your particular research question. In order to do this, you need to draw on literature that can argue the societal and scientific significance of your study. This generally involves readings that locate a topic and research question in a larger context. This literature can come from a variety of academic, Government, and popular sources, and provides the researcher with information needed to convince an audience of a question's worth.

Informing your study with theory

Theoretical reading can be highly difficult for students who perceive a large gap between research and theory – something not uncommon. For years, social 'scientists' engaged in research without strong links to theory, while social 'theorists' theorized without doing much research. This tendency to dichotomize, however, is diminishing and we are beginning to recognize the value of exploring quite tangible issues in relation to theory. For example, sociological research that touches on issue of power, class, and religion generally demand the exploration of theorists such as Weber, Marx, or Durkheim. Even applied scientists are beginning to appreciate how postmodern theorists such as Foucault can be instrumental in understanding how the social world is constructed, and what possibilities exist for a 'reconstruction' that might just facilitate sustainable change.

For some, theoretical reading is a passion and joy – and is therefore not problematic. For others, it can be an incredibly uncomfortable and laborious task. If you fall into the second category, it is important that you discuss the issue of theory with your supervisor and clearly negotiate the extent to which it is expected to inform your work.

Designing method

In order to design the methodological protocols for your own study, you need to engage in a fair amount of methodological reading. Obviously you are on the right track; you are reading this book and hopefully getting your head around research as a creative and strategic thinking process. Now it may pain me to say it, but this book alone is probably not enough. In order to appropriately design a study, collect the data, and engage in analysis, you generally need to do a lot of reading that includes: broad-ranging methods texts such as this; books focusing on particular research approaches, i.e. ethnography, action research, or statistics; and research articles on methods themselves. This book's recommended readings, references, and bibliography can be a great starting point for finding this type of literature.

You will also need to explore past studies in your topic area so you can: (1) critically evaluate the methods that may be standard for exploring your particular research question; (2) assess the need for alternate methodological approaches; (3) design a study that might overcome methodological shortcomings prevalent in the literature and; (4) generate ideas/get tips for finding samples, measuring variables, and analysing data appropriate to your field.

THE FORMAL 'LITERATURE REVIEW'

While the uses of literature in research are quite broad, a formal 'literature review' is a very specific piece of argumentative writing. It is a work that relies on scientific and academic discourse and debate to construct arguments about a current research project. A 'literature review' generally relies on articles published in well-established research journals and is usually a distinct and required section of any research write-up, including grant applications, research reports, and journal articles. Virtually all student theses require a literature review that should be relevant, critical, and comprehensive; in fact, the review should represent a level of engagement in the literature that indicates a readiness to contribute to the literature itself.

Conducting and writing a good literature review, however, is no easy task. You need to negotiate multiple purposes; decide on appropriate content; work towards a logical structure; and make convincing arguments that are neither hypercritical nor deferential. And while most supervisors certainly know a good literature review when they see one, many have difficulty articulating what it is and what it takes to construct one. In this section, I outline the basics of a good literature review. But keep in mind that constructing a literature review is a task that you learn through doing. Expect that it may take several drafts to get right.

The purpose

It would make a whole lot of sense if the purpose of a 'literature review' was to simply review the literature – but it isn't. Reviewing is a step along the way towards an end purpose, not the end purpose itself. Perhaps this can explain why the tendency for new researchers to simply review and report on past research falls far short of most supervisors' expectations. Within a 'literature review', the literature is reviewed or explored so that researchers can:

- *Inform* *readers of developments in the field* – not only should a research study provide your readers with information about your particular research question, it should also provide rich learning about the general topic. The inclusion of a strong literature review should provide readers with contextual learning through an up-to-date account and discussion of relevant contextual

TABLE 6.1 REVIEWING THE LITERATURE VS 'THE LITERATURE REVIEW'

Reasons for reviewing the literature	Purposes of the 'literature review'
• Informing yourself of what is happening in the field	☑ Informing your audience of what is happening in the field
• Gaining a level of topical and methodological knowledge and expertise	☑ Establishing your credibility as a knowledgeable and capable researcher
• Finding potential gaps in the literature that may point to potential research questions	☑ Arguing the relevance and the significance of your research question(s)
• Critically evaluating common/ typical methods	☑ Providing the context for your own methodological approach
• Facilitating the development of your own methodological approaches	☑ Arguing the relevance and appropriateness of your approach

theories, methods, and research studies that make up a particular topic's body of literature.

- ***Establish*** *their own credibility* – because researchers are responsible for the production of new knowledge, it is essential they can show they are abreast of the field; aware of relevant new developments; and conversant with academic and scientific discourse and debate within their research area. The literature review allows researchers to establish such credibility through rigorous and critical evaluation of relevant research works; a demonstrated understanding of key issues; and the ability to outline the relationship of their own work to the rest of the field.

- ***Argue*** *the need for, and relevance of, their study* – the literature review needs to make an argument for a researcher's own research agenda. It needs to set the current study within the context of past research. The literature review has the potential to identify 'gaps' that show the appropriate and significant nature of a study's research questions. It can also justify methodological approaches by critically evaluating methods generally accepted/typical for this type of research; highlighting the limitations that might be common to past studies; and uncovering the possibly unwarranted assumptions that can underpin method.

Table 6.1 attempts to break this down a bit further by highlighting the broader, more self-educative reasons for reviewing the literature, and the corresponding purposes of the formal 'literature review'.

Coverage

What's the most common question asked by students frustrated by the demands of doing a literature review? That's easy. 'What do I need to include?' Students

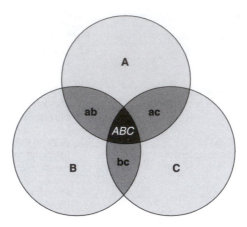

FIGURE 6.5   FOCUSING THE REVIEW

often follow this question with one of two comments. Either, 'I can't find anything! There is simply no research in this area', or 'There is just so much literature, how do I decide what I need to review?'

In both cases, I recommend that students clearly articulate their research question and see if the model introduced in Figure 6.3, and shown in a modified form in Figure 6.5, can be used to break the question down into relevant concepts, variables, theories, etc.

The struggle to find literature

If you are struggling to find anything, the first step is to check with those in the know to see if you are overlooking anything obvious. Your own search may not uncover what your supervisors know is out their, or what a trained librarian is able to find. If, however, a truly exhaustive search of the literature does not yield what Figure 6.5 refers to as highly relevant 'ABC' literature, then you can move to the literature that sits at the intersection of two or more relevant concepts, i.e. the literature that sits at 'ab', 'ac', and 'bc'. Finally, there is the rich contextual/ background literature on specific concepts/variables likely to be readily available, i.e. 'A', 'B', and 'C'. If you are struggling to find literature, it is important to recognize that studies do not have to directly mirror your particular research questions to be relevant, informative, and highly useful.

The struggle to limit literature

If you are feeling overwhelmed by a vast array of literature, the first task is to set boundaries and critically assess whether your reading is getting too broad. In other words, have you unnecessarily added circles D, E, F, and G to Figure 6.5? While such areas of reading may be interesting and informative, one study rarely covers it all, and some readings may be outside the realm of your study. Alternatively, it might be that your research question itself is too broad. If this is the case, you may need to reconsider/renegotiate it with your supervisor.

Okay, once boundaries are set and questions potentially redefined, you need to start with a more thorough review of highly relevant 'ABC' literature. This can involve: exhaustive coverage that cites all the literature; exhaustive coverage with only selective citation; representative coverage that discusses works that typify particular areas within the literature; coverage of seminal/pivotal works; or a combination of the above. You can then begin dipping into the intersecting (ab, ac, bc) and background (A, B, C) literature as needed to give depth and context.

If in the end you are still struggling with issues of coverage, I'd recommend taking the advice of your supervisor on what is most appropriate/required. Generally speaking, the coverage in your literature review should be broad enough to: inform your readers of the nature of the discourse and debate current to your topic; establish your own credibility as a researcher abreast of the field; and demonstrate the need for, and relevance of, your own research. But the topic area, the nature of the question, and the level of the project/thesis will also determine what is both suitable and required.

The writing process

Why is writing a good literature review a tricky endeavour? Because if you think a good way to write a literature review is to review the literature, you are likely to be on the wrong track. As shown in Box 6.1, what you really need to do in a literature review is to use the literature to *inform*, *establish*, and *argue*. The literature review needs to go beyond a he said/she said report. Remember that the literature review is an argumentative piece of writing that *relies* on a review of the literature rather than reports the review itself. In order to write a good literature review I'd recommend that you:

- *read a few good, relevant reviews* – have a look at the literature reviews in a number of theses and journal articles. You need to have a sense of what a good literature review is before you are in a position to construct your own. Your supervisor should be able to point you towards particularly good examples in your area.
- *write critical annotations as you go* – if you begin sorting and organizing your annotations by themes, issues of concern, common shortcomings, etc., you may find that patterns begin to emerge. This can go a long way towards the development of your own arguments.
- *develop a structure* – work on a potential outline for your literature review early; it is an important part of the thinking process. Remember that your structure can always be modified as your thinking evolves. Some suggestions are to structure your review by topical themes, the tasks that you need the literature review to accomplish, or the arguments you wish to make.
- *write purposefully* – the literature review is driven by the researcher and needs to have and make a point. You can review literature without an agenda, but you cannot write a formal 'literature review' without one. Your audience should be able to readily identify the 'point' of each section of your review. If your audience does not know why you are telling them what you are telling them, you need to reconsider your approach.

- *use the literature to back up your arguments* – rather than review, report, or even borrow the arguments of others, use the literature to help generate, and then support, your own arguments.
- *make doing the literature review an ongoing process* – your literature review will inform your question, theory, and methods, and your question, theory, and methods will help set the parameters of your literature review. This is a cyclical process. A literature review is often a moving target that should evolve in both thinking and writing as your study develops.
- *get plenty of feedback* – writing a literature review is not an easy task, and supervisors' expectations can vary widely. Don't wait until the last minute to begin the writing process or to get feedback. Be sure to pass a draft to your supervisor, or anyone else willing to read it, early on.
- *be prepared to redraft* – it would be nice if first drafts and last drafts were the same draft. Nice, but not likely. Whether you are a student or professional researcher, not many can get away without a redraft or two (or three or four).

Style and tone

Two common criticisms of student literature reviews are that they are either uncritical – the student has not shown enough reflective engagement with the literature – or that they are hypercritical – they have taken critical to mean disparaging and have conducted their review as a series of criticisms. When I mention this to students, they generally ask, 'Where is the line, and how can I navigate it?'

Well, I tell them that they shouldn't think of themselves as merely students at the feet of prominent academics. If you are in awe of those you are 'reviewing', you are likely to have difficulty in being critical and constructing relevant arguments. On the other hand, if you attempt to establish your credibility by showing that you are able to pick holes in the work of others, you run the risk of being judgemental, hypercritical, and unable to draw relevance and significance from the works reviewed.

Personally, I like using the analogy of a dinner party to try to get students to understand how they might manage their criticality. Imagine you are at a dinner party with prominent researchers in your area. You are just another guest, an equal, not someone in a disparate power position. You are conducting research in the same area, you pretty much know the field, and are able to engage in interesting and relevant conversation. Through the course of the night, you hear of research that you find interesting, exciting, and inspiring. But other studies seem old hat, premised on assumptions that you don't believe hold water, or lacking credibility due to some really questionable methods.

The most interesting part of the night, however, was the conversation you had with other researchers that had you learning, arguing, and developing your own ideas simultaneously. At home that night, you debrief with your partner, and find yourself saying, 'Hey!... You know what I should really look at...?', or 'I think I have figured out a way to find out...'. The rich engagement in the work of others has conspired to develop your ideas in a way that would have never happened in isolation.

The good dinner party conversationalist is neither hypercritical nor syco-phantic. Rather, the consummate dinner party conversationalist is an individual who engages, learns, debates, argues, contributes, and even evolves his or her own ideas. And this is exactly what needs to happen in order for you to develop and write a good literature review.

Further Reading

There are quite a few readings out there that can help you navigate your way through the complexities of working with research literature. You may find the following sources a good place to start:

Hart, C. (2000) *Doing a Literature Review*. London: Sage.

Hart, C. (2001) *Doing a Literature Search*. London: Sage.

Orna, L. (1995) *Managing Information for Research*. Buckingham: Open University Press.

CHAPTER SUMMARY

- Working with literature is an essential part of the research process that generates ideas, helps form significant questions, and is instrumental in the process of research design. It is a complex task that involves developing the skills to find, manage, use, and review the literature.
- Finding relevant literature can be made easier if you are able to readily access and draw on a wide variety of resources, including reference materials, books, journals, grey literature, official publications, and archives. In doing this, you should call on the expertise of librarians and supervisors, as well as other researchers.
- The ever-increasing availability of literature requires students to develop proficient search skills. Working with key words is the most common way to navigate the internet and relevant databases.
- Managing the literature requires efficient reading skills that allow you to cull through vast amounts of written work. It also pays to be organized and diligent when it comes to keeping references.
- Annotating your sources provides you with a record of relevant literature. It should include the citation, articulation of the author and audience, a short summary, critical

commentary, and notes on relevance that remind you of the significance, accuracy, and quality of the sources cited.

- Literature is used for disparate purposes throughout the research process. Whether it be focusing interests, defining questions, articulating a rationale, theoretically informing your study, developing appropriate design, or writing a formal literature review, every stage of the research process demands literary engagement.

- The formal literature review is a very specific piece of writing designed to inform your readers of your topic, establish your credibility as a researcher, and argue the need for, and relevance of, your work. Most find it a difficult task that takes patience, practice, drafts, and redrafts.

- Students are often unsure of what needs to be included in the literature review. Some have difficulty finding relevant literature, while others have difficulty focusing their reading. Organizing and searching for the literature according to various concepts/ variables can help manage the task.

- A good literature review is an *argument* that is more purposeful than a simple review of relevant literature. Writing a good review requires you to: read a few good reviews; write critical annotations; develop a structure; write purposefully; use the literature to back up your arguments; review and write throughout the research process; get feedback; and be prepared to redraft.

- Writing a good literature review can be likened to holding a good dinner party conversation. They both require individuals who can engage, learn, debate, argue, contribute, and evolve their own ideas, without being hypercritical or sycophantic.

7   Methodological Design

'What's the best way to design my study?'

Chapter Preview

- **Methodology, Methods, and Tools**
- **From Questions to Answers**
- **Three Key Prerequisites for Methodological Design**
- **Getting Down to the Nitty Gritty**
- **Thoughts on the Qualitative/Quantitative Divide**

METHODOLOGY, METHODS, AND TOOLS

For first-time researchers, the challenge of developing an appropriate methodological design can be made even more difficult by the haziness of 'methods' terminology. In this chapter, I have decided to start by offering a few 'methods' definitions in order to clarify the key distinguishing elements of each of these terms, and indicate how I am using these terms throughout this chapter.

Methodology: The *framework* associated with a particular set of paradigmatic assumptions that you will use to conduct your research, i.e. scientific method, ethnography, action research.

Methods: The *techniques* you will use to collect data, i.e. interviewing, surveying, participative observation.

Tools: The *devices* you will use to help you collect data, i.e. questionnaires, observation checklists, interview schedules.

Methodological design: The *plan* for conducting your study that includes all of the above.

Getting your head around these terms is an important preliminary step in the development of methodological designs that are logical, clear, and unambiguous.

FIGURE 7.1 THE PATH

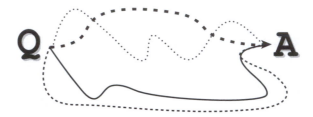

FIGURE 7.2 MULTIPLE PATHS

FROM QUESTIONS TO ANSWERS

Without a doubt, the most crucial step in developing a methodological design that will move you from questions to answers is making sure that you are working with a well-defined research question (or questions). If you think you are ready to move to methodological design, yet you are having a hard time articulating your question, or you feel the question is ambiguous or ill-defined, you really need to go back and work on the question itself. After all, not knowing where you want to go makes it awfully hard to get there. If you are still struggling with your question, it might be worthwhile revisiting Chapter 3, which is dedicated to the art of developing 'good' questions.

Finding a path

Assuming you are pretty happy with your research question(s), the next step is figuring out how to best go about getting the answers; in other words, defining the elements of your methodological design. Have a look at Figure 7.1. It represents a common conception of how we move from questions to answers. The arrow represents the methodological design that will best get you from Q to A. The assumption here is that there is a correct or best design, and students need to work in that direction.

Figure 7.2 offers an alternate representation of methodological possibilities. Here the assumption is that there might be numerous ways to move from questions to answers. Paths are varied and diverse, but they all have the potential to generate the data that can lead to credible answers. The trick is travelling down a methodological path that is appropriate for the question, the researcher, and the context.

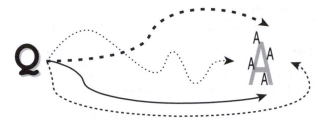

FIGURE 7.3 PATHS AND PERSPECTIVE

Figure 7.3 works on the same 'multiple path' assumption as Figure 7.2, but reminds us that both who we are and what we do can influence how we see and what we find. Each methodological design has the potential to draw out answers from a somewhat different perspective. I think Werner Heisenberg, the twentieth-century physicist who founded the area of quantum mechanics, said it best: 'It is worth remembering that what we observe is not nature itself, but nature exposed to our method of questioning' (in Shulman and Asimov 1988: 324).

The significance of the progression of these models is in the increased responsibility they represent for the researcher. As you move from finding the path, to choosing from a range of potential paths, to reflexive consideration of the implications of the paths themselves, the need to consider issues that can affect credibility increases. To view the development of methodological design in a manner similar to that in Figure 7.3 requires both creativity and strategy; methodological design becomes a real thinking game.

Designing creative and strategic methods

As discussed in Chapter 1, science certainly needs structure and logic, but it also needs unremitting injections of creativity. Put simply, there are times when you'll want to 'think outside the square'. Now this is not to say that all approaches to research need to be eclectic, eccentric, or unique. There is certainly a place for following the rules and adopting the recipes – many rules are derived from years of experience and expertise, while recipes are often followed because they are tried and true. One approach is not necessarily better than the other. What is important, and what I strongly advocate, is that all researchers work towards reflexive awareness and informed choice. There are no easy answers. Methodological design is about informed decision-making that involves weighing up pros and cons, and deciding what is best given your specific context.

Table 7.1 highlights some of the pros and cons associated with the development of conventional versus innovative methods, while Box 7.1 presents an example of 'thinking outside the square' in Vietnam.

TABLE 7.1 CONVENTION VS INNOVATION

Following the rules and adopting the recipes

Pros	Cons
☑ Drawing on the methodological expertise of the best researchers in the field	☒ Can lead to unreflexive acceptance of unwarranted assumptions
☑ Adopting methodological approaches that are tried and true	☒ Sometimes the accepted way of doing things is not necessarily the best way of doing it
☑ More time that can be spent on execution and analysis	☒ Can limit your creativity

Working with autonomy and innovation

Pros	Cons
☑ You are not limited by what others have/have not done	☒ It can be easy to get lost and confused
☑ You have the potential to break new ground	☒ It can take a lot of work to break new ground
☑ You can be very context-specific in your methodological design	☒ It can be quite difficult to show credibility

---

Box 7.1   *Being Creatively Strategic in Vietnam – Brent's Story*

I was stuck and I was a long way from home. The city was Haiphong, it was day one, and I had asked the focus group to create a vision for the future of the city. We had begun by talking together about the problems of the city and the barriers to change. Working with a translator, I found the progress slow and the participants hesitant. I felt that my data was limited to 'expected' answers.

On a hunch I turned to poetry. I asked if we could begin by writing some poems about the city. All of a sudden there were smiles and eyes lit up. What unfolded was amazing; there was a rush of activity and new-found enthusiasm as participants wrote of days gone by and ideas for the future. The poems were explained, shared, and celebrated in what became an unlocking of insight.

THREE KEY PREREQUISITES FOR METHODOLOGICAL DESIGN

It might seem obvious, but when it comes to methodological design, the number one prerequisite is that your design addresses your question(s). You'd be surprised just how often this can be an issue. It's not uncommon for me to tell students, 'That's an interesting plan, but I'm not sure how it gets at your question'. The second prerequisite is that you have, or are willing to develop, the skills and interests needed to undertake your plan. There are many ways to conduct research, each associated with a variety of skills that need to be called on. You need to give real

88

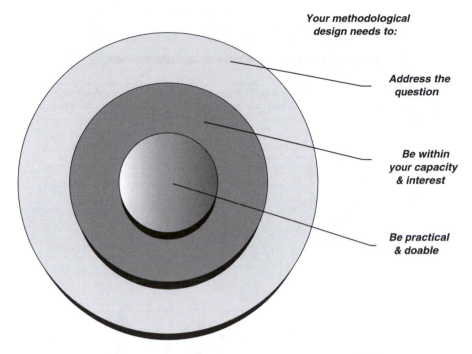

Your methodological design needs to:

Address the question

Be within your capacity & interest

Be practical & doable

FIGURE 7.4   GETTING YOUR METHODOLOGICAL DESIGN ON TARGET

consideration to your own abilities, limitations, and interests. The final prerequisite is that all the elements of your methodological design are 'doable'. Your design may be completely appropriate to your question and be within your comfort zone, but if you find yourself without ethics approval, enough time, adequate resources, or necessary access, your design won't be able to lead you to answers. Figure 7.4 illustrates how these prerequisites (discussed in more depth below) can be used to help get your methodological design on target.

Addressing the question

The Question

As discussed in Chapter 3, the development of clear and unambiguous research questions is an essential part of the research process; it is difficult to plan for a journey with destination unknown. Sure, you can take off and explore new territory, or take a 'grounded theory' approach (discussed later in this chapter), but you need to be able to articulate to yourself and to your audience that your desire to 'explore' and 'discover' is indeed part of your design or plan.

Additionally, knowing what you want to know does not mean your questions must be set in stone from their first articulation. I firmly believe research is an

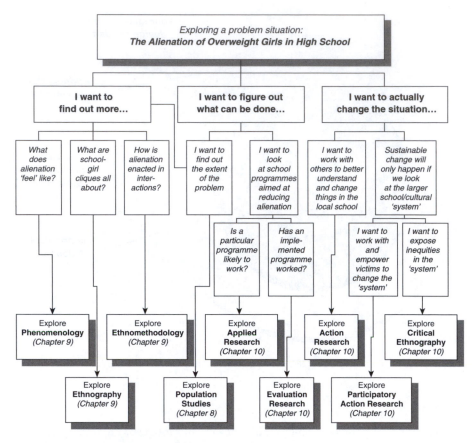

FIGURE 7.5 EXPLORING METHODOLOGIES

ongoing and iterative process of development and redevelopment that may see questions shift and change before taking on their final form. What I am stressing is that there needs to be a goodness of fit between your **final** questions and your methodological design. One, the other, or both may evolve but, in the end, your questions and your design need to have the tightest of relationships.

Exploring methodologies

The nature of your research question will be a key determining factor in your exploration of potential methodologies. As discussed in Chapters 8, 9 and 10, various methodologies have been developed in order to address research questions with objectives ranging from understanding populations to facilitating change. Having a sense of how your question(s) links to various methodological approaches is an essential first step in exploring relevant methodological literature.

Using an example of researching the alienation of overweight girls in high school, Figure 7.5 attempts to work you through the links between questions and methodology. While neither definitive nor exhaustive, it should point you to potential methodological areas that you may want to further explore.

Letting the question drive the methods

Once you explore potential methodologies, your research question can go much further in directing the nitty gritty of methods. Now many students seem to know how they'll conduct their study before they even know what they want to know. I, for one, don't believe you can start with 'I plan to do a survey', or 'I think I will do focus groups'. The goal needs to be developing the most appropriate methodological design for your particular inquiry, and not falling prey to belief in the superior nature of one particular way of doing things. Your methods need to fall from questions, and the better articulated the questions, the more readily this can happen.

Well-articulated questions can point to who you need to talk to; what you want to ask; and even what methods/tools you might use. For example, imagine that you want to do your research on the self-image of teenage girls. You can do one of two things. You can jump in and begin to design your study – after all you already know you want to do interviews. Or you can really think about what you want to know; go through some of the more relevant literature; work on the process of narrowing and clarifying; and clearly articulate your question before you attack the issue of methodological design.

In my experience, students who go for the jump-in approach and work from a topic rather than a question can really struggle. They often end up getting lost and confused. Things take a long time to fall into place (and sometimes never do), and they can end up with data they don't know how to use. Believe me, trying to retrofit a question to your data is not easy and rarely works!

On the other hand, if you have been able to narrow your question to let's say, 'Do parents somehow teach their daughters that worth is dependent on external beauty?', because you know what you want to know, deciding how to get your answers is only one small logical step away. You can consider whether you want to get the perspective of parents, children, or maybe health care professionals – perhaps those working in the area of anorexia or bulimia. You may want to do a large-scale survey comparing various socio-economic or cultural groups, or you may want to conduct interviews or focus groups in order to draw out rich descriptions. You could also do observation and see if and how this practice is occurring. Perhaps you will do a variety of the above. In any case, clarity and precision in your question can readily lead to a range of methodological possibilities; and once these possibilities are drawn out, you can consider which are likely to be right for you as the researcher, and of course, which are 'doable'.

Making it right for the researcher

Once you have a goodness of fit between your question and your potential methodological designs, you can begin to work on finding a similar goodness of fit between your designs and you as a researcher. Various designs require you to be comfortable with and willing to take on particular roles, and that you have or are willing to develop certain skills. Keep in mind that knowing your own approach to knowledge (see Chapter 2) can be invaluable in determining the right methodological path.

Roles

There is no shortage of metaphors for the role of the researcher. From theorist to scientist, choreographer to change agent, the range of metaphors used to depict the researcher points to the diversity of possibilities for approaching the research process. Have a look at the following researcher metaphors and consider which might suit you and your research process. Perhaps just as important, consider what roles might be uncomfortable or inappropriate for you and your methodological design. Also keep in mind that there is no need for these roles to be mutually exclusive, and of course there is nothing keeping you from creatively and strategically creating your own researcher role.

Theorist: The 'philosopher' or 'thinker'. The theorist metaphor suggests a researcher who can analyze critically and think abstractly. Theorists are likely to draw on the work of other theorists and are interested in new ways of seeing. In explaining a particular phenomenon or situation, theorists often attempt to develop understandings that lie outside the dominant paradigm.

Scientist: The 'objective expert'. The scientist metaphor suggests a researcher who works to a formula; is removed, precise, methodical, logical, highly trained; and is in control of the research process. Objectivity ensures that scientists do not have an undue influence on the research process.

Change agent: The 'emancipator'. The change agent metaphor suggests a researcher who not only acknowledges subjectivities, but is working to better a situation based precisely on these subjectivities. There is often devotion to the research/change process and sensitivity to the words and actions of respondents. Change agents often work in participatory and collaborative ways.

Bricoleur: The 'jack of all trades' or 'professional do-it-yourself person' (Lèvi-Strauss 1966: 17). The researcher as bricoleur sees methods as emergent and dependent upon both question and context. The bricoleur will employ a variety of methodological tools and even create new ones as needed to solve a puzzle or find a solution (Denzin and Lincoln 1998).

Choreographer: The 'coordinator of a dance'. The choreographer metaphor suggests a researcher who begins with a foundation of key principles, has vision, and tries to not have a limited view. The choreographer works by warming-up or preparation, exploration and exercise, and finally illumination and formulation (Janesick 2000).

Skills and interests

As a researcher, not only will you take on roles, you will also need to have, and/or develop, particular interests and specific skills. Are you a people person, or do you like sitting behind a computer? Are you comfortable having intimate chats with strangers, or are you better at more distant and formal communication? Do you like working with words or would you rather play with numbers? Can you handle a level of emotional investment or do you want to be 'objective'? Can you be objective or will you struggle to keep your opinions to yourself? Do you loath statistics, or is loath not a strong enough word!

Now you can develop new skills, and of course this is a worthwhile goal, but keep your timeline in mind. New skills are not always easy to master, and the number of new skills you would need to develop to be able to do it all is probably not practical. Have a good think about where your skills and interests lie. It would be kind of silly to go down the path of large-scale surveys if you know you hate stats and the thought of having to do it makes you break out in hives. On the other hand, even if you see the value of in-depth interviewing, without the right communication skills it might be a torturous route that ends up not doing justice to your research process. Not only do you need to consider your own comfort zone, you need to think about how your skills, or lack thereof, might affect the quality of the data you collect.

Making it doable

Assume your intended design addresses your research question and sits within your comfort zone. There's just one more question. Is it doable? Regardless of how appropriate your methodological design might be for you and your question, if you do not have ethics approval, or the resources, time, or access necessary to accomplish the task, you will need to rethink your approach.

Ethics approval

Anytime a study calls for interaction with human participants, you are likely to need ethics approval. Chapter 5 talks about power and ethics in some detail, but to reiterate, an ethical study (the only type that should proceed) is one that takes responsibility for integrity in the production of knowledge; acknowledges responsibility for the researched; and ensures that the mental, emotional, and physical welfare of respondents is protected. If your study is 'unethical' or does not have ethics approval, it should not be considered doable.

Resources

Doing research is not cheap, and university funding for student research projects generally ranges from non-existent to highly limited. It is important to develop a realistic budget for your study. You might be surprised at just how expensive your methodological plan is. Take, for example, travel expenses. The original plan for my doctoral thesis involved a comparative study in Ireland, Australia, and the United States. One look at my bank account and I realized I seriously had to rethink that approach. Surveys can also cost a packet. Say you wanted to gather 300 surveys. You might need to distribute over 2,000 surveys to get that many respondents. By the time you add up the cost of producing that many surveys, plus the cost of envelopes and postage (both to and return), your costs can be up in the thousands.

A smaller number of in-depth interviews can also be expensive. Did you know that a transcript for a one-hour interview can be over 50 pages long? If you plan on paying someone to type up a few of those, costs will add up really quickly. Books, computers, computer programs, equipment, interpreters, translators, training, etc., all need to be realistically considered. A practical methodological design from the start is much better than one that comes to a premature halt when funds run dry.

Time

Yes, ambitious is good, but ambitious yet realistic is better. If you have not given yourself enough time to do what your methodological design demands, you are likely to be headed down a very frustrating and stressful path. Ensuring that your design will fit within your timelines will help you avoid:

- applying for an extension
- compromising your study by changing your methodology mid-stream
- doing a shoddy, half-assed job with your original methods
- compromising the time that should be dedicated to self, work, and/or family
- giving up all together

Access

A major challenge for researchers is gaining access to data. Whether you plan to do document analysis, interviews, surveys, or observations, the best-laid methodological plans are worthless if you can't find a way to access people, places and/or records. Again it's about being realistic. Ask yourself how you will go about gaining access (tips for gaining access are included in Chapter 11), and whether your methods are truly feasible.

GETTING DOWN TO THE NITTY GRITTY

Now it may not seem extraordinarily clever, but getting down to the nitty gritty of your methodological design, i.e. specifically developing your methods and tools, is about: (1) being able to answer the basic questions of who, where, when, how, and what; and (2) being able to assess your answers in relation to the prerequisites above, i.e. addressing the question, being right for the researcher, and being doable.

Who, where, when, how, what

As they say, it's all in the details. It's amazing how well-defined a methodological plan can become once you work through the basic questions as outlined below.

Who

- *Who do you want to be able to speak about?* In other words, what is your 'population', or the realm of applicability for your results? Are your findings limited to only those you spoke to, or do you want to be able to speak for a broader group? For example, are your findings applicable to the children you interviewed, children from Philadelphia, children from the US, or children from the Western World? Or do your findings represent one rural community in Kent, all rural communities in England, or all rural communities in the UK?
- *Who do you plan to speak to/observe?* It is quite rare to be able to speak to every single person you wish to speak about. If who you wish to speak *about* is your 'population', then those you will actually speak *to* is your 'sample'. The key is that your sample is either intrinsically interesting or representative of a broader population. Chapter 8 discusses the issue of sampling and population in depth.

Where

- *What is the physical domain of your sample?* This relates to working out how far afield you need to go in order to carry out your methods. Will you need to travel to different geographic areas? Are there various sites you need to visit?
- *Are settings relevant to the credibility of your methods?* This involves considering how place can impact on method. For example, if you wanted to conduct job satisfaction interviews with construction workers, you would need to consider if an informal chat at the Friday night watering hole will generate data distinct from that gathered through informal on-site interviews.

When

- *How do your methods fit into your time frame?* There are plenty of students who underestimate just how long it takes to collect data, let alone analyze it, draw conclusions from it, and finally produce a finished product. The question of when needs to be framed in relation to your overall timeline.
- *Is timing relevant to the credibility of your methods?* If you were to conduct a survey or interview when it is most convenient to you, without considering how 'when' can affect your data, you can put your study's credibility at risk. For example, a community survey conducted from 9 to 5 is likely to lead to a large underrepresentation of workers. And if you conduct university subject evaluations on the same day that results are released, it is sure to affect your data.

How

There are numerous ways to collect data and Chapter 11 spends a fair bit of time discussing fundamental methods such as observation, interviews, surveys, and document analysis. Suffice it to say here that you will need to consider two key questions in relation to how:

- *How will I collect my data?* This involves deciding on the methods and tools you will use to collect, gather, and/or generate your data.

- *How will I conduct my methods?* Once you decide on your methods, thinking about how you will conduct those methods is an even deeper level of 'nitty gritty'. For example, you will need to consider whether you will tape record your interviews or take notes; or whether your observations will involve living in a community for a year, or making a defined number of visits (Chapter 11 covers such issues in some depth).

What

This is a tricky one because what you ask/what you look for will define the shape of your data. Now this is also discussed more thoroughly in Chapter 11, but I'll say here that you need to seek out a lot of support in developing your data collection tools.

- *What will you look for/what will you ask?* Depending on your methods, this might involve developing questionnaires, observation checklists, and frameworks for document analysis. Do not do this alone; make sure you get advice and support. These tools are difficult things to get right, and it may take a few trials or pilots to really develop them to a point where you are comfortable with the data they generate.

Table 7.2 provides an example of this who, where, when, how, what framework for developing the nitty gritty of your methodological design, and uses the 'prerequisites' discussed at the start of the chapter to assess the appropriateness of those elements. In the example provided, the use of this framework has lead to significant modifications to the original design that should make the quest for credibility much more achievable. Note that even in the second draft, there are a couple of question marks remaining. This highlights that beyond mere reflection, there is a need to pilot or trial certain aspects of your design before you can fully assess its appropriateness.

Emergent methodological design

Before leaving the 'nitty gritty' of method, I want to briefly discuss the issue of emergent methodological design. Now what I mean by this is a particular type of research design in which the researcher does not predetermine all of the details of his or her methodological protocols in advance of going into the field. This is quite distinct from haphazard or ill-defined designs. For example, in the case of both grounded theory and action research, emergence itself is a well-considered and planned part of the process. These methodologies require as much rigour as do more traditional approaches to research.

Grounded theory

Emergent methodological design is often central to grounded theory methodology. In grounded theory, researchers work inductively to generate theories strictly from the data. In the first phase of a grounded theory study a research question or topic is defined; a methodological protocol for initial data collection is implemented; data is coded and analyzed; and theories subsequently generated. Successive phases

TABLE 7.2   CHECKLIST FOR METHODOLOGICAL DESIGN

**'Do parents (mothers) teach their daughters
that worth is dependent upon external beauty?'**

A one-year research project

Methods – 1st draft	Methods – 2nd draft
WHO	*WHO*
Speaking about: parents of girls in Australia	**Speaking about:** mothers of young girls in Australia
Speaking to/observing: 30 mothers of 2–5 year-old girls in Western Sydney	**Speaking to/observing:** observe 30 mothers of 2–5 year-old girls in W. Sydney, interview 10 mothers in 2 focus groups
✗ True to the question (Not a tight match – parents/mothers Australia/Western Sydney – need to modify)	☑ True to the question (will modify question to mother and try to make a case of Australian applicability with the literature)
☑ Right for the researcher (Will enjoy working with the group)	☑ Right for the researcher (Will enjoy working with the group)
? Doable (I have access, but 30 interviews may be too many)	☑ Doable (10 in 2 groups is more realistic)
WHERE	**WHERE**
Domain: Western Sydney	**Domain:** Western Sydney
Setting: book room at University for interviews/observations	**Setting:** observe and conduct focus group at playgroup
? True to the question (maybe need a more natural setting)	☑ True to the question (more naturalistic observation)
☑ Right for the researcher (convenient)	☑ Right for the researcher (mothers live local)
☑ Doable (can book room)	☑ Doable (have checked with playgroup coordinator)
WHEN	**WHEN**
Timing: midday, midweek	**Timing:** during playgroup (4 weeks)
Timeframe: early May	**Timeframe:** March
? True to the question (mom's may be rushed/stressed – effect nap times etc.)	☑ True to the question (already in mom's weekly schedule)
☑ Right for the researcher (convenient)	☑ Right for the researcher (convenient)
? Doable (midday fine, May might not leave enough time)	☑ Doable (March should fit timeline)
HOW	**HOW**
Method: observation and individual interviews	**Method:** observation and focus group interviews
Use of method: will videotape mothers and children in simulated playgroup on four occasions and also videotape the interviews	**Use of method:** will use an observation checklist at playgroup and tape record focus groups

(Continued)

TABLE 7.2 CONTINUED

? True to the question (lots of detail with videotape, but mom's may act different if they feel under surveillance)	? True to the question (I think the checklist and tape will work, but I will need to trial the method before I really know – will pilot – may need to modify depending on pilot results)
? Right for the researcher (have made videos before – but not analyzed them – will need skill development)	☑ Right for the researcher (I have done some observation and group facilitating – but will work on developing skills)
✕ Doable (too many cameras needed to capture it all, a few mothers have said they do not feel comfortable being videotaped, 30 interviews may generate too much data)	☑ Doable (should be able to manage the data generated)
WHAT **Questions:** develop observation checklist and interview questions	**WHAT** **Questions:** develop observation checklist and focus group discussion topics
? Answers the question (will need to get support in development and pilot the tools)	? Answers the question (will need to get support in development and pilot the tools)
☑ Right for the researcher (skills that I would like to build)	☑ Right for the researcher (skills that I would like to build)
☑ Doable (have support of supervisor/methods lecturer in developing tools)	☑ Doable (have support of supervisor/methods lecturer in developing tools)

of the study are then emergent based on generated theories. This can involve re-examination of existing data, or the development and implementation of new methodological protocols for generating, coding, and analyzing additional data. In both cases, grounded theory researchers know from the planning phase of their study that much of *their* methodological protocol cannot be developed in advance, and is in fact dependent on what emerges from the initial data. This, however, is not meant to imply that grounded theory should be used as an excuse for 'qualitative' studies conducted without a well-defined methodological plan. Grounded theory may be flexible, iterative, and emergent, but it is never ill-defined, haphazard, or *ad hoc*.

Action research

Action research methodology (see Chapter 10) is also highly emergent. The goal of action research is to work with stakeholders to generate knowledge in order to action change. Because this process works towards significant change for the stakeholders, they take on the role of co-researchers. The main 'researcher' becomes a facilitator of a team that will develop the methodological protocols necessary for the action research process. This is a highly participative and collaborative type of research for which defined methodological approaches are outside the full control of the lead researcher. Rather, the process is emergent and often cyclical, and is based on collaborative input from the stakeholder/researcher team.

THOUGHTS ON THE QUALITATIVE/QUANTITATIVE DIVIDE

As a close to this chapter, I want to spend a bit of time discussing the qualitative/quantitative divide. For my money, the two most confusing words in the methods world are *quantitative* and *qualitative*. I must get asked a couple of times a semester if I am a quantitative or qualitative sociologist, which to my mind makes little sense. I do not believe that these terms are appropriate descriptors of a researcher, or for that matter a methodology or method. It is much more useful (and potentially liberating) to see these terms as simply adjectives for types of data and their corresponding modes of analysis, i.e. qualitative data – data represented through words, pictures, or icons analyzed using thematic exploration; and quantitative data – data that is represented through numbers and analyzed using statistics.

Assumptions and dichotomization

'Quantitative' and 'qualitative', however, have come to represent a whole set of assumptions that dichotomize the world of methods and limits the potential of researchers to build their methodological designs from their questions. For example, quantitative research is often described as an objective search for singular truths that relies on hypotheses and variables, and is large-scale. On the other hand, qualitative research is said to be a subjective, value-laden, biased, and *ad hoc* process that accepts multiple realities through the study of a small number of cases (Cavana et al. 2000; Creswell 1994; Neuman 1997). As shown in Figure 7.6, these beliefs can lead to unreflexive adoption of assumptions and protocols that can send a researcher down a narrow and predetermined methodological path.

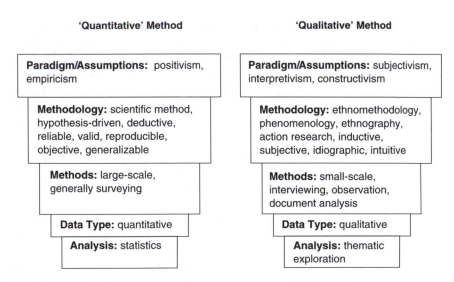

FIGURE 7.6 ASSUMPTIONS RELATED TO THE QUANTITATIVE AND QUALITATIVE

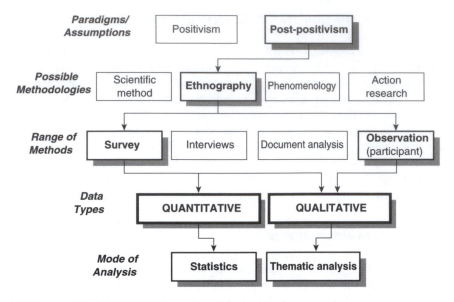

FIGURE 7.7   OPENING UP POSSIBILITIES

Opening up possibilities

The potential to develop your methodologies in the most appropriate and context-specific manner can open up tremendously if you systematically consider all the assumptions that are represented by the words 'quantitative' and 'qualitative'. Figure 7.7 gives an example of a researcher's reflexive consideration of his or her own positioning.

In the first instance, the researcher explores his or her own worldview and recognizes he or she is probably more post-positivist than positivist (see Chapter 1). The researcher then explores what accepted methodology (if any) might be appropriate for the study. In this case, the researcher decides that ethnography is a suitable methodology and moves on to consideration of data collection methods.

This researcher really wants to survey the entire population of the small community under study, but also wants to live in the community to get a more empathetic sense of the place. Now the survey will gather most data in a quantitative form, but one or two open-ended questions that will see some qualitative data also generated. It's expected that participant observation will be limited to qualitative descriptions. The plan is to then analyze the quantitative data with a statistics program like SPSS, and explore themes in the qualitative data with the assistance of a qualitative data analysis program like NU*DIST.

Now if you were to run a few different scenarios through this framework you quickly realize that the whole quantitative/qualitative divide makes little sense. You have to wonder why a positivist researcher using hypothesis-driven scientific methods would not ever want to consider anything other than numbers as a unit of analysis. On the other hand, you have to wonder why numbers are so often seen as an evil reductionist device by many post-positivist researchers. If you remove yourself from the assumptions of the quantitative/qualitative divide, your ability to develop eclectic yet logical methods that value all forms of data increases dramatically.

CHAPTER SUMMARY

- There are often a number of ways to credibly move from questions to answers with each path giving a different perspective.
- Methodological options may be diverse, but credible design is reliant upon three key 'prerequisites': the design addresses the question; it is suited to the researcher; and you have the ethics approval, resources, time, and access necessary to accomplish the task.
- The three prerequisites should not be seen as limiting creativity; rather, they are offered as a strategic safety net for exploring a range of methodologies and methods. It is worth considering whether your design can be imaginative yet focused, intuitive yet logical, flexible yet methodical, ingenious yet practical.
- Getting down to the nitty gritty of design involves being able to answer basic questions of who, where, when, what, and how, and being able to assess your answers in relation to whether they are right for the question, suited to the researcher, and are doable.
- The terms 'quantitative' and 'qualitative' have come to represent a set of assumptions that dichotomizes and limits the potential of researchers to let methodological design develop directly from their questions.
- The potential to develop the methodological design that is most appropriate to your particular context can expand if you systematically consider all the assumptions represented by the words 'quantitative' and 'qualitative'.

Exploring Populations

'How can I best understand and represent a population?'

Chapter Preview

- Population Research
- The Sampling Process
- Random Samples
- Non-random Samples
- Methods of Data Collection and Analysis

POPULATION RESEARCH

'USA Today has come out with a new survey – apparently, three out of every four people make up 75% of the population.'

–David Letterman

So what is a population, and how can you understand and 'speak' for one? Well a population is the total membership of a defined class of people, objects, or events. Now by far the best way to research any population is to gather data from every element within it. In order to do this you might conduct in-depth research on small, defined, and accessible populations. Or for larger-scale studies, you might consider conducting a 'census', which is basically a survey of every element of a defined population (often an expensive option). Most studies, however, involve populations for which it is impossible to name and access all elements.

The need to sample

Our inability to access every element of a population does little to suppress our desire to understand and speak for it. In our day-to-day lives we speak about and for populations all the time. We might talk about a chain of restaurants or a race of people, but rarely do we do this on the basis of a 'full data set'. We are unlikely to have eaten at every McDonald's, or to have chatted with every Asian person in the country. So what do we do? We gather information from a 'sample' and then apply our findings to a broader population. 'Research' works the same way. Rarely do we speak to everyone we wish to speak about, so we sample, investigate, conclude, and attempt to argue the broader applicability of our findings. The trick, however, is being able to apply our findings in a credible manner.

Working towards credibility

When researching populations, working towards credibility generally involves two distinct steps. This first is striving for 'validity' or 'authenticity' within the sample's findings. As discussed in Chapter 5, this means negotiating researcher subjectivities, approaching methods with consistency, and ensuring research processes can be audited, or even reproduced. This allows researchers to argue the credibility of their samples' findings.

To apply these sample findings to a larger population, however, requires a second level of consideration. Researchers need to consider if, and in what ways, findings might be applicable outside their immediate frame of reference. For small-scale, in-depth studies, the indicator of *transferability*, which highlights that lessons learned might be applicable in alternative settings, can be useful for researchers who, while not claiming representativeness, want their findings to be seen as more than idiographic. The goal of most population studies, however, is *generalizability* – to be able to show that findings are directly applicable to a larger population.

THE SAMPLING PROCESS

In order to generalize findings we look for samples to be representative. For example, in the real world, we wouldn't taste a spoonful of spaghetti sauce to determine if the entire pot needs more salt without stirring first. Nor do we go and see the latest Jennifer Lopez movie based solely on the comments made on her own website. We recognize that generalization requires both appropriate and representative sampling, and of course the same is true in selecting a research sample.

Far from a haphazard activity, sampling is a process that is always strategic, and sometimes mathematical. In studies with goals of generalizability, sampling will involve using the most practical procedures possible for gathering a sample that best 'represents' a larger population. At other times, however, the nature of the research question may find representativeness inappropriate or unassessable. In these cases, researchers will still strategically select their samples, but in ways that best serve their stated research goals. If these goals include transferability, researchers should be able to articulate how their sample is likely to, if not represent, then at least 'relate' to a larger population.

Regardless of any quest for representativeness, the process of sampling will still involve: naming your population; determining sample size; and employing an appropriate sampling strategy.

Naming your population

The first step in understanding and representing a population is to be able to name that population. Now populations are commonly made up of individuals, but depending on the nature of the research question, the 'unit of analysis' might be households, workplaces, or events.

Once you have identified the unit of analysis, you need to consider further defining characteristics. One common defining characteristic is geographic range. For example, you will need to consider if your population is restricted to all the people, events, or workplaces in a particular community, or whether it extends to the whole state or county, the entire country, or all developed or developing countries. In populations made up of individuals, additional defining characteristics might include age, class, gender, marital status, and/or race. Populations made up of organizations might be defined by number of employees, years of operation, type of business, etc., while events are often defined by both setting and time period.

Determining sample size

'How many people do I need in my sample?' This is an incredibly common question, with the unfortunate answer 'it depends'. Sample size, as well as appropriate sampling strategies, very much depends on the nature of your research and the shape and form of the data you intend to collect. I think the best way to come up with a figure is to consider: your goals (transferability or generalizability); the parameters of your population (how large it might be and how easy it is to identify and find its elements); and the type of data you plan to collect.

Working with qualitative data

Many researchers who collect qualitative data in order to understand populations are not looking for representativeness. Their goal is often rich understanding that may come from the few, rather than the many. Applicability comes from the 'lessons learned', that might – depending on context – be applicable in alternative or broader populations. Such studies are not so much dependent on representativeness and sample size as they are on the ability of the researcher to argue the 'relativeness' of any sample (even a single case) to a broader context.

There are, however, researchers who wish to gather qualitative data AND represent a defined population with some level of confidence, but they are often unsure how to do this because the nature of collecting qualitative data generally limits sample size. In this case, rather than rely on numbers, it will be up to the researcher to logically argue that their sample captures all the various elements/characteristics of the population under study.

Alternatively, researchers working with qualitative data can follow size guidelines required for minimal statistical analysis (covered below). This will allow them the option of quantitatively summarizing some of their qualitative findings in order to make more mathematical generalizations about their population.

Working with quantitative data

If your intention is to work with quantified data, the basic rule of thumb is to attempt to get as large a sample as possible within time and expense constraints. The logic is that the larger the sample, the more likely it can be representative, and therefore generalizable. As for minimum requirements, these are often determined by your anticipated level of statistical analysis.

Minimal statistical analysis: If your goal is to do just basic statistical analysis (sometimes used to support more qualitative data analysis), you will generally need a minimum of about 30 respondents. Because statistical analysis is based on probability, the use of smaller numbers can make it difficult to show statistical significance. This is particularly relevant for any findings with large standard deviations (widely distributed results). Keep in mind that with small samples, you will need to argue representativeness.

Intermediate statistical analysis: As you move to more sophisticated analysis, the use of any 'subdivisions' will require approximately 25 cases in each category. For example, you may have a sample of 500 members of a particular community, but only 263 females. Out of this, there are 62 mothers with children under 18, and only 20 mothers with children under five. Statistical analysis of mothers with children under five would be difficult. Similarly, if you want to show significance in multivariate analysis (the analysis of simultaneous relationships among several variables), you will need at least ten cases for each variable you wish to explore.

Advanced statistical analysis: If you want to represent a known population with a defined level of confidence, you can actually calculate the required size using the following formula:

$$n = ((K \times S)/E)^2$$

where K is desired confidence level, S is sample standard deviation, and E is the required level of precision.

If you, like me, have little desire to work the above formula, you can use a 'sample size calculator' where the only things you need to know are: the population size; the confidence interval – what range you will accept above and below the mean, say ± 5%; and the confidence level – how sure you want to be that your findings within your confidence interval are more than coincidental. Researchers usually shoot for a confidence level of 95% or 99% (see Chapter 12).

The calculator I used to produce Table 8.1 was found on the internet by typing 'sample size calculator' into the *Google* search engine, and was found at www.surveysystem.com/sscalc.htm. Table 8.1 gives you some idea of the required sample size for more commonly used confidence levels. Note that: (1) as the population increases, shifts in corresponding sample size do not increase as dramatically; (2) as you increase your levels of confidence, your required sample size will increase significantly.

Working with both quantitative and qualitative data

If you are working with both data types, you will find that the nature of collecting qualitative data will limit your sample size. However, any planned statistical analysis will require a minimum number of cases. The best advice is look above to determine the minimum size necessary for any statistical analysis you wish to do, then consider the practicalities of collecting and analyzing qualitative data from this sample. Unless you have unlimited time and money, there will usually be

TABLE 8.1 REQUIRED SAMPLE SIZE

Confidence levels / Population	95% C.L. ±5% C.I.	99% C.L. ±5% C.I.	99% C.L. ±1% C.I.
30	28	29	insufficient
100	80	87	99
500	217	286	485
1,000	278	400	943
5,000	357	588	3,845
10,000	370	624	6,247
50,000	381	657	12,486
100,000	383	661	14,267
1,000,000	384	665	16,369

some trade-off between the collection of rich, in-depth qualitative data and the level of statistical analysis that might be possible.

Remembering 'doability'

By now you are probably familiar with the term 'doable', and all the advice I just gave needs to be checked against the criteria of doability. Yes, large samples are likely to mean less 'error', but they also mean more money and more time. Now this does not mean that you can simply cut sample size and forget about 'generalizability'. On the contrary, the credibility of your research needs to be paramount in all methodological considerations. What doability does highlight, however, is the need for credible research to be designed with practicalities firmly in mind.

Employing an appropriate sampling strategy

Once you have named your population and thought through all the issues related to appropriate size, the problem of how you actually gather your sample still remains. Now sampling can be done in numerous ways, but these strategies are broadly divided into two types: those that find samples randomly selected and those that find samples strategically selected in non-random ways. Personally, I do not believe that one type of strategy is inherently better than the other. As with determining size, the strategy that is best for you will depend on the nature of your question; the make-up of your population; the type of data you wish to collect; your intended modes of analysis; and whether you are after representativeness.

RANDOM SAMPLES

Random sampling relies on random selection, or the process by which each element in a population has an equal chance of selection. For example, lottery balls scooped up while spinning in their machine, names drawn out of a hat, or computer-generated random numbers. It is a process that eliminates researcher bias and allows for statistical estimations of representativeness, and is the only choice for researchers wishing to do advanced statistical analysis.

Sounds like a straightforward process – but it does have its down side. First, relying on 'randomness' takes away the ability of the researcher to handpick a sample on the basis of any alternative criteria or theoretical considerations. Second, random sampling is a process that demands that all elements of a population are known and accessible. Finally, random sampling demands that all elements of a population are equally likely to agree to be part of a sample. When these criteria are not met, two types of error can occur:

Coverage error. This error occurs when the list you draw your sample from is not complete and therefore does not fully represent the population. For example, while every name in the hat has an equal chance of being drawn, if your name belongs in the hat but wasn't put in there, you have a coverage error. This was once a common problem when conducting telephone surveys of households. It wasn't long ago that many poorer homes did not have a phone, and of course there are still households where this is the case. Surveys reliant on e-mail addresses have a similar problem. Unless a population is defined by the fact that each individual within it has an e-mail address, coverage is likely to be incomplete.

Non-response bias: Unlike names in a hat or lottery balls in a machine, individuals randomly selected for inclusion in a sample have the right to decline. Now this is not necessarily problematic if the characteristics of those who accept and those who decline are basically the same. But that is often not the case. For example, when it comes to surveys, you often find that those who are most interested in a topic will be the ones willing to participate. Or you may offer an inducement that appeals to those with a particular need for, or interest in, what is being offered. In both cases your eventuating sample will not be representative of your population.

In order to control for these errors, it is important to consider whether the lists you draw your sample from (often called the sampling frame) are complete. If this is not the case, consideration needs to be given to any sector of the population that might miss inclusion. Similarly, your sampling design needs to explore any issues of non-response, with an attempt made to ensure broad population representation in the eventuating sample.

Simple random sampling

As the name suggests, this is the simplest type of random sampling because within a designated population all elements have an equal chance of inclusion. It is considered 'fair', and therefore allows findings to be generalized. Simple random sampling, however, is rarely used in practice because the process demands identification of all elements of the population, lists of all those elements, and a way of randomly selecting from this list – a tall order. Additionally, your sample may not capture enough elements of any subgroups you are interested in studying.

Systematic sampling

Systematic sampling involves selecting every nth case within a defined population. It may involve going to every 10th house or selecting every 20th person on a list. It is easier to do than devising methods for random selection, and offers a close approximation of random sampling as long as the elements are randomly ordered. For example, you would not have a random approximation if, say, you were to go to every 10th house which just happened to always be a stand-alone home on the corner in a neighbourhood with lots of duplexes.

Stratified random sampling

Stratified random sampling involves dividing your population into various subgroups and then taking a simple random sample within each one. This will ensure that your sample represents key subgroups of the population. Representation of the subgroups can be *proportionate* or *disproportionate*. For example, if you wanted to sample 100 nurses and the population consisted of 90% females and 10% males, a proportionate stratified sample would see you with 90 females and 10 males. In a disproportionate stratified sample you would use a different ratio which might see your sample made up of 50 males and 50 females. Keep in mind that stratification can be used in conjunction with systematic as well as random sampling.

Cluster sampling

Cluster sampling involves surveying whole clusters of the population selected through a defined random sampling strategy. Clusters might be schools, churches, or even geographic regions. These clusters are sampled so that individuals within them can be surveyed/interviewed. The thinking here is that the best way to find high school students is through high schools; or the best way to find church goers is through churches.

Multistage cluster sampling: Cluster sampling is often conducted in multiple stages. For example, say your population is high school students in the UK. First, getting a full list of this population could be really difficult. Second, if you wanted to do face-to-face surveys or interviews, you would end up all over the UK. In multistage cluster sampling you would: (1) use one of the random sampling strategies to select geographic regions in the UK; (2) from within these geographic clusters, you would then use a sampling strategy to select a number of high schools; (3) finally you would either survey all the students in these particular school clusters, or employ yet another sampling strategy to select your final student respondents. In this way your eventuating sample will be less geographically dispersed.

NON-RANDOM SAMPLES

Traditional scientists often view non-random samples as inferior because they cannot be statistically assessed for representativeness. For these researchers, 'non-random' implies samples that are gathered through strategies seen as second best or last resort. There is a growing belief, however, that there is no longer a need to 'apologize' for these types of samples. Researchers using non-random samples may be involved in studies that are not working towards representativeness or generalizability. They may be selecting their sample for other defined purposes. Further, there is growing recognition that non-random samples can credibly represent populations, given that selection is done with the goal of representativeness in mind.

This has led non-random samples to be labelled 'purposive' or 'theoretical', which highlights the importance of conscious decision-making in non-random sample selection. I, however, have chosen to not use these labels. While I certainly agree with the potential value of non-random samples, the use of the word 'purposive' implies that random samples are not purposive, which of course they are. All sampling strategies should be purposive and all purposive strategies should be of value as determined by their ability to meet stated research goals – whatever they may be.

Now if one of those research goals is representativeness, researchers using non-random samples will need to consider the main issues that often put a question mark over credibility; namely unwitting bias and erroneous assumptions.

Unwitting bias: This refers to the tendency to unwittingly act in ways that confirm what you might already suspect; and this can be quite easy to do when you are handpicking your sample. For example, you may want to conduct a focus group that can help evaluate a subject you are teaching. It can be just too easy to stack the deck in your favour (not that I would know!). Or in a study of sexually active teenagers, you may be drawn to those whose experiences tend to re-enforce your belief that, say, parental conflict is related to sexual promiscuity. You unwittingly seek out teenagers whose history matches your preconceived notions. In either case, your bias will affect your ability to generalize with any credibility.

Erroneous assumptions: This refers to sample selection that is premised on incorrect assumptions. Say, for example, you want to study Jewish women living in Detroit and you decide to go to Detroit's synagogues to look for volunteers. The problem here is that you have assumed all Jewish women go to a synagogue. This is an erroneous population assumption, and your resultant sample is not likely to be representative. Another example involves erroneous assumptions about particular elements of your sample. Say you want to study anger post-divorce and you select what you believe are extreme cases of 'anger'. If your assumptions are incorrect and what you see as extreme is actually quite average, the generalizations you make will not be valid.

In order to control for these sources of bias, it is well worth brainstorming and articulating your own ideas, assumptions, and expectations in relation to both your research questions and your proposed sample. You can then reflexively work towards developing a strategy that will best serve your project's stated goals.

Handpicked sampling

Handpicked sampling involves the selection of a sample with a particular purpose in mind. When looking for representativeness this might involve selecting cases that meet particular criteria; are considered typical; show wide variance; represent 'expertise'; or cover a range of possibilities. Other options for handpicked sampling include the selection of critical, extreme, deviant, or politically important cases. While not likely to be representative, the selection of such cases allows researchers to study intrinsically interesting cases, or enhance learning by exploring the limits or boundaries of a situation or phenomenon.

Snowball sampling

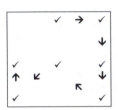

Snowball sampling is often used when working with populations that are not easily identified or accessed. Basically, the process involves building a sample through referrals. You begin by identifying someone from your population who is willing to be in your study. You then ask them to identify others who meet the study criteria. Each of those individuals is then asked for further recommendations. For example, it may not be possible to identify a population that consists of mothers of children with attention deficit disorder (ADD). Mothers of ADD kids, however, often know other mothers, who know even more mothers. While snowball sampling can quickly build a sample, there is no guarantee of representativeness. If this is a goal, you may want to combine snowball sampling with other sampling strategies. Another alternative is to develop a profile of your population from the literature, and assess representativeness by comparing your sample to your profile.

Volunteer sampling

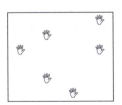

Volunteer sampling simply refers to the process of selecting a sample by asking for volunteers. This may involve putting an ad in the newspaper or going to local organizations such as churches, schools, or community groups. Now this method of sampling can be highly convenient, but it is not likely to be representative. In many ways you have a situation similar to non-response bias. That is, within any given population, the characteristics of those who volunteer are likely to be quite distinct from those who don't. Again, you'll find that those most interested, or those most susceptible to any offered inducements, will be most likely to participate. Arguments for representativeness will rely on strategies used to minimize the difference between volunteers and the rest of the population.

A note on 'convenience' sampling

In almost all writings on sampling, you will find something referred to as 'convenience' sampling, i.e. selecting a sample in a manner convenient to the researcher. Usually, convenience sampling falls under the heading of non-random or non-probabilistic sampling – and in fact, often heads up the list. But put simply, convenience sampling has no place in credible research. There needs to be more to a sampling strategy than just convenience. Sure, limited time and money may see convenience become *one* factor in any type of sample selection, but I do not believe that convenience should be the main criteria or descriptor of a sampling strategy. Regardless of type, all sampling strategies need to work towards the ultimate goal of research credibility.

METHODS OF DATA COLLECTION AND ANALYSIS

Before concluding this chapter, I want to briefly talk about methods of data collection and analysis appropriate to exploring populations. Now all of the relevant methods are covered in detail in Chapters 11 and 12, but I wanted to mention a range of methods here because I've found that as soon you mention populations and samples, students' minds jump to surveys and statistics.

Yes, under the positivist umbrella population studies usually involve: (a) the use of a standardized instrument, most often a survey questionnaire to; (b) collect quantitative data from; (c) a randomly drawn representative sample that can; (d) be statistically analyzed. In fact these parameters are often seen as criteria for arguing generalizability.

The narrowness of these 'criteria', however, have meant that studies that fall outside the above parameters, i.e. studies that: (a) might use a variety of methods to; (b) collect qualitative data from; (c) non-random samples that can; (d) be analyzed thematically, are often seen as simply idiographic and unable to make a contribution to broader understandings.

Such studies, however, are increasingly recognized as crucial to understanding populations. Consequently, a range of methods for data collection and analysis are now called upon to help us understand a world of complexity. Yes, surveys and statistics are appropriate methods for exploring populations, but observations, interviews, and documents analyzed statistically and/or thematically can also be called upon in population research.

Further Reading

Additional readings on methods of data collection/analysis appropriate to population studies can be found at the ends of Chapters 11 and 12. For further readings on sampling, you may find the following useful:

Levy, P. S. and Lemeshow, S. (1999) *Sampling of Populations: Methods and Applications*. New York: Wiley-Interscience.

Lohr, S. L. (1998) *Sampling: Design and Analysis*. Pacific Grove, CA: Brooks/Cole.

Rao, P. S. R. S., Rao, Poduri, S. R. S. and Miller, W. (2000) *Sampling Methodologies with Applications*. New York: Lewis Publishers.

Thompson, S. K. (2002) *Sampling*. New York: John Wiley and Sons.

Tortu, S., Goldsamt, L. A. and Hamid, R. (eds) (2001) *A Practical Guide to Research and Services with Hidden Populations*. Boston, MA: Allyn and Bacon.

Wainer, H. (2000) *Drawing Inferences from Self-selected Samples*. Mahwah, NJ: Lawrence Erlbaum Associates.

CHAPTER SUMMARY

- We don't often speak to everyone we wish to speak about, so understanding populations often involves sampling, investigating, concluding, and attempting to argue the broader applicability of our findings.
- Credibility in population studies relies on both striving for validity or authenticity within the sample's findings and appropriately applying those findings outside the immediate frame of reference.
- The process of sample selection involves naming your population, determining sample size, and employing appropriate sampling strategies.
- Random sampling refers to sampling strategies that give every element of a population an equal chance of selection. Strategies include simple random sampling, systematic sampling, stratified random sampling, and cluster sampling.
- There are two common errors in random sampling: coverage error – where the list you draw your sample from is incomplete and non-response bias – when the characteristics of those who accept and those who decline participation are distinct.
- Non-random sampling refers to strategic requests for 'volunteers', the use of informants that 'snowball', or 'handpicking' respondents. To select a sample on the basis of convenience alone can threaten a study's credibility.
- Non-random sampling strategies are not always used with a goal of generating representative samples. However, researchers with that goal need to consider the issues of: unwitting bias – drawing samples that confirm preconceived notions, and erroneous assumptions – sample selection premised on incorrect suppositions.
- Traditionally, population studies involved the use of survey questionnaires, quantitative data, random samples, and statistical analysis. However, a variety of methods, data types, modes of analysis, and the use of non-random samples have broadened possibilities for understanding populations.

9 | Investigating Complexities of the Social World

'I really want to understand what's going on here.'

Chapter Preview

- **Delving into Complexities**
- **Exploring Bounded Systems**
- **Exploring Cultural Groups**
- **Exploring Phenomena**
- **Exploring the Everyday**

DELVING INTO COMPLEXITIES

'The pure and simple truth is rarely pure and never simple.'

—Oscar Wilde

Trying to get an overview of a particular situation may find you surveying a wide array of individuals in order to seek 'statistically significant' findings. But there may also be times when you want to delve deeper into social complexities; times when you want to get below the 'pure and simple truth' – times when you want to explore the interactions, processes, lived experiences, and belief systems that are a part of individuals, institutions, cultural groups, and even the everyday.

Delving into such complexities is likely to find you working with small numbers, but generating 'rich' data. The goal is to gain an intimate understanding of people, places, cultures, and situations through rich engagement and even immersion into the reality you are studying. The goal of this chapter is to explore some of the issues that need to be managed in the quest to delve deeper, and introduce you to some of the cornerstone methodologies used for researching at this level.

Working towards credibility

While there are numerous strategies that allow researchers to 'investigate social complexities', many share elements that make the quest for credibility through the use of traditional positivist criteria difficult to establish. Studies that 'delve deeper', for example, often involve working with non-random samples; generating mainly qualitative data; conducting research in natural settings; searching for holistic meaning; and recognizing and managing the inherent biases of the researcher. Delving deeper can also involve emergent methodological design; inductive analysis; idiographic interpretation; and even the possibility of negotiated outcomes that recognize the need for the researched to be party to a researcher's constructed meanings.

Criteria

Often studies with these types of parameter are inappropriately assessed according to positivist criteria, and, as might be expected, fall short of expectation. But this is simply a matter of using the wrong criteria for the job. As discussed in Chapter 5, all studies, regardless of goals or even their paradigmatic positioning, need to consider whether: subjectivities have been managed; methods are approached with consistency; 'true essence' has been captured; findings have broad applicability; and, finally, whether findings can be verified. Criteria for such assessment, however, are likely to be neutrality or transparent subjectivity rather than objectivity; dependability over reliability; authenticity over validity; transferability over generalizability; and auditability rather than reproducibility (for a full discussion of indicators, refer to Chapter 5).

Strategies

Now I have a real love–hate relationship with quantitative data and statistics. All the numbers, coding, data entry, stats programs, knowing what tests to run, and understanding the meaning of various p-values (all of which are discussed in Chapter 12) can be a nightmare. The pay off, however, is that if this is done with diligence and rigour, you come out with this beautiful thing called 'statistical significance'. You actually get numbers that assess the reliability/validity/generalizability of your findings.

Unfortunately, this is not the case in smaller-scale studies using alternative indicators. In studies with small samples centred on thematically analyzed qualitative data, tests of statistical significance are irrelevant. Yet there is still a need to work towards credibility. A number of authors (Creswell 1998; Ely et al. 1991; Janesick 2000; Lincoln and Guba 1985; Morse 1998; Richardson 2000; Straus and Corbin 1998) have suggested that credibility for studies that attempt to 'delve deeper' can be established through strategies that ensure thoroughness and seek confirmation. Such strategies are summarized in Box 9.1.

Box 9.1   Strategies for Achieving Credibility

Techniques that can be used to ensure thoroughness and rigour include:

- **Saturation** – to finish collecting data only when additional data no longer adds richness to understanding or aids in building theories

---

- **Crystallization** – building a rich and diverse understanding of one single situation or phenomenon by seeing the world as multifaceted, and accepting that what we see depends on where we look, where the light is, etc.
- **Prolonged engagement** – investment of time sufficient to learn the culture, understand context, and/or build trust and rapport
- **Persistent observation** – to look for readings of a situation beyond an initial, possibly superficial, level
- **Broad representation** – representation wide enough to ensure that an institution, cultural group, or phenomenon can be spoken about confidently
- **Peer review** – external check on the research process in which a colleague is asked to act as a 'devil's advocate' in regards to all aspects of methodology

Techniques that can be used to obtain confirmation or verification include:

- **Triangulation** – using more than one source of data to confirm the authenticity of each source
- **Member checking** – checking that interpretation of events, situations, and phenomena gels with the interpretations of 'insiders'
- **Full explication of method** – providing readers with sufficient methodological detail so that studies are auditable and/or reproducible

EXPLORING BOUNDED SYSTEMS

There are many times when the desire to delve into complexities will involve the exploration of a 'bounded system', i.e. a particular instance or entity that can be defined by identifiable boundaries. While the goal here is unlikely to be representation of a population, an in-depth examination of one particular individual, institution, instance, or occurrence can add much illumination to a body of knowledge. The exploration of a bounded system is often referred to as a case study.

Understanding the case study

Case study: A method of studying elements of the social through comprehensive description and analysis of a single situation or case, for example, a detailed study of an individual, group, episode, event, or any other unit of social life organization. Emphasis is often placed on understanding the unity and wholeness of the particular case.

It is hard to know exactly how to class case studies. The 'case study' is often referred to as a methodology, but, literally, the term refers to the form and shape of 'participants'. The methodological approaches associated with case studies are actually eclectic and broad. Not only can they involve any number of data-gathering methods, i.e. surveys, interviews, observation, and document analysis, but they can also involve the use of a number of methodologies, including those that follow in this and the subsequent chapter.

The implication of studies concentrated on cases, however, does bring some unity to their study. As Goode and Hatt said over 50 years ago, the case study is 'a way of organizing social data so as to preserve the unitary character of the social object being studied' (1952: 331). Case studies therefore have much in common with methodologies generally used to 'delve deeper'. That is they allow for in-depth exploration; are an examination of subtleties and intricacies; attempt to be holistic; explore processes as well as outcomes; and investigate the context and setting of a situation.

The strength of case studies

There are a number of reasons why case studies are quite common in social and applied science. On a practical level, they concentrate research efforts on one case or one site, and therefore offer one set of boundaries for the study. This can minimize travel, ease access, and reduce costs – making the study 'doable'. On a more strategic level, case studies attempt to build holistic understandings through the development of rapport and trust. The goal is 'authenticity' and a richness and depth in understanding that goes beyond what is generally possible in large-scale survey research.

While an individual case study may not be generalizable, it can still offer much to the production of knowledge. Case studies can:

- *have an intrinsic value* – cases might be unique, interesting, or even misunderstood
- *be used to debunk a theory* – one case can show that what is commonly accepted might, in fact, be wrong
- *bring new variables to light* – exploratory case studies can often bring new understandings to the fore
- *provide supportive evidence for a theory* – case studies can be used to provide anecdotal evidence for a theory or to triangulate other data collection methods
- *be used collectively to form the basis of a theory* – a number of cases may be used to inductively generate new theory

The difficulties associated with case studies

While concentrating research efforts on one case or site can reduce costs, limit travel, and minimize issues of access, the trade-off is generally in-depth immersion and prolonged engagement. This can be 'expensive' for the researcher on a number of levels. First, the required level of access can be difficult to negotiate. Second, because case studies draw from only one or even a few, the demands on that one or few can be quite high. Third, the researcher can come to have an effect on the researched and vice versa. And finally, immersion can come with emotional costs for all parties involved.

On an other level altogether, you may also have to deal with those who aren't willing to give the time of day to any study not deemed to be 'generalizable'. Now you may not be able to convince every reader of the worth of a 'case study', but if you clearly articulate your goals and show how your study contributes to a particular body of knowledge, you are more likely to establish credibility and worth.

The process of doing case studies

As indicated, the process of doing a case study is not easily articulated because a case study is not really a 'methodology'. Rather, it is an approach to research that is predicated on in-depth case analysis. Accordingly, this section concentrates on the nature of cases and their selection, and only briefly outlines potential methodologies and methods for data collection and analysis.

Case selection

One of the most crucial determinations in conducting any case study is selecting the right case. Whether a case is of intrinsic value, or is seen to be representative of a larger population, it must provide the researcher with sufficient data to make relevant arguments. In order to select an appropriate case, you need to:

- *Define a 'case'* – this involves defining boundaries that separate some aspect of the case that makes it distinct. This might involve defining individuals on the basis of their job – say a police officer; their intrinsic characteristics – an aboriginal youth; or their experiences – a recovered anorexic teenager. It can also be a cultural group such as an immigrant family; a work team in a factory; or university students living in a college dormitory. You can also define cases by events, such as the implementation of an exercise programme in a workplace or the introduction of companion dogs in a prison. There are endless possibilities, but the key is to clearly articulate your boundaries, and be able to argue the importance of an in-depth study of a case within those boundaries.
- *Determine how many cases you will explore* – you may want to delve into only one case, or you may want to compare and contrast cases from two of more settings. You can also attempt in-depth analysis of a number of cases in a bid to argue representativeness and generalizability. The appropriate number of cases is highly dependent on your research goals and what you wish to uncover.
- *Select cases for study* – the selection of cases is generally non-random, with researchers handpicking cases on a pragmatic or theoretical basis. Pragmatic selection may involve commitment – the researcher is commissioned or sponsored to study a particular case; opportunity – the researcher takes advantage of a current event, i.e. farmers suffering through drought, or the rebuilding of a community after bushfires; or access – the researcher takes advantage of access that might normally be hard to get, i.e. a nursing home where they work part-time, or a school where they were once a student.

  Theoretical selection involves selecting cases for research-oriented purposes. For example, if the purpose is to attempt to argue generalizability, the researcher may select a case considered 'typical'. Alternatively, an extreme instance may be chosen in order to debunk a theory or highlight deviations from the norm. Another possibility is to seek wide variance in order to aid theory generation. Finally, selection may involve cases of intrinsic interest.

Methodology and methods

Since 'cases' in a case study can involve individuals, cultural groups, communities, phenomena, events and, in fact, any unit of social life organization, virtually all methodologies and/or data collection tools can be called upon dependent on the case at hand.

- *Methodologies* – this chapter, as well as the one that follows, discusses a number of methodologies suitable to case studies. For example, ethnography may be suitable for the study of a cultural group, while phenomenology might be appropriate for exploring the lived experience of a particular phenomenon. A case that explores doctor–patient interactions may call for an ethnomethod-ological approach, while a workplace attempting to change its focus may be suited to action research. The nature of your inquiry and the nature of your case will determine the most suitable methodology.
- *Methods* – methods used for data collection and analysis also run the full gamut and are rarely confined to one approach. Case studies are generally multi-method and often rely on interviews, observation, and document analysis in a bid to obtain rich qualitative data. In studies where a number of individuals form the case, for example, a community or workplace, surveying can also be used for the collection of qualitative as well as quantitative data. Chapter 11 covers data collection methods, while Chapter 12 covers qualitative and quantitative data analysis.

EXPLORING CULTURAL GROUPS

Conventional social scientists often rely on survey or interview processes to build understandings of cultural groups. These researchers are likely to make inquiries of a number of group members in a bid to understand their attitudes, beliefs, opinions, and/or behaviours. Delving deeper into cultures, however, can go beyond an exploration of simply what is, and may begin to explore why it is. Researchers can explore how cultural understandings are shaped, and how group members make sense of their experiences. Whether it be foreign cultures, marginal cultures closer to home, or even our own culture, delving into cultural complexities often involves an attempt to understand the world from the perspective of the participants, and often involves prolonged and participative cultural engagement. Ethnography, a research methodology with roots in cultural anthropology, can be quite powerful in building understandings at this level.

Understanding ethnography

Ethnography: To 'write a culture'. Involves exploration of a cultural group in a bid to understand, discover, describe, and interpret a way of life from the point of view of its participants.

Now on the surface this may seem fairly straightforward, but complexities become clear as you unpack the definition.

1. Ethnography is the study of *cultural groups*. This is significant because the term 'cultural' suggests that what binds the group is more than say genetics, biology,

or geography. 'Cultural' groups are bound together by social traditions and common patterns of beliefs and behaviours, for example, ethnic groups, community groups, or even workplace groups. Ethnographic studies are premised on the belief that how an individual processes the world is constructed and constrained by cultural experience. The study of cultural groups is thereby the study of shared understandings as well as the symbolic aspects of behaviour that can uncover cultural or normative patterns. In other words, ethnography explores the methods, rules, roles, and expectations that structure any given situation.

2. Ethnography explores a way of life *from the point of view of its participants*. It attempts to understand the symbolic world in which people live. The goal is to 'see' things the way group members do, and grasp the meanings that they use to understand and make sense of the world. In other words, ethnographers attempt to interpret meanings from within a culture, or build what Geertz (2000) refers to as 'thick descriptions'. This is significant because ethnography accepts multiple realities and requires cultural empathy. Rather than set understandings against a sometimes unrecognized Western worldview, ethnographers attempt to suspend judgement and understand from the perspective of the researched.

3. In ethnography, to *explore* is to *understand, discover, describe, and interpret*. Now a somewhat common critique of ethnography is that it is merely descriptive. But generating 'thick descriptions' that build an understanding of the underlying frameworks that produce both behaviour and meaning is an act of discovery as much as it is an act of description. And of course these descriptions are filtered through a researcher's worldview, inherent biases, and theoretical and analytical frameworks. Thus, in the words of Emerson, ethnographic descriptions are a researcher's 'theory informed re-presentations' (1983: 21).

The strengths of ethnography

The strengths of ethnography are quite readily revealed in its expanded definition. Ethnography offers:

*   rich and in-depth exploration of the values, beliefs, and practices of cultural groups through thick description of real people in natural settings. This may be a culture that is intrinsically interesting, or one that is explored to shed light on more fundamental cultural norms.
*   a way of exploring the working nature of culture, symbols, and norms. This can lead to a dialogue with existing theory, as well as insights that can lead to the development of new theory.
*   recognition of the importance of multiple worldviews. Ethnography offers an approach for building understandings from the perspective of the researched.

The difficulties associated with ethnography

Some of the difficulties associated with ethnography are shared by a range of studies that involve 'immersion'. These include: gaining access and building trust; emotional costs; the potential for the researcher to have an effect on the researched; and the demands placed on those being studied. But there are also concerns more specific to ethnography that need to be seriously considered and skilfully negotiated.

First, ethnographers need to guard against 'homogenization' that can give minimal recognition to divergence within a particular group. Ethnographers also need to be aware of a somewhat paradoxical dilemma in representing the reality of others. Ethnography has an explicit goal of building and interpreting understandings from the perspective of the researched. However, it also accepts that descriptions are necessarily interpretative, and that the basis of interpretation is the filtering of observations and inputs through theoretical and analytic frameworks that are, of course, imbued with a researcher's own worldview. This then begs the question, can an outsider (particularly one from a very divergent culture) ever truly know, describe, and interpret the reality of being an insider? Hmmmm....

How you manage this 'paradox' will depend on how you reflect on the above question, as well as your ability to mount arguments that will satisfy a sceptic's concerns over credibility. This will require you to reflexively consider and articulate: how you as a researcher have had an impact on the interpretative practices within your research; what strategies you have employed to seek thoroughness and confirmation (see Box 9.1); and the significance of your research findings to a particular body of knowledge.

The process of doing ethnography

Ethnographic studies attempt to understand the reality of the researched. They therefore involve the exploration of cultural groups within natural settings and often require 'immersion' through prolonged engagement and persistent observation. Data collection is generally multi-method and eclectic, and often continues until saturation. The research process is flexible and emergent, and likely to evolve as lived realities within the cultural group are revealed. While ethnography is a methodology commonly used in anthropological studies, its principles can be used in a wide range of contexts.

Selecting a cultural group

Just as there was a need to define a 'case', there is also a need to define a 'cultural group'. As discussed, a cultural group is defined by more than biology or geography. A cultural group needs to meet the prerequisite of a shared culture. It may be an exotic foreign culture (for example, a native 'tribe'), or a culture closer to home (for example, a migrant community or a boarding school). It is also possible to study a 'dominant' cultural group, which can be quite revealing because it is often dominance itself that causes privileged knowledge and governing ideologies to go unseen.

The selection of any particular cultural group will be driven by pragmatics, intrinsic interest, theory, or any combination thereof. As with case studies, pragmatics might involve research commitments, timely opportunities, or accessibility. Cultural groups can also be selected to increase idiographic understanding, i.e. selecting groups that are: unique and unfamiliar; misunderstood or misrepresented; marginal and unheard; or dominant, yet not reflexively explored. Finally, cultural groups can be selected on the basis of theory. For example, if the goal of a study is to understand how meaning is constructed, or to explore the interpretative and/or symbolic practices that define 'cultures', then the selection of a particular group might, on the judgement of the researcher, be made on the basis of being typical, atypical, extreme, or rare.

Regardless of how a cultural group is selected, it is essential that an ethnographic researcher has a very high level of access within the group. The researcher must believe that it will be possible to build rapport and trust. Credible ethnographic studies require that researchers are able to get below the surface, break through the pleasantries, and observe cultural actors and actions that are not performed solely for the benefit of the researcher.

Methods of data collection and analysis

The goal of the ethnographer is thick description and rich and reflexive interpretation, and few ethnographers would want to limit themselves to only one method of data collection. In order to gather a rich picture, most will use an array of tools, including observation, interviews, and document analysis (as discussed below and in more detail in Chapter 11). Now while the data generated can include the quantitative, the preponderance of ethnographic data is likely to be qualitative so that the richness of the symbolic world can be fully described (qualitative data analysis strategies are covered in Chapter 12).

- *Observation* – participant observation is common to most ethnographic studies and tends to involve deep cultural immersion. Ethnographers attempt to build cultural empathy and 'live' the reality of the other. Ethnographers can also engage in non-participant techniques in order to generate more structured observations.
- *Interviews* – these are generally in-depth and unstructured, and, in line with participant observation, often take the form of 'conversations'. Such 'interviews' can involve key informants, and/or individuals who represent cross-sections of the cultural group, i.e. men, women, children, the elderly, new members, foundational members, etc.
- *Document analysis* – sometimes a good way to understand the reality of the researched is to examine the texts that they themselves produce. Depending on the nature of the cultural group being explored, this might involve an examination of local newspapers, locally produced television, and/or radio broadcasts. Or it may involve analysis of local art, the poetry and essays of schoolchildren, journals and diaries, and/or doctrine and dogma.
- *Surveys* – while surveys are often critiqued by those conducting ethnographies for being too reductionist, I do not believe they should be unilaterally dismissed as a potential data-gathering tool. While studies based solely on survey research would not qualify as ethnography, a survey instrument, such as a questionnaire, may be the best way to canvas widely within a particular cultural group.

EXPLORING PHENOMENA

There are plenty of methods that can be used to acquire a better understanding of populations, individuals, and social/cultural groups. We can conduct a survey, do an interview, or run a focus group. We can also observe people in action, or we can explore and interrogate what they write and what is written about them. Such methods might also help illuminate 'constructs'. Take power, for example, the methods listed above can help us understand what it is, who has it, how it is wielded, and where it is found.

But what if you don't want to explore people, and you are not particularly interested in drawing out the who, what, why, and wherefore of a construct. What if your interest lies is in 'phenomena' or an individual's 'lived experience' of a particular 'object'. For example, rather than an interest in refugees or migration, your interest lies in understanding the lived experience of displacement; or rather than a particular desire to study athletes or the construct of competition, you want to understand the lived experience of victory; or more than understanding leaders and leadership, you want to delve deeper into the lived experience or 'phenomenon' of power.

Now phenomenology is literally the 'study of phenomena', but various forms of phenomenology, for example, social, philosophical, existential, empirical, hermeneutical, psychological, and transcendental, which are all highly theory-dependent, make it exceedingly difficult to succinctly describe the field and/or its methods. This, therefore, is not my intention. Instead, my intention is to draw on some of the theory and methodological approaches that might help you delve into the exploration of 'phenomena'. If you want to go further into the theory and processes of phenomenology, some suggestions for further reading are provided at the end of this chapter.

Understanding phenomenology

Phenomenology is premised on a world that is: (1) 'constructed' – people are creative agents in building a social world; and (2) 'intersubjective' – we experience the world with and through others. Therefore, to really understand and make sense of the world, you need to explore human phenomena without worrying about their causes, truth-value, reality, or appearances. You need to know how individuals go about making sense of their direct experiences. A concise definition might therefore be:

Phenomenology: Study of phenomena as they present themselves in direct experience.

This definition begs the question: What exactly is a phenomenon and how can you best go about studying it? I think the easiest way to explain this is to go over the basic elements in a phenomenological study and highlight the role each element plays in defining, understanding, and researching phenomena.

Phenomenological studies are highly dependent on individuals. Individuals, either through interviews or their cultural products, i.e. what they write, paint, etc., are used to draw out the experiences of a particular phenomenon. For example, refugees, athletes, or leaders might be called upon to provide descriptions of the experience of displacement, victory, and power, respectively. Individuals are therefore central to the conduct of phenomenological studies. But it is their descriptions of lived experience, rather than they themselves, that are the focus of phenomenology.

Phenomenological studies are also highly dependent on constructs. Constructs such as displacement, victory, and power are central to the phenomenological experience being explored. In phenomenological studies, however, the 'reality' of the construct is not of concern and should, in fact, be 'bracketed', i.e. they should be explored as free as possible from what the world says they are supposed to be, or supposed to mean. In phenomenology, a construct freed from its constructed meaning is often referred to as an 'object'.

Phenomena, which are the focus of phenomenology, actually sit at the intersection of people and 'objects', and centre on an individual's lived experience of these 'objects'. Rather than ask what causes X, or what is X, phenomenology explores the experience of X. In other words, phenomenology is the study of the experience of the relationship between the individual and the object. It is the study of a phenomenon as it presents itself in an individual's direct awareness.

The strengths of phenomenology

I think the main strength of phenomenology is that it offers a way of exploring these things called 'phenomena', something I believe is highly important in understanding our social world. Yet phenomena are often ignored in studies of the social. We explore the demographics, opinions, attitudes, beliefs, and behaviours of people, and we study the ideas, ideologies, and constructs that make up the social world. The study of phenomena, however, has never really moved into mainstream social science research, and often goes undiscussed as a potential research strategy available to student researchers.

Phenomenology reminds us that: (1) there are things called phenomena in the social world; (2) that these things can be researched; and (3) they are a worthy object of inquiry. Now taken to its philosophical extreme, the value of phenomenology might be understanding consciousness, pure truth, or existential knowing. If this is your interest, it is well worth reading the more philosophical works listed at the end of this chapter. But given that you are reading a social science research methods text, I'm going to highlight the value of studying more day-to-day phenomena. For example, understanding and describing the lived experience of critical illness. This would be essential reading for anyone wishing to develop appropriate protocols for mental health workers dedicated to the critically ill. Or what about capturing the essence of what it is like to live with AIDS – that description could be invaluable to someone recently diagnosed. And any study that explored stress would not be complete without understanding its lived experience.

The difficulties associated with phenomenology

In many ways, I can understand why the study of phenomena is relatively uncommon in the social sciences. The literature on the topic is thick and hard to read; is theoretically and conceptually divergent; and does not offer much clear guidance when it comes to actual 'methods'. Besides, most research methods books don't cover the topic at all, or do so by merely pulling out bits from the literature in ways that are not necessarily logical or helpful. The same goes for teaching and learning. In my 'training' as a social scientist, phenomenology was not a method that was discussed, and when it was covered in my philosophy classes, it was not done in a way that would help me in conducting a phenomenological study. The implication is that unless you have a supervisor or mentor experienced in phenomenology, 'doing' a phenomenological study is likely to go unconsidered or be uncharted terrain.

The process of studying phenomena

There are three basic elements to most methodological approaches used in the social sciences. These are your participants, your data collection methods, and intended modes of analysis. And of course, the end product is your 'report'. Well, it doesn't quite work that way in phenomenology. The product of phenomenological studies is phenomenological descriptions; and gathering descriptions, making sense of those descriptions, and writing-up those descriptions are not necessarily discrete activities.

Producing phenomenological description

Okay, so what do I mean by 'not discrete activities'. Well let's assume you have identified the phenomenon you wish to study. The next step involves gathering rich descriptions of that phenomenon. You can do this in a couple of ways. First, you can conduct in-depth interviews. This will involve finding people who have experienced the phenomenon you wish to study. How many? Well there may be more than one way to experience a phenomenon, and a common goal of phenomenology is to describe distinct experiences of the same phenomenon. So while your sample is unlikely to be very large or representative, you will probably want to conduct a number of interviews that ensure variation or lead to saturation.

The goal of the interview or 'conversation' is to draw out rich descriptions of lived experience. In other words, rather than explore how or why something is, you would ask your respondents to tell you what it feels like, what it reminds them of, and how they would describe it. This is often done in a dialogic manner where the interviewee is encouraged to further reflect on various aspects of their descriptions. This might involve digging below the surface of words to understand the meaning behind them. For example, the phenomenon of rejection first described as 'horrible' might be further described as 'like having absolutely no worth' or 'it's like I'm drowning'. In this way, the researcher and the researched are co-creators of a narrative that is both descriptive and interpretative, and is often rich, poetic, and full of metaphor. The produced text is therefore both the phenomenological process and its product.

Now I mentioned that there is another way to gather phenomenological description, and that is by exploring pre-produced texts. Beautiful, rich phenomenological descriptions abound in letters, journals, books, movies, poetry, and music. Take for example (and I'm not being facetious here), the phenomenon of being 'dumped'. Imagine the rich and poetic phenomenological descriptions you might be able to gather from popular music alone.

A second cycle

The second cycle in conducting phenomenological studies and producing phenomenological description is the synthesis of generated or located texts. Here what is being explored is the potentially different ways of experiencing a phenomenon. So rather than describe variations between individuals, this second cycle looks for a range of experiences related to the phenomenon itself. This is generally done through a process of identifying themes that reduce unimportant dissimilarities and integrate the essential nature within various descriptions. To do this, researchers might engage in an iterative writing and rewriting process (hermeneutics), or more traditional qualitative data analyses that involves thematic exploration (more on these processes in Chapter 12). Regardless of specific method, reflection and analysis cycles between the texts and eventuating themes. In my own study of apostasy, for example, which by the way is the process of giving up religion, 80 in-depth interviews led to a phenomenological description of apostasy that had three major and distinct themes. Those were the phenomenon of apostasy as 'resentful reaction', 'melancholic introspection', and 'spiritual exploration' (O'Leary 1999). And while this study was not strictly phenomenological, the generation of these themes were both process and product.

EXPLORING THE EVERYDAY

We wake up, we get ready to face the day, and throughout that day we have interactions – with our parents, with our children, with our work colleagues, with our partners, with the check-out person at the grocery store. And all day long we make judgements, sometimes conscious but mainly subconscious, about how we should act and what we should say. And we generally do this without too much stress because we are socialized with an appropriate repertoire of rules, norms, and patterns that help us wade through interactions of the 'everyday'.

Ethnomethodology, the approach most closely associated with delving into the interactions of the everyday, can be traced to the work of Harold Garfinkel in the 1960s. But there is actually an even more famous 'ethnomethodologist' – Jerry Seinfeld. Yes, Jerry Seinfeld the comedian. A man who makes his living by exploring and deconstructing the minutiae of the everyday. *Seinfeld*; the 'show about nothing', is actually a show about what we take for granted as we manage the interactions that make up the everyday. I'll get back to *Seinfeld* later on, but first I'll try to work you through the meaning of ethnomethodology.

Understanding ethnomethodology

Ethnomethodology: Study of the methods that individuals use to make sense of their social world and accomplish their daily actions.

So what does this mean? It means that individuals engage in interpretative work every time they interact with the world. In order to do this in a sensical manner, they engage in what Garfinkel (1967) refers to as '*documentary method*'. This involves '*indexicality*' – or selecting cues from a social interaction that conforms to a recognizable pattern – and then making sense of that interaction in terms of that pattern. I know this sounds confusing, but in practice it's pretty simple because it's something you do 'automatically' everyday. For example, if someone said, 'I couldn't help but notice you', you take cues from the social interaction to find the likely pattern, and formulate an appropriate response. So if you were in a nightclub and the person speaking to you was of the opposite sex, the pattern might be 'the pick-up' and you might reply with a disgusted, 'get lost, you loser' or a seductive, 'yeah … I noticed you too'. The other party has to then subconsciously find the right pattern, in this case let's say 'rejection' or 'flirtation', and form the appropriate response. Through the use of '*reflexivity*' you then use that response to generate your next response and so on and so forth until the interaction ends. In this way the pattern is emergent, but is consistently used in its most recent formulation to interpret new elements of the interaction.

Ethnomethodology is the study of these methods or the systematic discovery processes that individuals use to negotiate their way through the everyday. Ethnomethodological focus is on uncovering the 'rules' that direct ordinary life. It's not interested in whether what is said or done is right or wrong, true or false. In fact, ethnomethodology ignores the question of 'what' altogether and concentrates on 'how' interactions are performed.

The strengths of ethnomethodology

I think ethnomethodology offers quite a bit to the study of the social, including:

- recognition of the interpretative work of the individual, as well as methods for exploring that work. Ethnomethodology explores how individuals make sense of, and make sense in, the social word, and recognizes that individuals are not passive in making meaning and establishing social order.
- recognition that the actual process of interacting ('how' questions) are worthy topics of investigation, and that the topic of verbal interactions ('what' questions) and the reason for interactions ('why' questions) are not the only types of question that a social scientist can ask.
- another way to study culture. Ethnomethodology can be used to explore how members of a particular cultural group make meaning and engage in interpretative work. This can offer much to our understanding of the nature of communication and social structure within a culture.
- a way of investigating how particular types of interaction are performed. For example, how juries deliberate and draw conclusions, or how medical practitioners can best deliver bad news in ways that minimize negative reactions.

The difficulties with ethnomethodology

As with any methodological approach that sits outside the mainstream, there are a number of issues that can make using its methods quite difficult. This includes the difficulty of getting experienced support, and having to explain and justify your choice of methodology to those who may not know much about it.

Now a common misconception of ethnomethodology is that it doesn't make a significant contribution to understandings of fundamental social issues. It is assumed that because ethnomethodology doesn't explore the meaning of utterances or actions, it doesn't help us understand constructs such as race, class, gender, etc. But ethnomethodology can explore the interpretative work that individuals engage in to produce racism or sexism. This, however, is not always recognized or appreciated as a significant contribution to knowledge.

Another misconception is that understanding interpretative works is limited to conversation analysis or intricate exploration of transcribed verbal data (see Chapter 12). This mode of analysis can mean that ethnomethodological studies do not give much consideration to non-verbal aspects of communication and inter-action. Now while conversation analysis is the most well-defined and frequently used method for the analysis of ethnomethodological data, it is important to remember that this is but one of its potential methods. Interpretation of the non-verbal is, arguably, as important to ethnomethodological understandings as is interpretation of the spoken word.

The process of doing ethnomethodology

The goal of doing an ethnomethodological study is to draw out how individuals go about the interpretative work necessary to make sense and make meaning in everyday interactions. Approaches for drawing out meaning include 'breaching experiments'; exploring the building of shared interpretation and; exploring interpretative miscues. Now remember I said I'd get back to *Seinfeld*. Well I think *Seinfeld* provides some very insightful examples of all of these approaches. As it turns out, there is something very funny about exposing the taken-for-granted rules that we use to structure our everyday interactions.

Breaching experiments

In breaching experiments (something Garfinkel often had his students attempt), the goal is to expose the rules of the everyday by breaking them and taking note of your own reactions as well as the reactions of others. In this way, what is taken for granted can become apparent, for example, facing the back of a full elevator, or speaking to your family as though you just met them. Not only are you able to document the confusion, frustration, uncomfortableness, etc., of those around you, you can also reflect on how it feels to break taken-for-granted rules. Logically, facing the back of a full elevator shouldn't be an exceedingly stressful task, but it can make some 'experimenters' exceptionally uncomfortable.

As for *Seinfeld*, one of my favourite breaching experiments is undertaken by George. George, a self-confessed 'loser', has decided that every instinct he has ever had has been wrong, so as an experiment he decides to become 'Mr. Opposite'. He decides to breach as many of the 'rules' he has traditionally used to conduct his interactions as possible. So instead of saying yes, he says no; instead of hiding the truth, he exposes himself. But of course the joke here is that rather than alienate the other, George's interactions with others, including women, suddenly go right.

Exploring the building of shared interpretations

George and Jerry (back to *Seinfeld*) are often doing this at the coffee shop. They make explicit and deconstruct the 'rules' of interpretative practice. For example, they discuss the 'rules' for breaking up: how many dates constitutes the need for the face-to-face break-up (I think they actually come up with a number), or when can you get away with a telephone message or letter; what excuses (for example, 'It's not you it's me') can be used to break up in the most gracious manner; and why and when you might end with, 'let's stay friends'.

As an ethnomethodological research strategy, exploring the building of shared interpretations involves the collection of raw naturalistic data that captures everyday interactions. These interactions are often specifically defined, i.e. interactions between doctor and patient, family members, friends, members of a particular cultural group, etc. Data is then captured by audio tape, or if analysis will go beyond speech, video tape. This data is then faithfully transcribed, often including hesitations, comments on tone, attitude, use of sarcastic pitch, non-verbal cues, etc.

Analysis then turns to a search for the collaborative and constantly emerging nature of the interaction or conversation. The goal is to identify the 'rules' that underpin the interactions or how individuals manage action or conversation. Ethnomethodologists attempt to uncover the methodical, structured ways in which order in interactions is built. Because interpretative practices are indexical, that is indexed and dependent on a particular context or situation, the analysis will often include an exploration of the categories, classifications, and typifications used by individuals as they engage in interpretative practice.

Exploring interpretative miscues

A final method that can be used to uncover the taken-for-granted nature of communication and interaction is the exploration of conflicts or miscues – essentially, when it simply doesn't go right. It is often easier to spot, deconstruct, and understand the 'taken for granted' when it is exposed by 'conflict'. I'll turn to Seinfeld's Elaine for a final example. In one episode, the 'rules' for interacting with mothers of newborns is exposed through Elaine's internal conflict over the matter. While she well knows that the 'rules' mean that she's 'gotta see the baby' (always said in a whiney New York accent!), she has absolutely no desire to do so. And when she finally submits, she struggles to follow the 'rules' that demand she say just how cute this hideous creature is, even though she recognizes that this a 'must lie' situation. Through this inner conflict over building an acceptable interpretative practice, cultural expectations are exposed.

Further reading

I hope this chapter has got you thinking about all the possibilities associated with delving into some really fascinating aspects of the social world. If that's the case, you'll undoubtedly want to get into some of readings dedicated to particular approaches.

Case studies

Ragin, C. C. and Becker, H. S. (1992) *What is a Case? Exploring the Foundations of Social Inquiry.* New York: Cambridge University Press.

Stake, R. E. (1995) *The Art of Case Study Research.* Thousand Oaks, CA: Sage.

Stake, R. E. (2000) 'Case Studies', in N. K. Denzin and Y. S. Lincoln (eds), *Handbook of Qualitative Research.* Thousand Oaks, CA: Sage. pp. 435–54.

Yin, R. K. (2002) *Case Study Research: Design and Methods.* Thousand Oaks, CA: Sage.

Ethnography

Geertz, C. (1973) *The Interpretation of Cultures.* New York: Basic Books.

Grills, S. (ed.) (1998) *Doing Ethnographic Research.* London: Sage.

Hamersley, M. and Atkinson, P. (1995) *Ethnography: Principles in Practice.* London: Routledge.

Schensul, J. and LeCompte, D. (eds) (1999) *The Ethnographer's Toolkit* (7 vols). London: Sage.

Phenomenology

Berger, P. and Luckmann, T. (1967) *The Social Construction of Reality: A Treatise in the Sociology of Knowledge.* New York: Anchor.

Elliston, F. and McCormick, P. (eds) (1977) *Husserl: Exposition and Appraisals.* Notre Dame, IN: Notre Dame University Press.

Heidegger, M. (1996) *Being and Time: A Translation of Sein and Zeit.* Trans. J. Stambaugh. New York: State University of New York Press.

Moran, D. (2000) *Introduction to Phenomenology.* London: Routledge.

Moustakas, C. (2000) *Phenomenological Research Methods.* London: Sage.

Schutz, A. (1967) *The Phenomenology of the Social World.* Trans. G. Walsh and F. Lehnert. Evanston, IL: North Western University Press.

Sokolowski, R. (2000) *Introduction to Phenomenology.* New York: Cambridge University Press.

Spielberg, H. (1982) *The Phenomenological Movement.* Dordrecht: Kluwer Academic Press.

Ethnomethodology

Button, G. (ed.) (1991) *Ethnomethodology and the Human Sciences.* New York: Cambridge University Press.

Coulon, A. (2000) *Ethnomethodology.* London: Sage.

Garfinkel, H. (1967) *Studies in Ethnomethodology.* Englewood Cliffs, NJ: Prentice-Hall.

Sacks, H. (1992) *Lectures on Conversation.* Oxford: Basil Blackwell.

CHAPTER SUMMARY

- Investigating complexities of the social world can involve exploring the interactions, processes, lived experiences, and belief systems that can be found within individuals, institutions, cultural groups, and the everyday.
- Methods that allow researchers to delve into social complexities often involve parameters not likely to lend themselves to assessment by 'positivist' criteria. Appropriate criteria are likely to be neutrality or transparent subjectivity, dependability, authenticity, transferability, and auditability.
- In studies that 'delve deeper', strategies for achieving credibility include working towards thoroughness, i.e. saturation, crystallization, prolonged engagement, persistent observation, broad representation and peer review, and seeking confirmation, i.e. triangulation, member checking, and full explication of method.
- The exploration of bounded systems (case studies) involves studying elements of the social through comprehensive description and analysis of a single situation or case. While not technically a methodology, the implication of studying cases does bring some unity to their investigation.
- Case studies concentrate research efforts on one site, and while not necessarily representative, they can add to new knowledge through their ability to debunk theory, generate theory, and support existing theory.
- The process of doing case studies involves defining a case, selecting a case or cases for study, and being open to a range of methodological approaches that can draw out meaning.
- Exploring a cultural group through ethnography involves discovering, understanding, describing, and interpreting a way of life from the point of view of its participants.
- Ethnographic studies offer: thick descriptions of cultural groups; a methodological approach for exploring cultures, symbols, and norms; and an acceptance of multiple realities. However, they often involve 'immersion', and all the problems thereof. Ethnographic researchers also need to manage their own subjectivities when understanding from the perspective of the researched.

- Ethnographic studies involve: the selection of a cultural group; data collection through multiple methods that often demand prolonged engagement and persistent observation; and analysis that demands a high level of reflexivity.
- Exploring phenomena (phenomenology) involves generating descriptions of lived phenomena as they present themselves in direct experience.
- Phenomenology offers a way to study phenomena, something often neglected in the social science research. However, the literature on phenomenology can be thick, divergent, and not 'methods'-oriented.
- Studying a phenomenon involves gathering, making sense of, and writing rich phenomenological descriptions. Descriptions are drawn from individuals through a dialogic process, and are then synthesized to offer a range of distinct possibilities for the experience of a particular phenomenon.
- Exploring the everyday (ethnomethodology) explores the methods that individuals use to make sense of their social world and accomplish their daily actions.
- Ethnomethodology recognizes the interpretative work of the individual; offers a method for exploring 'how' questions; allows comparisons of divergent cultural norms; and allows exploration of specific forms of interaction. However, it can be critiqued for not addressing 'significant' questions, and being too focused on verbal aspects of communication.
- Doing ethnomethodology involves a search for the collaborative and constantly emerging nature of interaction or conversation. This can be done through breaching experiments; the exploration and deconstruction of building shared interpretations; and exploration of interpretative miscues.

Facilitating Change through Research

'I don't just want to research something – I want
to make a difference.'

Chapter Preview

- From Knowledge to Action
- Paving the Way for Change
- Creating Knowledge and Actioning Change
- Striving for Critical Emancipation

FROM KNOWLEDGE TO ACTION

'The world can only be grasped by action, not by contemplation …
the hand is the cutting edge of the mind.'
–Jacob Bronowski

According to the *American Heritage Dictionary*, research is 'scholarly or scientific investigation or inquiry'. Now this might tell us what research is, but it doesn't tell us why we would do it. So why do we do research? Is it to produce knowledge for knowledge's sake, or is it to make the world a better place? Is there value in simply knowing, or should that knowing always be linked to progress?

As shown in Figure 10.1, the goals of research can be placed on a continuum from knowledge to change. At one end of the spectrum is basic or 'pure' research that attempts to produce and expand knowledge in order to better understand the world. Technically, pure research is based on theoretical interests that need not be applied. At the other end of the spectrum is research that is conducted for the purpose of critical emancipation of those suffering repression at the hand of the dominant. Now I realize that these two ends of the spectrum may seem light years apart, but I'd argue they are not diametrically opposed.

As far as the pursuit of basic or 'pure' research goes, I really can't think of too many 'ivory tower' researchers who conduct their research without some practical purpose in mind. In fact, virtually all research proposals demand a rationale that highlights the scientific/social significance of the research questions posed. On the other end of the spectrum are your 'critical emancipators' who must necessarily be engaged in a research process that will generate new knowledge if they wish to distinguish their work from social activism. Most researchers want their

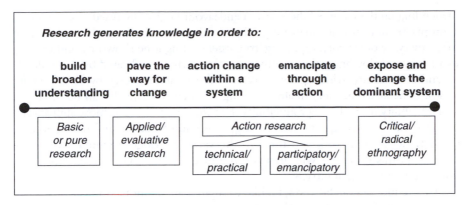

FIGURE 10.1 FROM KNOWLEDGE TO CHANGE – THE GOALS OF RESEARCH

research to be useful at least at some level in the real world. The question is whether that usefulness involves the production of knowledge that may some day lead to change, or whether change itself will be a direct product of the research process.

If you have a look at Figure 10.1, you will notice that above the line I have not boxed the different change-oriented research goals. And that's because the world is not discrete, and neither are the boundaries between what we want to know and what we want to accomplish. Your goals may fall on any point on the continuum, on two or more points on the continuum, or may encompass the entire continuum from end to end. What is 'boxed' in Figure 10.1 are the research approaches that have evolved paradigmatically in an attempt to address these various goals. Now its important to keep in mind that these approaches are constructions, and while there is tremendous debate about the right approach, the best approach, the nature of the approaches – what we are really after is not pre-scriptive rules, but tried and true frameworks that can help us best answer our questions and meet our aims and objectives.

This chapter discusses a number of methodological approaches commonly used in the quest to facilitate change through research. The approaches range from mainstream positivist to fairly 'out there' post-positivist methodologies. And unfortunately, such strong paradigmatic divergence has meant that these approaches suffer from a lack of dialogue, and are rarely brought together when looking at the research/change rubric. By starting with goals rather than paradigms, and working logically up to the various approaches, this chapter attempts to legitimize any and all approaches to knowing (and change) that are negotiated in ways that best assure credibility.

Working towards credibility

Change-oriented research is more about a distinct set of goals than a unique approach to research or even a particular paradigmatic positioning. Thus showing credibility need not be limited to indicators derived from the positivist domain.

Depending on the nature of the research endeavour (and as discussed in Chapter 5), appropriate indicators for managing subjectivities might be neutrality, transparent subjectivity, or objectivity; capturing 'true essence' might be shown by authenticity or validity; employing methods with consistency can be indicated by dependability and/or reliability; wider applicability of findings can be shown by transferability and/or generalizability; and finally ensuring research is verifiable can be indicated by auditability as well as reproducibility. The indicators that are most appropriate will depend on paradigmatic positioning, aims and objectives, and methodological approaches. As I work you through the various change-oriented approaches covered in this chapter, I will discuss some of the more salient credibility issues associated with each approach.

Before moving on, however, I'd like to suggest an additional indicator that can be used to assess credibility in change-oriented research, and that is 'usefulness'. If a research objective is the facilitation of change, then a measure of success or credibility will be how useful that research is in facilitating, driving, or implementing that particular change. Now the criterion of 'usefulness' addresses the political dimensions of change-oriented research and is often best determined by reflective practice that incorporates evaluative feedback from concerned stakeholders.

PAVING THE WAY FOR CHANGE

A common critique of basic or pure research is that it is 'too academic'. It may add to our scientific/social knowledge, but it doesn't necessarily improve situations. And even when the production of new knowledge has the potential to affect programmes, policy, procedures, practice, or even our personal approaches to the world, the critique is that this knowledge is all too likely to sit on the shelf. Research may help us understand the situation and may even lead to ideas/ recommendations for change, but change itself does not automatically spring from knowledge. Enter applied research.

Applied research

The immediate purpose of applied research is to produce knowledge that will help find real solutions to real problems. It is conducted to facilitate or pave the way for change by providing information for an immediate change-oriented purpose. Applied research is therefore often client-based, and commissioned by a change agent or a sponsor (government, non-government organization, workplace, etc.) who wishes to implement a change strategy. Now while results of applied research can be published in journals, change-oriented goals mean that the first point of dissemination is to those for whom the research is intended to aid informed decision-making.

Applied research can take many forms, but some of the more common applied studies attempt to:

- *Assess a problem* – these studies can provide an overview of a problem situation, explore prevalence, look for 'at-risk' subgroups, attempt to identify potential causes, and/or attempt to create a 'vision' for action. This is done in a bid to determine the need for potential change interventions and is sometimes called a 'needs assessment' or 'front-end analysis' in evaluation studies. Such studies can involve anything from wide-scale surveying to case studies, and might draw on any range of research methods/tools.

- *Assess potential interventions* – these studies attempt to explore the strengths/ weaknesses and costs/benefits of potential change interventions. Studies might look at whether the intervention is likely to be accepted by various stake-holders, whether there are likely to be any problems with implementation, and/or look at the success/cost of such programmes in alternative settings. Such studies are often called 'feasibility studies' and can be included as a preliminary stage in evaluation research. Given this wide range of possibilities, methods are developed in accordance with researcher/client goals and are not limited to any particular type.
- *Evaluate change initiatives* – these studies are conducted to assess the effectiveness of change intervention programmes and policies, and are considered crucial in rational and informed decision-making. Whether it be evaluation of new teaching strategies, the effectiveness of anti-smoking campaigns, or the impact of new anti-discrimination policies, unless the level and effectiveness of change can be assessed, it becomes impossible to know: (1) if the strategy was successful; (2) whether it is cost-effective; (3) whether it should be continued (or scrapped); (4) whether it needs to be modified; or (5) whether it should be expanded. In fact, change intervention proposals increasingly require evaluative components.

Evaluation research is therefore becoming quite prevalent, but the conduct of such studies can be difficult to negotiate because evaluations can be highly political in nature. For these reasons, evaluation research is discussed in more detail in the following section.

Evaluation research

As stated above, evaluation research attempts to assess the effectiveness of change intervention programmes and policies, and is related more to a research purpose or goal than a particular methodological approach. Now it's important to recognize that these goals tend to be political and tied to vested interests. Thus, clearly identifying a study's purpose and goals, and using rigorous protocols that are likely to stand up to both criticism and controversy, is essential.

Types of evaluation

While there are any number of options for evaluation research, evaluative studies can be broken down into two general types: formative or process evaluation and summative or outcome evaluation.

Formative evaluation: Also called process evaluation, the goal is to provide information that will aid the development of particular change intervention programmes. Such studies investigate programme delivery and ask how, and how well, a programme is being implemented. They can assess strengths, weaknesses, opportunities, and threats, and often work to assess barriers and lubricants to implementation. Results are expected to inform decision-making related to programme improvement, modification, and management. Now while these studies are often case-specific, 'transferable' findings (see Chapter 5) will allow other organizations interested in the use of any similar programmes to apply 'lessons learned'.

Summative evaluation: Also called outcome evaluation, the goal is to provide information that can assess the effectiveness, efficiency, and ethicality of the change strategy in question. These studies investigate whether the programme has met its aims and objectives, and might also assess the overall effects of the programme both intended and unintended. Summative evaluation may also consider cost-effectiveness and include a cost–benefit analysis. Results are expected to inform decision-making related to programme funding, continuation, termination, expansion, and reduction. While findings are often case specific, results can be of interest to any number of stakeholder groups and, depending on the nature of the change intervention, might be of interest to the wider population as well.

Research designs

Evaluation research is categorized by the objective of evaluation rather than any particular methodological approach, and as such calls on any number of research strategies. In formative or process evaluation, research is generally in the form of a 'case study' that might involve focus groups, interviews with key stakeholders, a stakeholder survey, observations, review of minutes and protocols, etc. Now regardless of methods used, the key is to clearly identify the aims and objectives of the formative evaluation, i.e. to clearly articulate what it is you are trying to assess, so that your study matches the expectations of your client/stakeholders.

In summative evaluation, the main goal is to evaluate effectiveness, and that effectiveness will often be related to the aims and objectives of the change intervention. In this way each aim can be considered a research question, i.e. has objective #1 been met, has objective #2 been met etc. Each of these 'questions' may then require different methodological protocols. Now generally the objectives, and therefore what you will try to evaluate, is some measure of real change. There are a number of ways you can do this:

1. Ask those involved (various stakeholders) if they believe a change has occurred. Do they see a difference, how and why? Individual interviews, focus groups, or surveys might be appropriate here.
2. Look at before and after data. This is often called 'time series analysis' and requires that: (a) similar data be collected before and after the intervention; and (b) any change is directly related to the intervention itself and not to anything else that might be happening. As you can imagine, meeting these requirements

can be tricky. For one, good 'baseline data', i.e. data from before the intervention, may not exist. Second, in the real world it can be difficult, if not impossible, to control for all extraneous variables that may effect change.

3. Compare two groups – one that has undergone the intervention and one that has not. The challenge here is to find a 'control' group that is as similar as possible to the 'change' group in every way except that it has not undergone the intervention. The greater the divergence between the two groups the harder it is to say that any difference is the result of the programme being evaluated.

Regardless of approach, conducting summative evaluation is difficult because you are not just looking for a correlation between intervention and change. You are actually trying to establish cause and effect, and your methods will need to attempt to control for any other factors that may be causal to any perceived change or difference.

Issues to consider

There are a couple of sticky issues related to evaluation research that you will need to consider and negotiate. These include:

*   *Unrealistic client/stakeholder expectations* – there is often a need, desire, or requirement (often within a funding period) for summative evaluation that is: (a) related to change that is hard to measure and/or hard to correlate to the intervention; and (b) subject to deadlines that might come before you'd expect to see any real change. Take, for example, a workplace that begins an exercise programme with the aim of reducing the risk of heart disease. Now to evaluate this programme you would need good medical baseline data, the collection of medical data at various points after the initiation of the exercise programme, and a research protocol that could control for any other factors that are known to have an effect on heart disease, i.e. genetics, diet, stress, etc. This takes a level of expertise, cooperation, time, and money that is likely to exceed your capacity. The lesson here is that before taking on an evaluative research study, you need to clearly consider and articulate what is, and what is not, possible.
*   *The pressure of vested interests* – some people honestly want to know if their programme is working; they want that information for informed decision-making. Others, however, are simply meeting requirements, or only want validation of what they're already doing. This can put researchers in a tough position. Say, for example, you are commissioned to conduct an evaluation. There might be an unspoken expectation that your results will confirm the client's hard work and large investment. Their expectation of you as a 'consultant' may be at odds with your ethical responsibilities for the production of knowledge (see Chapter 4). And even if their expectations are for an objective view, you yourself might find that hard to do. For example, what if you are evaluating the initiative of a really dedicated, terrific person with a really crappy, ineffective programme – and his or her job is on the line. There are more than a few researchers who have 'softened' their findings in that situation.

The only way to negotiate these dilemmas is to consider whether you have the 'stomach' to put it on the line regardless of controversy, criticism, or consequence. If you don't – best not undertake that particular research project. But if you do – I'd recommend you clearly set out your expectations, aims, and objectives; and document a well thought out and defined methodology that can stand up to the possibility of intense scrutiny.

CREATING KNOWLEDGE AND ACTIONING CHANGE

Applied science may pave the way for change, be directly linked to change, and have an immediate goal of facilitating change, but the *product* of applied research is knowledge. On the other side of the coin, if the product of a study is simply change itself, you don't have research; what you have is consultancy, change agency, or social activism. But when the product of a study is both knowledge *and* change you have what is broadly known as action research.

Getting a handle on action research

It is quite difficult to give a concise overview of action research because there are so many varieties, offshoots, perspectives, and approaches. There is action research, action learning, action science, action inquiry, participative inquiry, cooperative inquiry, participatory rural appraisal, practitioner research, and participatory action research. And while they may all owe something to the work of Kurt Lewin, who coined the term (Lewin 1946), recent perspectives from the fields of organizational behaviour, education, and rural extension have led to great diversity in both the goals and methodological approaches related to this mode of inquiry.

For example, one of the things students find highly confusing in action research literature is the distinction between action research, which has stakeholder participation as a central tenant, and 'participatory action research', which you would imagine should be basically the same thing. But as a methodological approach, 'participatory action research', as compared to action research that is participatory (I told you it was confusing), is actually distinguished by more defined emancipatory goals (which is why some refer to it as emancipatory action research and why I take it up later in the chapter).

Now the last thing I want to do is get into a debate over the 'correct' terminology, what action research should or shouldn't be, or what its appropriate uses are – and believe me that debate is out there. What I am interested in is the general principles of action research and how those principles can be instrumental in the conduct of studies that want to integrate the production of knowledge with on-the-ground change. If your goals go beyond the production of knowledge and include change implementation, it is well worth getting a handle on action research.

The basic tenets of action research

Action Research: A research strategy that pursues action and knowledge in an integrated fashion through a cyclical and participatory process. In action research, process, outcome, and application are inextricably linked.

Regardless of any academic debate on the precise nature of action research, there are some basic tenets (discussed below) that both define the process and outline its procedures.

Addresses practical problems

Action research is grounded in real problems and real-life situations. It generally involves the identification of practical problems in a specific context and attempts to seek and implement solutions within that context. Action research is often used in workplaces where the ownership of change is a high priority or where the goal is to improve professional practice. It is also considered an effective strategy when there is a strong desire to transform both theory and practice.

Generates knowledge

Action research is more than just change implementation and relies heavily on both the production of knowledge to produce change and the enacting of change to produce knowledge. Action research rejects the two-stage process of knowledge first, change second, and suggests that they are highly integrated. Action research practitioners believe that enacting change should not just be seen as the end product of knowledge; rather it should be valued as a source of knowledge itself.

Enacts change

Action research goes beyond knowledge generation and incorporates change into its immediate goals. Whether it be developing technical skills, building more reflexive professional practice, or emancipation and liberation, action research works towards situation improvement based in practice, and avoids the problem of needing to work towards change after knowledge is produced.

Is participatory

A central tenet of action research is 'democratization' of the research process. This refers to a rejection of research as the domain of the expert, and calls for participation of, and collaboration between, researchers, practitioners, and any other interested stakeholders. There is an attempt to minimize the distinction between the researcher and the researched, with high value placed on local knowledge. Contrary to many research paradigms, action research works *with,* rather than *on* or *for*, the 'researched', and is therefore often seen as embodying democratic principles. The key is that those who will be affected by the research and action are not acted upon.

Now the nature of participation and collaboration is varied and based on the action research approach adopted; the particular context of the situation being studied, and the goals of the various stakeholders. This might find stakeholders involved in any or all stages and cycles of the process. Meanwhile the researcher's role is to facilitate a sustainable change process that can find the researcher acting as planner, leader, catalyzer, facilitator, teacher, designer, listener, observer, synthesizer, and/or reporter at various points throughout the project.

Relies on a cyclical process

Action research is a cyclical process that takes shape as knowledge emerges. Cycles converge towards better situation understanding and improved action implementation; and are based in evaluative practice that alters between action and critical reflection. Action research can therefore be seen as an experiential learning approach to change. The goal is to continuously refine methods, data, and interpretation in the light of the understanding developed in the earlier cycles.

Now the cycles themselves can be defined in numerous ways and, in fact, are often defined through collaborative decision-making. However, as shown in Figure 10.2, they generally involve some variation on observation, reflection, planning, and action.

The exact nature of the steps in each part of the cycle is emergent and developed collaboratively with stakeholders. Research for the 'observation' part of the cycle is likely to be in the form of a case study and, as with all case studies, might involve a variety of approaches, methodologies, and methods in a bid to gather data and generate knowledge (refer to case studies in Chapter 9). The 'reflection' part of the cycle can be informal and introspective, or can be quite formal and share many elements with formative evaluations discussed earlier. The steps related to 'planning' and 'action', however, are likely to go beyond reflection and research, and may require practitioners to delve into literature on strategic planning and change management.

Issues in action research

While stakeholder collaboration is central to democratization of the research process, it can also pose significant challenges to the researcher. Yes, participation and collaboration can lead to empowerment and ownership, while hopefully creating sustainable change that will outlive a traditional research project. The participatory nature of action research, however, can also lead to a number of management issues. For example:

- The ultimate direction of the project is not in your hands. Decisions made about the direction of the research and the probable outcomes should be collective – and this is true even if you think the process is headed off course.
- It can be difficult to control the pace of the project. Getting stakeholders together, achieving consensus, and actioning real change can be slow, particularly in multiple cycles. Additionally, in a long-term project, key stakeholders

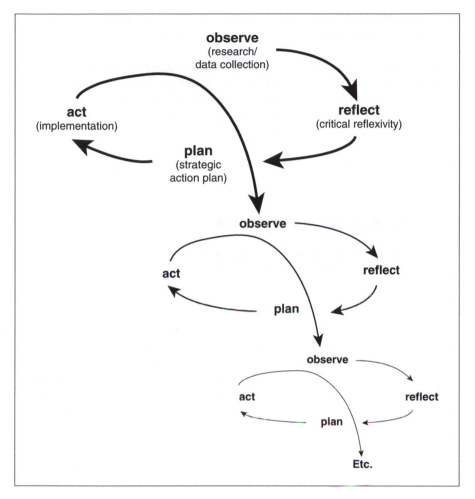

observe
(research/
data collection)

act
(implementation)

reflect
(critical reflexivity)

plan
(strategic
action plan)

observe

act

reflect

plan

observe

act

reflect

plan

Etc.

FIGURE 10.2 CYCLES IN ACTION RESEARCH

may also come and go, potentially changing the project's dynamic, pace, and direction.

- Facilitating collaboration is not always easy. Overbearing, powerful (sometimes obnoxious) individuals can usurp the democratic procedures; various stakeholders can feel unheard, ignored, and/or marginalized; and personal agendas can mean that strategic plans do not logically flow from observation and reflection.

- While stakeholders have a hand in the development of research and action protocols, unless otherwise negotiated, it is the researcher who carries the burden of ethical responsibility for both the production of knowledge and for the welfare of the researched (see Chapter 4).

- Finally, the researcher needs to negotiate ownership of research outcomes, which may include rights to publish, issues of authorship, etc.

In addition to methodological 'expert', the action researcher must also be a consummate organizer, effective communicator, skilled negotiator, conflict resolution specialist, well-organized time manager, strategic planner, efficient documenter, and be willing to get his or her 'hands dirty' as an on-the-ground implementer – all of which might require the development of specialist skills. As you begin to see practice evolve and change occur, action research can be exceedingly rewarding. It is, however, a process that demands a tremendous amount of skill, learning, and patience.

STRIVING FOR CRITICAL EMANCIPATION

> **'The philosophers have only interpreted the world in various ways;**
> **the point, however, is to change it.'**
> **–Karl Marx**

It is one thing to want to improve skills and practice, or to endeavour to change how things are done in a workplace, a school, or a community, but what if you believe that the only path to sustainable change is through fundamental transformation of larger social systems. What if you believe that it will take more than working within the system, and that at the heart of the social issue or social problem is injustice or inequity in the system itself, i.e. the repressive school system, the authoritative nature of the workplace, or the hierarchical structures of the community. Or underpinning even this, the underlying ideologies of, say capitalism, patriarchy, development, globalization, etc.

To strive for critical emancipation is to expose these underlying structures through astute political analysis in a bid to liberate those oppressed by them. It is argued that this requires:

Criticality: Challenging taken-for-granted ways of knowing. Asking not only what it is, but why it is, who benefits, and what are the alternate possibilities.

Radical views: Advocating fundamental or revolutionary changes in current it practices, conditions, institutions, or ideologies.

Emancipatory goals: To remove obstacles to understanding dominant social ideologies in a bid to open up potentialities and work towards new possibilities.

Critical emancipation thus refers to fundamental or revolutionary changes in current thinking, practices, conditions, or institutions that can free people from the constraints of dominant social structures that often limit self-development and self-determination. For those whose research includes goals of critical emancipation, research is likely to proceed on the assumption that if social problems arise from a system, they are unlikely to be solved within that system. Critical emancipation research necessarily delves into the underfelt of social systems. It is laden with political purpose and does not claim to be value free. It seeks transformation of society such that individuals are liberated and empowered towards action that opens up possibilities for improved situations.

Now in its radical extreme this might mean exploring the disempowerment and injustice created by industrialized societies, investigating the economic impacts of mass globalization, or exposing the patriarchal structures that act to disadvantage women. In terms of smaller-scale research, however, the application might be as 'ordinary' as exploring workplace stress, bullying in the playground, or low self-esteem in young girls. The 'critical' end of such studies comes from exploring the ideologies that create systems in which: workplace stress becomes an expected product of well-entrenched practices of authority, power, and control; low self-esteem in girls can be seen as 'ordinary' given the cultural emphasis on the body image of women in the public eye; bullying in the playground can be seen as quite reasonable given the legitimization of power through other forms of aggression readily accessible to youth (movies, video games, sport, etc.) This criticality is then applied to emancipation through the production of knowledge and/or implementation of change that exposes dominant and repressive ideologies and opens up alternate possibilities.

In the social sciences, these critical emancipatory goals have led to variations on ethnographic and action research. 'Participatory' action research has an explicit goal of emancipation through action, while 'critical' ethnography seeks to change existing social systems by exposing their dominant and repressive ideologies.

'Participatory' action research

Participatory action research (PAR), sometimes referred to as emancipatory action research or 'southern' participatory action research (which comes from the notion of working in developing countries often in the Southern hemisphere) falls under the action research umbrella. It has goals of emancipation, but maintains the action research dedication to cycles of knowledge and action that produce on-the-ground change. Now action research can certainly have emancipatory goals, but PAR makes these goals much more explicit. It works in participatory ways that value local knowledge, and attempts to empower communities to expose and liberate themselves from repressive systems and ideologies. PAR is often found in international development research that strives towards social transformation of the 'marginalized' through advocacy and action.

Cycles of knowledge and action
PAR pursues action and knowledge in an integrated fashion through a cyclical and participatory process. It attempts to facilitate exploration and unmasking of the ways dominant ideologies and systems shape and constrain thinking and

action, and works towards interventions that can liberate the marginalized from those forces that contribute to poverty, oppression, repression, and/or injustice. PAR relies on the same basic tenants as action research, but with a more specific emancipatory agenda:

- *Addresses practical problems* – as with action research, PAR works with real problems in order to produce knowledge and action directly useful to stakeholders. In PAR, this often involves the empowerment of the 'marginalized' as they act to construct their own knowing, and attempt to create and action their own strategic plan for emancipation.
- *Generates knowledge* – PAR attempts to challenge not only things within the system, but the system itself. It attempts to unmask the political aspects of knowledge production that often sees knowledge as an instrument of power and control.
- *Enacts change* – as is common to all action research processes, PAR goes beyond knowledge generation and incorporates change into its immediate goals. In PAR, these goals are directly related to emancipation and liberation by changing inequitable power relations.
- *Is participatory* – PAR works *with* the researched, rather than *on* or *for* them. It recognizes that the knowledge and experience of the 'marginalized' should be respected and valued, and it attempts to capitalize on capabilities and cultural practices that are often ignored. PAR also attempts to work towards 'conscientization' (Freire 1970) or 'enlightenment and awakening' (Fals Borda and Rahman 1991) of the oppressed, and acts to strengthen their capacity to generate knowledge and action from their own perspectives and in their own interests. Methods used to generate knowledge and action are broad, eclectic, and emergent, and need not be limited to traditional Western ways of researching. Song, poetry, art, drama, and storytelling might emerge as appropriate ways to draw out and generate knowledge.
- *Relies on a cyclical process* – as with all forms of action research, PAR converges towards better situation understanding and improved action implementation through cycles of observation, reflection, planning, and action.

Critical ethnography

Ethnography can be defined as 'the exploration of cultural groups in a bid to understand, describe, and interpret a way of life from the point of view of its participants' (see Chapter 9). Critical ethnography, also referred to as radical ethnography, adds a political agenda of exposing inequitable, unjust, or repressive influences that are acting on 'marginalized' cultural groups, in a bid to open up alternate, more liberating possibilities. Critical ethnography works towards conscientization, empowerment, and liberation of the 'marginalized' through in-depth critical analysis of underlying social fabrics.

Exposing the dominant system
Critical ethnography explores and critiques existing systems in a bid to serve the interests of the 'marginalized' group. There is thus an assumption that the dominant

or existing system is indeed repressive or unjust, and needs to be exposed in order to open up possibilities for change. Critical ethnography attempts to expose the political nature of knowledge and unmask the dominant forces that shape our view of the world. By critical examination of worldviews, ideology, and power, critical ethnography attempts to contextualize the current situation in a larger socio-historic framework that offers, and encourages others to engage in, critical reflection.

While traditional ethnographic techniques can, and many would argue should, consider how interpretations are influenced by dominant paradigms, critical ethnographers have an express goal of understanding and interpreting situations from both within and outside the dominant. By naming and then distancing themselves from cultural assumptions in a bid to work through a series of alternative conceptions, critical ethnographers expose dominant paradigms. The goal is to present alternative and potentially more liberating realities.

An example comes from a student of mine who conducted an ethnographic/phenomenological study of first-year university students who were subjected to hazing or bastardization. The study attempted to understand the reality of bastardization from the perspective of the 'victims'. Through observations, interview, and document analysis, the student wanted to be able to give a thick description and interpretation of both the phenomenon of bastardization and the culture in which it thrived. As she progressed in this work she realized that understanding the culture and how it might shift could not be done without a critical examination of the forces that allow this culture to continue, and in fact, flourish. She thus found herself immersed in exploration of the socio-historic context of the campus in a bid to expose and deconstruct notions of patriarchy, myth, aggression, mateship, cultures of silence, power, and control. In the end, her work had shifted to a strongly critical study that attempted to expose the broader social systems that had created a particular cultural reality.

Working towards change

Clearly, the highly political goals of critical ethnography link exposure of the dominant system to emancipation; to bring about change is a defined objective. According to Thomas (1993), ethnography as action can be seen in its ability to:

- change cognitive functioning of researchers
- offer a 'voice' to the marginalized
- instigate interactions with others that raise social awareness
- create networks of those with common goals
- become a starting point for legislative and/or policy reform

Issues in emancipatory research

There is a level of debate around the intertwining of research goals and political agendas – basically because it flies in the face of one of the most well-entrenched 'positivist' rules of research, namely objectivity. And although both critical ethnography and PAR sit under a 'post-positivist' umbrella, they nevertheless suffer from this critique and are accused of confusing social activism with research. For those wanting to conduct such studies it will be important to clearly outline your methodological protocols, and call on literature that legitimizes, and acknowledges the importance of, critical agendas in research. Luckily, the proliferation and acceptance of post-positivist methodologies makes this task ever easier.

This said, there is still a need to manage subjectivities. It is one thing to have and work towards a political agenda, but it is another to have it bias the interpretation and analysis of your research. Political agendas may be acceptable, but to have it colour your perception in unrecognized ways will put a question mark over research credibility.

Another perhaps more problematic critique is the risk of dedicated and motivated researchers imposing their political agenda on the 'marginalized'. Are problems necessarily problems if they are not recognized as such by the researched? Is it the researcher's right to stir this up, even if the goal is liberation and emancipation? Is 'conscientization' always justified? There are many cultures that can be defined as marginal by Western researchers that are not self-identified in that way. A huge responsibility in emancipatory research is thus negotiating political agendas that can 'arise from', be 'assigned to', or 'imposed on' the researched.

Further Reading

While most student researchers choose their topics with the ultimate goal of social change in mind, the majority do not give much consideration to research strategies that see change as a more instrumental goal of the research process itself. I hope this chapter has inspired you to at least consider some approaches that link knowledge and action. If so, have a look at some of the reading listed below. They represent a large range of possibilities for linking research and change.

Applied/Evaluation Research

Berk, R. A. and Rossi, P. H. (1999) *Thinking about Program Evaluation.* Thousand Oaks, CA: Sage.

Bickman, L. and Rog, D. J. (1997) *Handbook of Applied Social Research Methods.* Thousand Oaks, CA: Sage.

Chen, H. (1999) *Theory Driven Evaluations.* Thousand Oaks, CA: Sage.

Rossi, P. H., Freeman, H. E. and Lipsey, M. W. (1999) *Evaluation: A Systematic Approach.* Thousand Oaks, CA: Sage.

Action Research

Greenwood, D. and Levin, M. (1998) *Introduction to Action Research: Social Research for Social Change*. Thousand Oaks, CA: Sage.

McNiff, J. and Whitehead, J. (2002) *Action Research: Principles and Practice*. London: Routledge.

Reason, P. and Bradbury, H. (2001) *Handbook of Action Research: Participative Inquiry and Practice*. London: Sage.

Stringer, E. (1999) *Action Research*. Thousand Oaks, CA: Corwin Press.

Zuber-Skerritt, O. (ed.) (1996) *New Directions in Action Research*. London: Falmer Press.

Critical Research

Freire, P. (1970) *Pedagogy of the Oppressed*. New York: Herder & Herder.

Participatory Action Research

Fals Borda, O. and Rahman, M. A. (1991) *Action and Knowledge: Breaking the Monopoly with Participatory Action Research*. New York: Intermediate Technology/Apex Press.

Kemmis, S. and McTaggart, R. (2000) 'Participatory Action Research', in N. K. Denzin and Y. S. Lincoln (eds), *Handbook of Qualitative Research*. Thousand Oaks, CA: Sage. pp. 567–605.

Rahman, A. (ed.) (1994) *People's Self-Development: Perspectives on Participatory Action Research: A Journey Through Experience*. London: Zed Books.

Smith, S., Willm, D. G. and Johnson, N. A. (eds) (1997) *Nurtured by Knowledge: Learning To Do Participatory Action Research*. New York: Apex Press.

Whyte, W. F. (ed.) (1991) *Participatory Action Research*. Newbury Park, CA: Sage.

Critical ethnography

(Also see recommended readings on ethnography offered at the end of Chapter 9.)

Denzin, N. K. (2003) *Performance Ethnography: Critical Pedagogy and the Politics of Culture.* London: Sage.

Quantz, R. A. (1992) 'On Critical Ethnography (with some postmodern considerations)', in W. L. Millroy, J. Preissle and M. D. LeCompte (eds), *The Handbook of Qualitative Research in Education.* New York: Academic Press. pp. 470–505.

Thomas, J. (1993) *Doing Critical Ethnography.* Newbury Park, CA: Sage.

CHAPTER SUMMARY

- Facilitating change through research can range from the production of knowledge that may lead to change, to applied research conducted for the express purpose of enabling effective change, to research that attempts to embed action and change into the actual research process.
- Research that facilitates change can be considered highly 'political' and, as such, credibility will involve careful consideration of issues of power, objectivity, subjectivity, and bias.
- In addition to both positivist and post-positivist indicators of credibility, change-oriented research can also look to 'usefulness' as an indicator of success.
- Applied research paves the way for change. It is often linked to policy/programme development and can include studies that assess a problem situation, assess potential interventions, or evaluate change initiatives.
- Since change intervention strategies often require formal review, evaluation research has become increasingly common. This can involve both formative evaluation conducted to provide developmental feedback and summative evaluations conducted to assess effectiveness.
- Evaluative research is often conducted in the form of a case study. For formative studies, methods tend to be eclectic and diverse and driven by research objectives, while summative designs often involve comparative analysis of groups and/or time series analysis.
- Issues in evaluative research include both unrealistic client/stakeholder expectations and the potential pressure of vested interests.
- Action research covers a broad array of research strategies that are dedicated to the integrated production of knowledge and the implementation of change. Action research addresses practical problems, generates knowledge, enacts change, is participatory, and relies on a cyclical self-reflective process.
- While the participatory and collaborative nature of action research can be highly rewarding and productive, it can also result in a number of management issues, including a lack of control over the project's direction and pace, the potential for stakeholder conflict, and the sole burden of ethical responsibility.

- Striving for critical emancipation relates to goals that require more than just change within a 'system'; it requires radical change to the system itself. Two strategies for achieving such goals through research are participatory action research and critical ethnography.
- Participatory action research attempts to expose dominant and repressive systems, and has an express goal of emancipation through action. It encourages the oppressed to control their own knowledge production and emancipatory change interventions through an action research process.
- Critical ethnography also attempts to expose dominant systems in the interest of the 'marginalized'. Change comes from the voice offered to the oppressed, as well as the starting point it offers for action at individual, legislative, and policy levels.
- A common issue in emancipatory research is the intertwining of research and political agendas. In addition to managing subjectivities, researchers need to guard against imposing their own political agendas on the researched.

<table>
<tr><td>**11**</td><td>**Data Collection**</td></tr>
</table>

'So what's the best way to go about collecting my data?'

THE QUEST FOR CREDIBLE DATA

What do large-scale surveying, ethnomethodology, phenomenology, ethnography, evaluation research, action research, etc., all have in common? Well, they may differ on any number of dimensions, but what they have in common is a need for credible DATA. Sources of data may vary, and means of accessing and gathering it may differ, but all methodologies are reliant on data and the basic methods and tools used to collect it.

Now as you read through this chapter, you may be surprised at just how many issues and complexities are associated with any particular method of data collection. Collecting credible data is a tough task, and it is worth remembering that one method of data collection is not inherently better than  another. Each method needs to be weighed up and considered in light of your own research goals, as well as the method's inherent pros and cons.

Gaining access

The first step in collecting data is access. Whether it be written records, workplaces, survey respondents, or interviewees, without access, obtaining credible data becomes impossible. As highlighted in Box 11.1, tips for gaining access include doing your background homework (it can help if you are knowledgeable and well-informed), conducting yourself in a professional manner, and offering to give something back. Keep in mind that those willing to assist often have a genuine interest in what you are doing and appreciate being kept in the loop.

Box 11.1   Gaining Access

DO YOUR HOMEWORK
- **Be prepared to talk about your research** – the ability to clearly articulate the rationale, aims, objectives, and methods of your project can be instrumental in getting the right doors opened.
- **Prepare a brief outline of your project** – certain individuals or organizations may want to have a document they can consider and/or present to 'gatekeepers'.
- **Have a letter of introduction** – a letter of introduction from your supervisor can professionally answer questions like, 'So who are you and where are you from?'
- **Find out about appropriate protocols** – sometimes the contacts that are most willing to help do not have the authority to authorize access. Finding out about appropriate protocols can help avoid awkward situations.

BE PROFESSIONAL
- **Go through the appropriate channels** – going through a 'backdoor' is both risky – it is more likely to be shut prematurely – and unethical.
- **Be respectful** – choose the right time for your approach, be prompt, dress appropriately, and be modest in your initial requests.
- **Plan for the unexpected** – very rarely does the research process run smoothly, especially when you are dealing with individuals – be prepared for glitches.
- **Leave doors open** – many researchers swear they've collected all the data they're going to need, but later wish they could go back and ask just a few more questions.

OFFER SOMETHING BACK
- **Don't disappear** – let your contacts know how things are progressing and/or send a note of thanks.
- **Make results available** – it is quite natural to have a sense of curiosity about studies of which you are a part; results of your study can be quite valued by those who have facilitated your research.

Access and power

Generally we think of research ethics in terms of our impact on subjects, respondents, or participants. It's quite easy to forget that ethics need to be considered even when you are dealing with 'gatekeepers' or those who might be in a position to grant you access. Researchers are in a power position that can see the

TABLE 11.1   ACCESS AND POWER

Using power	Abusing power
➤ Using official channels and protocols	➤ Avoiding and skirting around official channels and protocols
➤ Establishing points of contact	➤ Going around or above the appropriate person's head
➤ Using gatekeepers and insiders	➤ Asking gatekeepers and insiders to act unethically or to go behind management's back
➤ Building rapport	➤ Ingratiate yourself to the point of becoming sycophantic
➤ Leaving doors open	➤ Becoming a nuisance
➤ Offering something back	➤ Making promises you cannot or do not intend to keep

researched abused at any stage in the research process. As articulated in Table 11.1, if the subtleties of gaining access are not managed appropriately, it can be easy to abuse relationships and take advantage of individuals.

SURVEYING

First, a point of clarification … in its broadest sense, *to survey* (v) means 'to look at or examine', while *a survey* (n) means 'an observation or an overview'. Now some research methods texts use these definitions and group a number of approaches/methods under the survey heading. However, when I use the word 'survey', both as a noun and a verb, I am using more specific definitions that relate to a particular social science method.

Survey (n): Information gathered by asking a range of individuals the same questions related to their characteristics, attributes, how they live, or their opinions.

Survey (v): The process of collecting such information.

Knowing what to expect

Now students often tell me they've decided to conduct a survey; after all, they've heard they are a relatively simple, straightforward, and cost-effective means of gathering credible data. Well I hate to break it to them, but this is a long way from the truth. Yes, a good survey does have the potential to:

- reach a large number of respondents
- represent an even larger population
- generate standardized, quantifiable, empirical data

- be confidential and anonymous and
- generate qualitative data through the use of open-ended questions

But there seems to be a belief out there that just about anyone can construct a survey instrument, and conduct a survey. You just need to know who you want to target; what you want to ask; and have some modicum of common sense about you. But I'll tell you what … social science surveying really needs to be considered a specialist activity. Constructing and administering a survey that can generate credible and generalizable data is a truly difficult task. There are a whole lot of really crappy surveys out there that aren't worth the paper they're printed on, yet the data they generate is often reported as truth and used in all kinds of decision-making processes.

If it is your intention to gather data using a survey and a survey instrument, you will need to have good support. In addition to getting a handle on the information presented here, it's worth talking to your supervisor and working through some of the recommended readings at the end of the chapter. Another option is to look into survey software. 'Sphinx', accessible at www.scoalri.com, is a program designed to help you with all main aspects of surveying, including questionnaire construction and data analysis.

Basic survey types

A survey is a survey. Well not quite. There are actually a few distinct types of survey, each suited to a different purpose. But if you are familiar with the various types, and know what you want to know (thereby knowing what you want your survey to do), choosing appropriate types will be a relatively easy task.

Surveys can describe and/or explain:

Descriptive surveys: These surveys pretty much do what they say – they describe. This might involve basic demographic information like age, socio-economic status, and gender; or more personal information such as voting patterns, how often respondents have sex, or how frequently they spank their children. They can also gather attitudinal information such as attitudes towards war, euthanasia, or abortion. The goal is to get a snapshot – to show or to describe your 'respondents' – and, if a representative sample is used, to be able to generalize that description to a larger population.

Explanatory surveys: These surveys go beyond description (although they do gather descriptive data) and attempt to establish why things might be the way they are. For example, not only would an explanatory survey want to describe a population's attitude towards abortion, but it would also seek to establish what might shape and form those attitudes, i.e. the effect of family values or personal experience. An explanatory survey attempts to build more complex understandings and goes beyond description, or even correlation, in an attempt to determine cause and effect.

Surveys might target full populations or samples of populations:

Census: This is a survey that does not rely on a sample. A census surveys every single person in a defined or target population.

Cross-sectional surveys: This type of survey uses a sample or cross-section of respondents selected to represent a target population. The goal is to be able to generalize the findings of the sample to the population with a high degree of confidence.

Survey can also be longitudinal and explore changing times or changing people:

Trend surveys: A trend survey asks similar groups of respondents, or the same cross-section, the same questions at two or more points in time. For example, conducting three surveys over a 20-year period (1984, 1994, 2004) that asks teenagers about perceived personal and professional opportunities. This allows you to assess whether the attitudes of teenagers have changed over the past two decades – in other words, are teenagers the same now as they were in the 1980s.

Panel study: A panel study involves asking the same (not similar) sample of respondents the same questions at two or more points in time. Using the example above, if you were to survey 18 year-olds in 1984, then you would survey these same individuals in 1994 when they were 28, and again in 2004 when they were 38. You would then be able to assess whether there was a shift in respondents' attitudes as they get older.

Finally, surveys can be administered in a number of ways:

Face-to-face surveys: This mode of surveying allows surveyors the opportunity to establish rapport, build trust, motivate respondents, clarify questions, read non-verbal cues, and probe appropriately. The response rate also tends to be good. However, face-to-face surveying is often a lengthy and expensive process, does not assure anonymity or even confidentiality, requires surveyor training, and may be affected by interviewer bias.

Telephone surveys: Telephone surveys are relatively inexpensive and take minimal time, allow for coverage of a wide geographic area, and offer some assurance of anonymity and confidentiality. On the down side, the response rate, while better than self-administered surveys, is still lower than face-to-face surveys; it's easy to catch people at a bad time; respondents can hang up on you if they have had enough; and you are limited to surveying only those with a telephone.

Self-administered surveys: These surveys can offer anonymity and therefore confidentiality. They also allow coverage of a wide geographic area, and give respondents the opportunity to complete questionnaires in their own time. Response rates, however, can be really low (unless you can distribute your survey through an organization that lets respondents fill out the surveys as part of the school/or work day). And of course respondents cannot seek clarification. Self-administered surveys are often mailed, but can also be sent and received electronically. This can potentially save you thousands, but you are limited to surveying those with e-mail addresses or populations likely to be online.

The survey process

Conducting a 'good' survey is a process that involves a whole lot of steps. Surveys require you to: plan the approach, process, tools, and all the contingencies; construct the survey instrument; run a trial or pilot; redevelop as appropriate; send out the survey; manage the responses; and finally analyze the data. Box 11.2 outlines the 25+ steps (some you will need to do more than once) involved in surveying. You may find this box helpful as both a guide and a checklist.

Box 11.2   Steps (and there are a lot) for Conducting a 'Good' Survey

PLAN

1. Realistically consider issues of sampling, distribution, reminders, response rates, and data management so that you are relatively sure a survey/questionnaire will work.
2. Develop a plan you can implement if response rates are low.
3. Consider what aspects of your research question(s) are likely to be answered through a questionnaire.
4. List, group, and categorize these 'aspects'.
5. Explore whether there might be existing questionnaires or sets of questions that address these 'aspects' that may be appropriate.

CONSTRUCT

6. If relevant questionnaires or sets of questions exist – adopt, adapt, and modify.
7. If your questionnaire requires the construction of any new questions, have a shot at drafting them.
8. Decide on the response categories for each question, considering both the effect of response categories on responses themselves and how various types of response category translate to different data types that demand quite distinct statistical treatment.
9. Carefully read each question and response choices, and think about whether your questions might be considered ambiguous, leading, confronting, offensive, based on unwarranted assumptions, double-barrelled, or pretentious.
10. Rewrite the questions in relation to the considerations above and run them past a few peers/supervisors for their assessment. Repeat this step as many times as necessary to get each question as right as possible.

---

11. Attempt to put your questions in an order that will be logical and ease respondents into your survey.
12. Write instructions for your respondents and ask your peers/supervisor whether they seem clear and unambiguous. Rewrite as necessary.
13. Construct a clear, logical, professional, and aesthetically pleasing layout and design.
14. Write a cover letter.

PILOT

15. Pilot your questionnaire with a few people who are similar to those in your sample.
16. Get feedback from the pilot group in relation to the questions themselves (see step 9); the overall layout and design; the effectiveness of the cover letter; the usefulness of the instructions; and the length of time it took to complete the questionnaire.
17. Attempt to create variables, code the pilot responses, and then plug it into a statistical program (or qualitative data analysis program) to see if you are likely to encounter any issues when you input your main data.

REDEVELOP

18. Make modifications based on both the feedback of the pilot group and the quality of the data generated.
19. If modifications are substantial, start again from step 15.
20. Get ethical clearance for the final version of your questionnaire.

EXECUTE

21. Distribute questionnaires; be sure to include instructions for return (address and return date) and possibly a self-addressed stamped envelope.
22. Send out a reminder letter if response rates are low.
23. Put low response rate plan (see step 1) into action if not enough data has been gathered by your deadline.
24. Record and manage responses as they are received.

ANALYZE DATA

25. Turn to Chapter 12 to work through management and analysis of the data!

The survey instrument

When it comes to conducting a survey, what students struggle with most is constructing the actual survey instrument. From drafting the questions through to layout and design, students are quite surprised at how much thought and work goes into the development of an instrument capable of generating credible data.

Formulating questions

The first step in writing your questions is knowing what you want to ask. By the time you are ready to construct your survey instrument you should know what aspects of your research questions can be answered by your respondents. The second step is to attempt an initial drafting of questions related to each of these aspects.

Now there are about 762 ways to ask the same question, and each of these ways has potential to generate quite different data, so knowing how to best draft your questions can be a real challenge. While there are volumes written on crafting survey questionnaires, a few basic rules can be applied that can help you avoid the pitfalls of leading, offending, or confusing your respondents. Using a number of examples, Box 11.3 covers these basic rules.

Box 11.3 Questions to Avoid

Writing good questions is about clarity and specificity, but there are plenty of ways to make sure this doesn't happen. It is easy to construct questions that are:

POORLY WORDED

- **Complex terms and language** – big words can offend and confuse. If they're not necessary, why use them? Compare the two following agree/ disagree statements: '*Polysyllabic linguistic terminology can act to obscure connotations*' vs '*Big words can be confusing*'.
- **Ambiguous questions** – it's very easy to write ambiguous questions because frames of reference can be highly divergent. For example, consider the questions: '*How big is your family?*' or '*Do you use drugs?*' Families can be nuclear or extended, or for children of separated parents, may include two households. Similarly, 'drugs' can be an ambiguous term. Some respondents will only consider illegal drugs, while others may include prescription drugs. And of course, it would be impossible to know whether alcohol or cigarettes were also considered.
- **Double negatives** – a significant proportion of respondents get confused when faced with double negatives. Consider the following agree/disagree statement: '*You are not satisfied with your job*'. To state that you are satisfied in your job means that you need to choose disagree, which can be quite confusing.
- **Double-barrelled questions** – this is when you ask for only one response to a question with more than one issue. For example, take the question: '*Do you consider the President to be an honest and effective leader?*' Respondents may think yes, effective – but definitely not honest.

BIASED, LEADING OR LOADED

- **'Ring true' statements** – these are statements that are easy to agree with simply because of their 'ring true tone'. A couple of examples might be '*You really can't rely on people these days*' or '*Times may be tough, but there are generally people around you can count on*'. Both of these are likely to get a high percentage of agree responses.
- **Hard to disagree with statements** – these are statements where your respondent is likely to think 'yes that's true, but…' They are not, however, given a chance to elaborate and are forced to either agree or disagree. For example, '*The elderly are often a burden to society*'.
- **Leading questions** – leading respondents towards a particular response can be a simple task (one often done for political purposes). Consider how the wording of the following questions on abortion might affect responses: '*Do mothers have the right to murder an unborn child?*' vs '*Do women have the right to make choices about their own bodies?*'

PROBLEMATICAL FOR THE RESPONDENT

- **Recall dependent questions** – these are questions that rely on memory. For example, '*How many jobs have you held?*' Without boundaries such as an occupational field or timeframe, this question can be easy to answer 'incorrectly'.
- **Offensive questions** – if respondents take offence to a question or a series of questions, not only are they likely to skip those items, they may just throw out the entire survey. Offensive questions can range from '*What did you do to make your husband leave you?*' to '*How old are you?*'
- **Questions with assumed knowledge** – be careful not to assume your respondents know about, or are familiar with, the same things as yourself. For example, the agree/disagree statement '*Postmodern art is exciting and dynamic*', could easily meet with a, 'What the *#@% is postmodern art?' response.
- **Questions with unwarranted assumptions** – respondents are likely to be at a loss when it comes to answering a question that contains an assumption they do not agree with. For example, the question '*What aspect of this course did you enjoy most?*' assumes that the respondent enjoyed something.
- **Questions with socially desirable responses** – this is more likely to be an issue in face-to-face surveying where the respondents may not want to 'look bad' to the survey administrator. For example, respondents may be uncomfortable disagreeing with the statement *I am for affirmative action* because they don't want to come across as a racist.

Response categories

Determining response categories is as crucial to generating credible data as is setting the questions themselves. First, response categories influence the answers that are given. For example, if you add an 'I'm not sure' option to a controversial yes/no question, it will have a definite impact on your findings. Second, different types of response category generate various data types that demand quite distinct statistical treatment. In fact, understanding the various data types (nominal, ordinal, interval, and ratio – discussed in Chapter 12), definitely facilitates the process of survey construction, particularly response category determination. Most students, however, don't really get their heads around variable types and the significance they have for survey instrument construction until they begin the process of analyzing their data.

This makes conducting your first survey really tricky. Many lecturers find that 'doing' is the best way of learning, and that struggling with analysis in a first survey is the best way to learn what to do when it comes to constructing your next. Now I happen to agree, but if your first survey 'needs to count' and credible data is a high priority, you'll need to: (1) turn to Chapter 12 to familiarize yourself with the basics of data management and analysis; and (2) become familiar with various response options before finalizing your questions (see below).

Survey questions can either be open or closed:

Open questions: These questions ask respondents to construct answers using their own words. Respondents can offer any information/express any opinion they wish, although the amount of space provided for an answer will generally limit the response. Open questions can generate rich and candid data, but it can be data that is difficult to code and analyze.

Closed questions: These questions force respondents to choose from a range of predetermined responses and are generally easy to code and statistically analyze. As shown in Box 11.4, closed questions come in many forms, each associated with particular issues.

> ### Box 11.4 Common Response Categories for Closed Questions
>
> **YES/NO – AGREE/DISAGREE**
>
> 1. *Do you drink alcohol?*   *Yes/No*
> 2. *Is drinking bad for your health?*   *Agree/Disagree*
>
> While it can be easy to work with 'binomial' data (or data with only two potential responses), you need to consider whether respondents will be comfortable with only two choices. For example, in Q1, a respondent might be thinking 'Not really (I only drink when I go out, which is hardly ever)', or for Q2, 'It depends on how much you're talking about?' A potential strategy is to offer a *don't know/no opinion* option, but this allows for a lot of 'fence sitting'.
>
> **FILL IN THE BLANK**
>
> 3. *How much do you weigh?* _____

Even a simple question like this (assuming your respondents know the answer and are willing to tell you) can lead to messy data. Will respondents write 90 kgs, 198 lbs, or 14 stone? Of course you can convert these answers to one system, but that isn't going to be possible if they just put 90.

CHOOSING FROM A LIST

4. *What would you drink most often?*

Beer   Wine   Spirits   Mixed drinks   Cocktails

There is an assumption here that there will not be any 'ties'; you need to consider what you will do if more than one option is circled. You also need to make sure all options are covered. A potential strategy is to offer an '*other*' or '*other._____*' option.

ORDERING OPTIONS

5. *Please place the following drinks in order of preference*

Beer   Wine   Spirits   Mixed drinks   Cocktails

These questions have been found to be quite difficult for respondents, particularly if lists are long. It is worth remembering that if respondents get frustrated trying to answer your question, they are likely to leave the question blank, leave it half finished, or just write anything at all.

LIKERT TYPE SCALING:

6. *It is normal for teenagers to binge drink*

1	*2*	*3*	*4*	*5*
Strongly disagree	*Disagree*	*Unsure*	*Agree*	*Strongly agree*

Likert scales offer a range of responses generally ranging from something like 'strongly disagree' to 'strongly agree'. In Likert scaling you need to consider: the number of points you will use; whether you will force a side; and whether you think respondents will 'get on a roll' and keep circling a particular number.

Information and instruction

Providing clear background information and lucid instructions is an essential part of good survey instrument construction.

* *Offering information* – surveys need to include some background information that identifies the sponsor/university; clarifies the survey's purpose; assures anonymity/confidentiality; provides return information, including deadlines and return address; and offers thanks for time/assistance. This information can be included at the start of the survey or as a cover letter or e-mail.

- *Providing instruction* – what might be self-evident to you, may not be so obvious to your respondents. Your instructions should introduce each section of the survey instrument; give clear and specific instructions for each question type; provide examples; and be easy to distinguish from the actual survey questions – in fact it's a good idea to use a different font. It may take a couple of drafts to get your instructions as clear and helpful as possible, and it's advisable to ask your peers/supervisor if your instructions do the job. However, the real test will come when you pilot the instrument, review the data, and seek feedback from your pilot participants.

Organization and length

Once the elements of your survey are complete, you need to think about putting it together in a logical order that covers it all without being overly lengthy.

- *Length* – instruments considered too long can be abandoned, returned incomplete, or filled in at random. I once filled in a survey for a gourmet chicken shop in order to get a free piece of chicken (well I was a poor student at the time). This thing turned out to be, no lie, nine pages long. How many finger-licking chicken questions can you answer? For me it turned out to be all of them (I wasn't leaving without my Kiev), but I think I was supposed to actually read the questions before ticking the boxes!
- *Organization* – you are likely to find contradictory advice on whether to start or end with demographics, and where to place your most important questions. A lot of this depends on the nature of both your questions and your respondents; and you may want to pilot two different versions of your questionnaire if you are unsure how to lay it all out. One tried and true piece of advice, however, is that you don't want to start your survey with any questions that might be considered threatening. It is important to ease your respondents into your survey and save sensitive question for near the end.

Layout and design

You'd think that all of the intense intellectual work that has gone into writing clear and unambiguous questions with appropriate, well thought out response categories that are accompanied by clear instruction and organized into a sensitive, logical, and manageable form would be enough to ensure a 'good' survey. Not quite. Aesthetics counts!

If your survey looks unprofessional (for example, poor photocopies, faint printing, messy and uninteresting layout etc.), two things can happen. First, respondents will be less likely to complete a survey that is unprofessional and lacking an aesthetically pleasing layout and design. Second, the potential for mistakes increases dramatically if surveys are cluttered, cramped, or messy.

INTERVIEWING

I'm going to start my discussion of interviewing with another point of clarification. When I talk about interviewing, I am referring to a process with the following definition:

Interviewing: A method of data collection that involves researchers asking respondents basically *open-ended* questions.

The reason I want to make this clear is that some methods texts class any verbal researcher–respondent questioning process as an interview, including the administration of telephone and face-to-face questionnaires. Now while in its most structured form an interview can be quite similar to a face-to-face survey, interviews tend to rely on open-ended questions for the majority of data collected.

Interviewing in all its complexity

If you've just finished reading the section on surveying, you may be thinking, 'Ok, that's pretty involved. Interviewing may be an easier option.' Well, not really. First, interviewing needs to be the right method for addressing your particular research question. And assuming that it is the right method, it's important to realize that interviewing has its own issues and complexities, and demands its own type of rigour.

The complexities of people

What's the biggest barrier to gathering credible data through the interview process? That's easy – it's people. People (researchers included) are complex, complicated, and sometimes convoluted; and the interview process demands a high level of engagement with others. In an interview, the researcher is reliant on the interviewee to provide honest and open answers, yet we know that people want to be liked, want to maintain a sense of dignity, and want to protect some level of privacy. If respondents feel judged, ashamed or offended, or, on the other hand, deferential or awestruck, gathering credible data is far from assured. Basic attributes such as race, gender, ethnicity, class, and age, of interviewer and interviewee alike, can also affect the interview process (see Chapter 4). The bigger the 'gulf' between interviewer and interviewee the greater the chance it will influence the interview process.

Complexities of communications

Interviewing is often aligned with conversation. But in actuality, interviewing is a very specific form of communication that is much more complex than simply asking a question and taking note of an answer. Questions move from the mind to the lips of the interviewer, before moving to the ears of an interviewee, who filters the question through mental processes, before articulating any answers. The interviewer must then hear what has been said, and use their own mental processes to take in and interpret meaning. From forming ideas to the articulation of those ideas, from hearing others to making sense of what they are saying, the question and answer (Q&A) process is rife with the potential for miscommunication. Box 11.5 highlights how difficult it can be to ensure that the interview process does not lead to misunderstandings and misinterpretation.

Box 11.5   It's just Q&A, isn't it?

		From A to K	**Getting lost along the way…**
The Interviewer		A. formulates a question	**A to B:** Your thoughts and words do not always match up.
		B. asks the question	**B to C:** Respondents can simply mishear. Accents, language difficulties/interpreters can make this quite common.
		C. hears the question	**C to D:** Respondents don't always share the same understandings as the interviewer.
The Respondent		D. interprets the meaning	**D to E:** Respondents can intentionally filter/hide/lie or simply forget.
		E. considers a response	**E to F:** Again, words do not always capture thoughts.
		F. articulates an answer	**F to G:** Interviewers also have the potential to mishear. If taping, make sure audio is of adequate quality.
		G. hears the response	**G to H:** The more 'foreign' the culture the more potential for divergent interpretation.
The Interviewer		H. interprets the meaning	**H to I:** Note-taking is not easy. You can miss significant information. You can also lose data in the transcription process.
		I. takes notes	**I to J:** Judgements/interpretations need to be made by the interviewer.
		J. synthesizes/analyzes	**J to K:** The interviewer reports back understandings as truth!!!
		K. reports	

Interview basics

When it comes to conducting an interview there are a number of options, each with its own strengths, weaknesses, opportunities, and limitations. An early challenge is determining what type of interview is most suited to your research question.

Interviews can range in type from fixed to free:

Structured: At one end of the spectrum is the fully structured interview that uses pre-established questions, asked in a predetermined order, using a standard mode of delivery. Means for prompting and probing the interviewee are predetermined and used in defined circumstances. Researchers attempt to be objective, neutral, and removed, and try to minimize personal interactions. The goal is standardization without improvisation.

Semi-structured: As the name suggests, these interviews are neither fully fixed nor fully free, and are perhaps best seen as flexible. Interviewers generally start with some defined questioning plan, but pursue a more conversational style of interview that may see questions answered in an order more natural to the flow of conversation. They may also start with a few defined questions but be ready to pursue any interesting tangents that may develop.

Unstructured: At the other end of the spectrum is the unstructured interview that attempts to draw out information, attitudes, opinions, and beliefs around particular themes, ideas, and issues without the aid of predetermined questions. To do this, interviewers use a more conversational style and attempt to prompt, probe, and develop questions on the spot as is appropriate to the ongoing conversation.

Interviews also vary in their level of formality:

Formal: A formal interview is just that, formal. Perhaps the best analogy is the classic job interview that includes: the office setting; the formal handshake; appropriate attire; order and structure; and best professional behaviour. There are defined roles and there is deference to those roles. The interviewer role includes being somewhat removed from the interviewee and maintaining neutrality/objectivity. While it is possible to conduct an unstructured interview in a formal manner, formal interviews are generally structured.

Informal: An informal interview attempts to ignore the rules and roles associated with interviewing in an attempt to establish rapport, gain trust, and create a more natural environment conducive to open and honest communication. It is a casual and relaxed form of interviewing that attempts to close the gulf between the researcher and the researched. The setting for an informal interview is not limited to an office and might occur over a beer at the pub, or while having a cup of coffee at a mother's group. Informal interviews are often unstructured, but this varies with the style, comfort zone, and goals of the researcher.

Finally, interviewing can be done one–on–one, or in groups:

One-on-one: Most interviews are an interaction between the interviewer and a single interviewee. It is thought that 'one-on-one' allows the researcher control over the process and the interviewee the freedom to express his or her thoughts. At times, however, the interviewer may require the assistance of a translator or decide to use a note-taker, or video cameraperson. One-on-one interviews are generally face-to-face, but can also be done over the telephone. The advantages of phone interviewing are researcher convenience and unlimited geographical range. The disadvantages include an inability to read non-verbal cues and less control throughout the interview process.

Group: Group interviews involve interviewing more than one person at a time. This can be done in a formal structured way, or may involve a less structured process where the researcher acts more as a moderator or facilitator than an interviewer. In this less structured approach, interviewees are often referred to as a focus group. Since group interviews can be difficult to follow, they are often taped so that raw data can be sifted through at a later time.

The interview process

As with surveying, conducting a 'good' interview is a process that requires a lot more steps than you may realize. Interviewing involves the need to: plan for all contingencies; prepare an interview schedule and data recording system; run a trial or pilot; modify the process as appropriate; conduct the interviews; and, finally, analyze the data. Box 11.6, which can be used as both a guide and a checklist, outlines the steps involved in interviewing.

Box 11.6   Steps in the Interview Process

PLAN

1. Realistically consider issues of representation and access.
2. Develop a contingency plan in case key interviews fall through.
3. Familiarize yourself with, and plan for, any potential language and/or cultural issues likely to affect the process. Find and trial a good translator if necessary.
4. Consider the presentation of self, including what role you will take and how involved you will be in conversations.
5. Decide approximately how long you think the interviews should take.
6. Make appointments early. Plan travel time, interview time, AND wait around time.

PREPARE AN INTERVIEW SCHEDULE AND DATA RECORDING SYSTEM

7. Draft relevant questions or develop thematic areas to explore.
8. Carefully read any questions and consider whether they might be considered confusing, leading, or problematic in any way for the interviewee.
9. Rewrite the questions in relation to considerations above and run them past a few peers/supervisor for their assessment. Repeat this step as many times as necessary to get each question as right as possible.
10. Attempt to put your questions into an order that is logical and will ease respondents into the interview.

---

11. Consider and develop any instructions, prompts, or probes you feel are appropriate to the interview.
12. Decide on recording methods. If note-taking, consider/develop a form that can aid this process. If audio or video-taping, be sure to acquire and become familiar with the equipment.

PILOT

13. Attempt a pilot interview with a couple of respondents whose background is similar to those in your 'sample'.
14. Note any difficulties encountered, i.e. access, time taken, pacing, comfort zones, recording/note-taking, roles, objectivity, conversational flow, ambiguities, etc.
15. Get feedback from the interviewees on the above and anything else they wish to discuss.
16. Attempt to make sense of your notes and/or transcribe your data.

MODIFY

17. Make modifications based on your own reflections, the feedback from the interviewees, and the quality of the data generated.
18. If modifications are substantial, start again from step 13.
19. Get ethical clearance for the final interview schedule/question/themes.

INTERVIEW

20. Be on time, set up, and check any equipment.
21. Establish rapport, introduce the study, and discuss 'ethics'.
22. Ease into main questions/themes.
23. Keep on track and/or explore interesting tangents.
24. Manage the process, wind down the interview, and bring to a close.

ANALYZE DATA

25. Turn to Chapter 12 to work through data management and analysis!

Conducting your interview

No matter how well prepared you are for your first interview, you are still likely to feel nervous at the beginning and wish you did things differently at the end. Interviewing is not easy; and I think that's because you are actually trying to do three things at once. First, you are trying to listen to the interviewee and make sense of what they are saying. Second, you are attempting to question, prompt, and probe, in ways that will help you gather the 'best' data. Finally, you are trying to manage the overall process so that you know how much time has passed, how much time is left, how much you still need to cover, and how you might move it all forward.

There is a real skill to conducting a good interview. But if you are aware of the key issues (outlined below) and are able to reflect on your experiences, it is a skill that can develop over time.

Presentation of self

It's not just a matter of what you say, but it's how you say it and how you present yourself in general. Whether it be appearance, demeanour, or the words you use, you will usually need to strike a balance between formality and rapport. For example, think about your appearance. Is your interview style/goal better suited to formality or is it one more suited to developing a sense of comfort where matching the attire of your respondent may make more inroads than going conventional? Of course if you are too causal, you run the risk of looking non-professional.

There is also the issue of body language. As you probably know, a whole lot of everyday communication is non-verbal; and just as you will read the non-verbal cues of your respondents, your respondents will be reading your own non-verbal cues. The SOLER model (Egan 1994) provides a framework that allows you to consider how your own body language might affect the communication process, while simultaneously allowing you to assess your respondent's level of ease and comfort. The SOLER elements are:

Square on – if you are both facing each other it connotes that you are paying full attention.

Open posture – for the interviewer this indicates a willingness to accept, for the interviewee it is a posture that suggests they are non-defensive.

Lean forward – shows involvement and interest – too far forward, however, can be read as aggressive.

Eye contact – this varies by culture, but little eye contact generally means little interest, while too much can be unnerving.

Relax – this refers to a relaxed flow of information accompanied by smooth and non-jerky movements.

Preliminaries

A fair few things need to be attended to before you even ask your first question. Preliminaries include the need to:

- *BE ON TIME!* – if you keep someone waiting, building rapport can be a nightmare. Miss an appointment altogether, and you may not get a second chance.
- *Set up and check equipment* – if you think this will require a significant amount of time, organize in advance. If not, do it quickly and efficiently while you establish rapport.
- *Establish rapport* – this includes the introduction, handshake, small talk, and expressions of appreciation. This is a crucial step, but doesn't have to take a lot of time.
- *Introduce the study* – this includes reviewing who you are; the purpose of the study; why his or her involvement is important; and approximately how long the interview will take.
- *Explain ethics* – this generally involves assurances of confidentiality, the right to decline to answer any particular questions, and the right to end the interview upon request.

The questioning process

When it comes to interviewing, you generally get a lot of advice on what to say and how to say it, but much more important is your listening skills. Perhaps the golden rule of interviewing is to:

Listen more than talk

The main game in interviewing is to facilitate an interviewee's ability to answer. This involves easing respondents into the interview by asking the right questions; prompting and probing appropriately; keeping it moving; and finally winding it down when the time is right.

- *Easing your respondents into the interview* – as with surveying, it is important to ease into main questions and themes. If you start off with a 'sensitive' question or one that might be considered threatening, you may find yourself facing an uphill battle for the remainder of the interview. In fact, it can be easy to get an interviewee off-side, so it's well worth considering how you might handle such a situation.
- *Ask strategic questions* – this refers to asking questions that can open up conversations and draw out rich responses. Peavey (2003) suggests that this requires questions that create possibilities, open up options, avoid yes/no answers, dig below the surface, and lower defences by avoiding any tone of judgement. Strategic questions also avoid the pitfalls of leading, offending, or confusing respondents. Box 11.3, earlier in this chapter, provides a fuller discussion and examples of problematic questions.
- *Keep it flowing* – this involves the use of prompts (giving the interviewee some ideas that might jog a response) and probes (comments and questions that help you dig for more, i.e. 'tell me more', 'really', or 'why'). Sometimes probes can be an inquisitive look or a few moments of silence.
- *Keep on track/explore tangents* – if you have a limited amount of time and your interview is quite structured, you will want to make sure you are keeping your interviewee on track and moving at a decent pace. You may find yourself saying, 'That's really interesting, but I really want to know more about …', 'When you mentioned …' If your interview is less structured, you may find yourself wanting to explore interesting tangents as they develop. The trick here is to be mindful of the time and be sure you end the interview with the full range of data you aimed to gather.
- *Be true to your role* – how you keep it flowing, keep it on track, or explore tangents needs to be considered in light of the role you have chosen to adopt as an interviewer. If you are using a formal procedure and working towards objectivity, you will want to use standardized prompts and probes, and will need to consider how you can direct the process without directing responses. On the other hand, if you accept that your own subjectivities will be part of the interviewing process, you will need to consider and openly report how your engagement in the process might influence a conversation.
- *Wind down/close* – there is generally a flow to an interview that ends with wind down and closure. The wind down involves questions that 'round off' an interview and asks respondents if there is anything else they would like to cover, contribute, or clarify. The interview then ends by thanking your interviewee

and asking if it might be possible to contact him or her again if you need to ask any further questions or need to clarify any points.

Recording responses

You may be adept at asking good questions, and in fact be an exceptional listener, but if you can't read your own handwriting or make heads or tales of your recordings ... you are in a whole lot of trouble. Recording responses can be done in a number of ways; you may need to trial a couple of recording methods in order to assess what is best for you and your research process.

- *Note-taking* – this can range from highly structured to open and interpretative. Highly structured note-taking often utilizes a form that can be filled in as the interviewee speaks. It may even include a list of codes for common responses. On the other end of the spectrum is unstructured note-taking that may take the form of a concept map or involve jotting down interpretative ideas directly after an interview. Remember that if you're going to take notes during an interview, be sure you practise talking, listening, and note-taking simultaneously – and that you can read your own writing. You also need to keep in mind that note-taking is actually a preliminary form of analysis that does not provide raw data, and that you may want to consider taking notes in conjunction with audio/video recording.
- *Audio recording* – audio recording allows you to preserve raw data for review at a later date. It therefore allows you to focus on the question/answer process at hand. The disadvantages of taping are: the unease it can cause for the interviewee; its inability to capture non-verbal cues; the fallibility of equipment (see Box 11.7); and the enormous time and financial cost of transcribing data.
- *Video taping* – video-taping offers the added bonus of being able to record visual cues, but is more intrusive, is prone to more technical difficulties, and can generate data that is hard to analyze.

Box 11.7   Tape-recording Dilemmas

SOME THINGS YOU DON'T WANT TO FIND YOURSELF SAYING...

To your interviewee:

- 'Oh jeez, wait – hold on. I don't think the silly thing's recording.'
- 'Sorry, but I didn't realize the tape finished, do you mind repeating everything you said for, let's see ... the last 43 minutes.'

To yourself:

- 'Damn – all I can hear is that stupid lawnmower.'
- 'I knew I should have stopped at the 7–11 for more batteries.'
- 'Oh nooo. ... I think I recorded over the interview I did last week.'

AND ONE THING YOU MIGHT WANT TO CONSIDER SAYING…

To your interviewee when you are sensing 'wariness':

- 'Would you feel more comfortable if I turned it off and just took notes?'

A note on translators

Finally, a quick note on translators. If you need to use a translator, there are a number of issues you will need to consider in the quest for credible data. First, you need to make sure your translator is experienced. Just being bilingual doesn't guarantee the necessary skills – be sure to trial and/or seek references. You then need to decide how you will use the translator. Will you ask them to translate your questions literally, or would you like them to use their own judgement in an attempt to convey your meaning? Will they translate for the interviewee during the interview, or will you tape the interviewee in their native language and have the translator transcribe into English at a later time? You also need to think through issues of structure and formality. Gaining casual rapport or being highly flexible can be tough to do through a translator. There are no easy answers here, and perhaps the best advice is that you definitely need to have a run through. This is probably the only way to assess whether your translation process is going to work for you.

OBSERVATION

Observation is a word we might use on any given day, in any multitude of situations. In day-to-day language, *to observe* means 'to watch or notice', while *observation* refers to 'the act of watching or noticing'. The problem is that these day-to-day definitions cannot be directly transferred to the world of research methods. As a methods term, 'observation' needs to be identified as a systematic methodology; while the term 'observe' needs to connote more than input from just visual cues.

Observation: A systematic method of data collection that relies on a researcher's ability to gather data through his or her senses.

Observe: To notice, using a full range of appropriate senses. To see, hear, feel, taste, and smell.

What you see isn't always what you get

Because students are often familiar with the general concept of observation, they tend to think that conducting an observational study will be pretty straightforward.

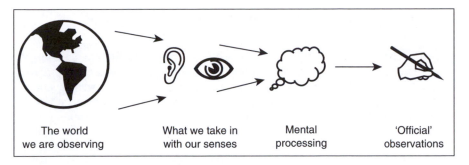

| The world we are observing | What we take in with our senses | Mental processing | 'Official' observations |

FIGURE 11.1   FILTERING OBSERVATIONS

They will simply observe and take note of what is happening in a given situation or context. What I try to stress to these students is that observation needs to be considered a systematic data collection method. The challenge is taking something done on a daily basis and converting it into a rigorous research tool. This can be quite difficult because observation requires that researchers continually consider and negotiate how their own inherent biases might: (1) colour their observations; and (2) have a potential impact on the observed.

You and you alone
A major obstacle in the quest for credible data through observation is the way in which your own history, biases, interests, experiences, and expectations can colour what you observe. As highlighted in Figure 11.1, a world exists that we observe. That world is narrowed by what we can manage to take in of it through our senses. Sensory input is then filtered and processed by a brain that has been socialized into thinking and understanding through very structured, defined, and indeed limited frameworks. Finally, our constructed understandings are condensed into our official observations. This process puts a lot of responsibility for the generation of credible data squarely on the thought processes of the researcher, and highlights the need for observational studies to be systematically planned and, if possible, confirmed through the use of other methods.

You and them
Do people ever act the same when they know they are being observed? What are the ethics of observing people without telling them? Are there any potential threats posed to researchers who immerse themselves into the cultures they are observing? The respective answers to these questions are not really, highly suspect, and lots. The more entwined you become with the researched, the more difficult it is to navigate the process. Box 11.8 gives a nice example of the difficulties researchers can face when they observe without reflexive consideration of their own impact and positioning.

> **Box 11.8   Come for Miles, Will They? – Timothy's Story**
>
> I remember a documentary I saw in an anthropology class where researchers were conducting an observational study of a small community somewhere in South America. They were filming an old woman that they described as a local 'guru', and decided to film her doing her 'Sunday ritual'. This was the first time the researchers had been to this event and talked about how far people were coming just to see this woman. I watched this film and thought … 'Hold on, what if these people are coming here to see you. You know, white people with cameras, lights, and sound booms'. My suspicions became even greater when the camera briefly panned on a couple of laughing children trying to pat the big fuzzy microphone. The researchers never mentioned the potential impact they had on what they were observing, and ended up attributing all they observed to the local context.

From objectivity to immersion

A common feature of all observational studies is that they attempt to document what people actually do, rather than what they say they do. Observational studies rely on actual behaviour. But of course, how natural those behaviours are can depend on the role of the observer and the nature of the observational study.

In conducting observations, researchers can be anything from removed to immersed:

Non-participant: In this role, researchers do not become, or aim to become, an integral part of the system or community they are observing. This may involve watching interactions through a one-way mirror, sitting in the corner of a room observing a meeting, or hanging out in the local park. Observers are physically present but attempt to be unobtrusive. Non-participant observation tends to occur over a fixed time period and is often aligned with a structured format.

Participant: In this role, researchers are, or become, a part of the team, community, or cultural group they are observing. They may be part of a workforce, they may live in a particular community, they may join the church, etc. The goal is to attempt to preserve a natural setting and to gain cultural empathy by experiencing phenomena and events from the perspective of those observed. Participant observation can involve large time and emotional commitments, and is often aligned with a less structured, often ethnographic, process.

It is important to note, however, that these roles are not necessarily discreet and often overlap, which can cause difficulties for the researcher. For example, when non-participant observers begin to participate, they can influence and contaminate their research settings. On the other hand, observation is still the goal of the 'participant', and the more immersed the participant becomes, the harder it may be to maintain the role of researcher.

In conducting observations, researchers also need to carefully consider the advantages and disadvantages of full disclosure:

Candid: With candid observations, researchers offer full disclosure of the nature of their study; the role the observations will play in their research; and what they might expect to find through the observation process. This allows observers to take notes on site, but it can also create an uncomfortable situation where the observed feels under surveillance, and is therefore less likely to act naturally. Nevertheless, full disclosure is often an ethics requirement.

Covert: Covert observation can be non-participant, i.e. watching pedestrian behaviour at an intersection or watching interactions at a school playground. In these types of observational study, interaction between the observer and the observed is minimal and there is often an attempt to ensure the anonymity and confidentiality of those observed.

Covert studies can also be participant. This involves researchers going 'undercover' in an attempt to get a real sense of a situation, context, or phenomenon. Observers may be outsiders who attempt to become insiders, or they can be insiders who decide to study their own. This type of covert observation can be necessary when attempting to study fringe, marginal, or illegal groups/activities, i.e. biker gangs, cults, or cockfights. While the naturalness of the setting is maintained and the ability to develop trust and rapport is maximized, participant covert studies can be highly problematic. First, observers may find themselves immersed in a culture that may be dangerous; they may feel pressured to become involved in immoral/illegal activities. Second, as observers become immersed in the group, they may have difficulty maintaining the covert nature of their activities, or may feel guilty about their deception. Third, observers must eventually leave the setting and report findings, which may take its own emotional toll. Finally, for all the above reasons, getting ethics approval for covert participant observation can be highly problematic.

Finally, as with interviewing, observational techniques can range from highly structured to unstructured. Keep in mind, however, that irrespective of the level of structure, observation of any sort demands systematic planning.

Structured: Structured observational studies can collect both qualitative and quantitative data; are highly systematic; and often rely on predetermined criteria related to the people, events, practices, issues, behaviours, actions, situations, and phenomena being observed. Checklists or observation schedules are prepared in advance and researchers attempt to be objective, neutral, and removed with a goal of minimizing personal interaction.

Semi-structured: In semi-structured observations, observers generally use some manner of observation schedule or checklist to organize observations, but also attempt to observe and record the unplanned and/or the unexpected.

Unstructured: Unstructured observation involves observers attempting to observe and record data without predetermined criteria. Observers either attempt to record all of their observations and later search for emergent patterns, or they make judgement calls on the relevance of initial observations and attempt to focus subsequent observations and reflections on those areas deemed most significant.

The observation process

Observing as a social science method requires as much forethought and planning as any other data–gathering technique. Observation involves the need to plan for all issues and contingencies; observe the setting; record observations; review the process; refine as appropriate; and finally, analyze the data. Box 11.9 outlines the steps involved in observation. As was the case for surveying and interviewing, you may find this box helpful as both a guide and a checklist.

Box 11.9   Steps in the Observation Process

PLAN

1. Realistically consider access/acceptance to the group/situation/activities you wish to observe.
2. Familiarize yourself and plan for any potential language and/or cultural issues likely to affect the process.
3. Consider the presentation of self, including what role you will take and how involved you will be.
4. Decide approximately how long you think you will be observing and whether the process will be covert or candid.
5. Consider strategies for ensuring credibility (see Chapter 9, Box 9.1.)
6. Brainstorm preconceived ideas and expectations and also brainstorm alternatives.
7. Prepare an observation schedule/checklist or, if unstructured, consider any relevant themes to explore.
8. Seek ethics approval.

OBSERVE

9. Ease into the observation situation. If structured and candid, this will be similar to the opening stages of an interview where you need to be on time, set up and check any equipment, introduce the study, and establish rapport. If your study involves greater immersion into a culture, early stages will require you to sit back, listen, attempt to gain trust, and then establish rapport.
10. Use all your senses, and possibly your intuition, to gather data.
11. Because you will not be directing the process, you need to be prepared to invest significant time in your observations.
12. Look for saturation (your observations no longer yield new knowledge) before ending the process.

RECORD

13. Observations need to be recorded in a timely manner. If using schedules, they should be filled in while observations occur. If you are more immersed in your research context, you may want to record your observations when removed from the situation either on data sheets or in a journal. Your record may also include photographs and video/audio recordings.
14. Attempt to record your data in a systematic fashion that will ease future analysis.

REVIEW

15. Review the process and note any difficulties encountered, i.e. access, time taken, engagement, cultural 'ignorance', comfort zones, recording/note-taking, roles, objectivity, etc.
16. Review your observation records and note any difficulties you might encounter in making sense of your record.
17. See if you can confirm your record by checking with an insider, asking another observer to compare notes, or triangulating your observational data with other data types.

REFINE

18. Make modifications based on your own review of the process and the quality of the data generated.
19. Observation takes practice. Keep reviewing and refining until you are comfortable with the process and data collected.

ANALYZE DATA

20. Turn to Chapter 12 to work through data management and analysis!

Receiving, reflecting, recording, authenticating

As highlighted above, what sets observational methods apart from those of interviewing and surveying is that there is no tool used to generate particular responses from the observed. There are no 'questions'; it is simply the observed doing what they do, and observers taking that in, noting it, and making sense of it. While the perceived advantage is 'genuineness', the disadvantage is how complicated it can be for researchers to work through the process of receiving, reflecting, recording and authenticating their observations.

Receiving

We do not all take in or perceive the world in the same way. As outlined in Chapter 2, individuals can be predominately right-brained or left-brained. A right-brained individual is likely to hear music, see vivid images, and process the whole rather than the parts, i.e. see a park, while a left-brained person is likely to see sequences, be tuned into language, and process components, i.e. see a river, a swing, a grassy area.

Similarly, individuals can be identified by their predilection for a particular type of sensory input. Visual learners tend to gather data through sight; auditory learners gather data through hearing; while kinesthetic learners tend to gather data by moving, doing, and touching. It is, therefore, not only possible, but in fact likely, that two observers in the same situation will take in quite different sensory inputs.

This 'bias' has obvious implications for the credibility of data collected through observation. Within structured observations this can be controlled for by using observation schedules that require information gathered though a variety of senses. In less structured formats, it is important for observers to: be aware of their own learning styles (see Chapter 2); be conscious of the need to compensate for any 'weaker' areas; reflect on their observation process; critically assess the data they are collecting; and attempt to modify their techniques accordingly.

Reflecting

Once sensory data is taken in, the potential for bias continues. It is exceptionally difficult for researchers, particularly those who choose to immerse themselves within the research setting, to be objective. Our worldviews are embedded within us. We carry with us the biases and prejudices of both our attributes and our socialization. They are a part of how we understand and make sense of the world, and how we might go about observing it. And as discussed in Chapter 4, if we do not recognize and attempt to negotiate our subjectivities, our research will be imprinted with our own biases and assumptions. This can lead to observations that are interpreted through the perspective of the observer, rather than the observed; are insensitive to race, class, culture, or gender; have difficulty hearing marginalized voices; tend to dichotomize what is seen; and do not respect the power of language.

Another difficulty in unbiased reflecting is your own expectations. Put simply, you are more likely to see the things you expect to see, and hear the things you want to hear. It's like when you get a new car and you suddenly see that model everywhere you go; the cars were always there – you just never noticed them before. And I know that much of the feedback I give students is positive, but every bit of (constructive!) criticism seems to loom ten times larger in their brain. Before going out in the field, it is well worth consciously brainstorming your own expectations. You can then brainstorm a range of alternatives, so that you're less likely to unconsciously reflect on your observations in ways that find you confirming what you already suspect.

Recording

Your method of recording will vary depending on the level of participation, openness, and structure you will adopt in your observational processes. There are two quite different strategies for recording observations that somewhat overlap with strategies discussed in surveying and interviewing; and your study may see you adopt one or both of these methods:

- *The capture of raw data* – this can involve audio and video-recording, as well as still photography. The advantage here is that raw data is preserved for review and use at a later date. The major disadvantages are that it can be seen as intrusive; equipment can be fallible; and costs can be high.

- *Note-taking/journaling* – content can range from purely descriptive and formal accounts of space, actors, acts, and events, to much more interpretative narrative accounts or 'thick descriptions' (see Chapter 9) that include goals, feelings, and underlying 'stories'. The form also varies and can range from coded schedules and quantitative tallying to stories, poems, pictures, concept maps, and jotted ideas.

Authenticating

For all of the reasons listed above, the question mark that looms over the credibility of observational data can be quite large. It is therefore particularly important to include credibility checks into your methodological plan. As covered in Chapter 9 (Box 9.1), ensuring credibility includes both thoroughness and confirmation. In relation to thoroughness, your observational method should involve broad representation, prolonged engagement, persistence, crystallization, saturation, peer/supervisor review of your process, and full explication of method. Strategies for confirmation include: informant/member checking and triangulation.

DOCUMENT ANALYSIS

The final data collection method discussed in this chapter is document analysis. Now this can be a bit confusing on a number of counts. First, the term 'document' can refer to more than just paper, and can include photographs, works of art, and even television programmes. Often the word 'text' is used to represent this range of data. Second, document analysis refers to these 'texts' as a primary data source – or data in its own right. It does not refer to an overall review of literature as discussed in Chapter 6. Finally, document analysis refers to both a data collection method and a mode of analysis.

Document analysis: Collection, review, interrogation, and analysis of various forms of text as a primary source of research data.

The focus of this chapter is on the collection, review, and interrogation of documents, and does not cover analysis. Issues of analysis are covered in Chapter 12.

Going to the source

In document analysis, we are talking about documents as a source of data, similar to data gathered in surveys, interviews, and observations. This can take the form of previously gathered census data, newspaper articles, historical archives, or company minutes – the list goes on and on. The main point of distinction, however, is that the 'documents' are pre-produced texts that have not been generated by the researcher. Rather, the researcher's role is limited to gathering, reviewing, and interrogating relevant documents.

The difficulty here is that you actually need to consider two potential sources of bias. First is the author's bias. Because you are working with pre-produced texts, the credibility of the data you generate will, in part, be dependent on recognition of the bias/purpose of the author. It may be tempting to treat the printed word as truth, but if you do, you need to ask whose truth? The second source of bias lies with you as the researcher. As with any method (and as discussed in Chapter 4 and in the above section on observation), how you read and draw from the documents will be coloured by your own researcher reality.

Working through document types

Documents suitable for analysis are wide and varied. They can contain numbers, words, or pictures, and can range from love letters to television commercials, or from children's books to the US census. The following schema may help you sort through the various types of text available for review.

Authoritative sources: These include documents that by their authorship or authority attempt to be unbiased and objective. This can include censuses, surveys, books, journals, independent inquiries, and reports. The common denominator is that these documents are produced by authorities with an explicit goal of unbiased knowledge. Of course some documents that profess to be official and unbiased, can be very subjective. Biographies and autobiographies are a case in point.

The party line: These documents have an 'agenda'. For example, political campaign paraphernalia, promotional materials, or even surveys produced by those with a vested interest in the outcomes. Analysis of these documents needs to take the interest of the author into account.

Personal communication: This can be letters, e-mails, memoirs, sketches, drawings, photographs, diaries, memos, journals, etc., that are, by their very nature, personal and subjective. These are often a rich data source that can be used on their own or in conjunction with interviews and/or observational data.

Multimedia: Multimedia can refer to newspaper or magazine columns/articles, current affairs shows, news reports, TV sitcoms, commercials, etc. These types of 'texts' are often examined in relation to questions of portrayal, i.e. how often female characters are given starring roles in cartoons, or how often the issue of salinity has made the national news over the past two years.

Historical documents: This can refer to an organization's records, minutes, and policy documents, or to any of the materials mentioned above that have been authored or produced within a particular historical period of interest to the researcher.

The document analysis process

Because document analysis does not involve document production, the steps involved somewhat differ from other methods of data collection. In order to carry out document analysis you need to: plan for all contingencies; gather your documents;

review their credibility; interrogate their witting and unwitting evidence; reflect and refine your process; and finally analyze your data. Box 11.10 provides the steps/checklist for the process of document analysis.

Box 11.10   The Steps in Document Analysis

PLAN

1. Create a list of documents you wish to explore.
2. If any documents are considered 'sensitive', seek ethics approval.
3. Do preliminary groundwork to determine whether they will be accessible.
4. Consider and plan for any translation needs.
5. If there are too many documents for analysis, develop an appropriate sampling strategy (see Chapter 8).
6. Consider what types of data you wish to gather from the documents.

GATHER

7. Gather relevant documents – be prepared for hiccups.
8. Develop and employ a scheme for organizing and managing the documents.
9. Make copies of original documents that can be annotated.

REVIEW

10. Assess the authenticity and credibility of the 'text'.
11. Explore the 'agenda' of the document and look for any biases.

INTERROGATE

12. Extract background information on author, audience, purpose, style.
13. Explore content – this can be done by occurrence, or by themes and issues (see Chapter 12).
14. Look for 'witting evidence' (what the document was meant to impart) and 'unwitting evidence' (everything else you can glean from the documents).

REFLECT/REFINE

15. View document analysis as an iterative and ongoing process.
16. Reflect on any difficulties associated with gathering the data, reviewing the sources, and exploring the content.
17. Modify the plan based on your reflections.
18. Gather, review, and interrogate additional documents as needed.

ANALYZE DATA

19. Turn to Chapter 12 to work through analysis and management of the data!

From documents to data

Once you locate, acquire, and assess the credibility of your documents, you are ready to extract (sounds like you are at the dentist's office) the data. Now the first step is to ask yourself questions *about* the document. This refers to questions related to the author, audience, circumstances of production, document type, whether it is a typical or exceptional example, the style, tone, agenda, political purpose, whether it contains facts, opinions, or both; basically any background information related to the document. This is sometimes called 'unwitting' evidence. Answers to these questions may lie within the document itself, i.e. document type, tone, and style, or may require further investigation, i.e. information about the author or the document's genre.

The next step involves exploration of the 'witting' evidence or the contents *within* the document. There are a couple of ways you can do this. The first is by using an interview technique. The second involves noting occurrences, a method akin to formal structured observation.

- *The interview* – in interviewing your documents, you are, in a sense, treating each document as a respondent who can provide you with information relevant to your inquiry. The questions you ask will be dependent on the nature of your inquiry and on document type. As with an interview, you will need to determine what it is you want to know, and whether your 'respondent' or document can provide you with the answers. You then need to 'ask' each question, and highlight the passages in the document that provide the answer. Organizing your responses can be done by using a colour-coded highlighting system and multiple copies of your document, or you can turn to qualitative data management programs such as NUD★IST that can help you with document indexing.
- *Noting occurrences* – noting occurrences is a process that quantifies the use of particular words, phrases, and concepts within a given document. As in formal structured observations, the researcher determines what is being 'looked for' and notes the amount, the frequency, and perhaps the context of the occurrence. This can also be referred to as content analysis, and is taken up in more depth in Chapter 12.

THE FINAL WORD

There's a lot of information in this chapter, so I thought I'd end with a few final thoughts …

- All data collection methods are capable of gathering quantitative and qualitative data, although some may be better suited towards one task or the other.
- There is no single data collection method that can guarantee credible data.
- All data collection methods can be consciously manipulated.
- All data collection methods can be 'contaminated' by unrecognized bias.
- All data collection methods require conscious deliberation on the part of the researcher to ensure credibility.

Remember, in the words of Mark Twain:

Get your facts first, and then you can distort them as much as you please.

… on to analysis!

Further Reading

While this chapter should give you a good idea of what is involved in each data collection method, getting right down to the nitty gritty of each approach can require more information and advice than I can give here. You may find the following readings helpful in your quest for credible data.

Surveying

Converse, J. and Presser, S. (1986) *Survey Questions: Handcrafting the Standardized Questionnaire.* Newbury Park, CA: Sage.

Oppenheim, A. N. (1999) *Questionnaire Design, Interviewing and Attitude Measurement.* London: Pinter.

Schuman, H. and Presser, S. (1996) *Question and Answers in Attitude Surveys: Experiments on Question Form, Wording, and Context.* San Diego: Academic Press.

Singleton, R. and Straits, B. C. (1999) *Approaches to Social Research.* New York: Oxford University Press. (Good chapter on survey instrumentation.)

Interviewing

Fielding, N. (2002) 'Qualitative Interviewing', in N. Gilbert (ed.), *Researching Social Life.* London: Sage. pp. 135–53.

Fontana, A. and Frey, J. H. (2000) 'The Interview: From Structured Questions to Negotiated Text', in N. K. Denzin and Y. S. Lincoln (eds), *Handbook of Qualitative Research.* Thousand Oaks, CA: Sage. pp. 645–72.

Kvale, S. (1996) *Interviews: An Introduction to Qualitative Research Interviewing.* Thousand Oaks, CA: Sage.

Peavey, F. (2003) *Strategic Questioning.* San Francisco: Crabgrass. Available at: http://www.crabgrass.org.

Rubin, H. J. and Rubin, I. S. (1995) *Qualitative Interviewing.* Thousand Oaks, CA: Sage.

Observation

Angrosino, M. V. and Mays de Perez, K. A. (2000) 'Rethinking Observation: From Method to Context', in N. K. Denzin and Y. S. Lincoln (eds), *Handbook of Qualitative Research*. Thousand Oaks, CA: Sage. pp. 673–702.

Bakeman, R. and Gottman, J. M. (1997) *Observing Interaction: An Introduction to Sequential Analysis*. Cambridge: Cambridge University Press.

Lofland, J. and Lofland, L. H. (1995) *Analyzing Social Settings: A Guide to Qualitative Observation and Analysis*. Belmont, CA: Wadsworth.

Robson, C. (2000) *Real World Research*. Oxford: Blackwell.

Document Analysis

Duffy, B. (2000) 'The Analysis of Documentary Evidence', in J. Bell (ed.), *Doing Your Research Project: A Guide for First-time Researchers in Education and Social Science*. Buckingham: Open University Press.

Finnegan, R. (1996) 'Using Documents', in R. Sapsford and V. Jupp (eds), *Data Collection and Analysis*. London: Sage. pp. 138–51.

Holder, I. (2000) 'The Interpretation of Documents and Material Culture', in N. K. Denzin and Y. S. Lincoln (eds), *Handbook of Qualitative Research*. Thousand Oaks, CA: Sage. pp. 703–16.

Prior, L. (2003) *Using Documents in Social Research*. London: Sage.

CHAPTER SUMMARY

- Virtually all methodologies are reliant on the collection of credible data, and the first step in any form of data collection is gaining access.
- Your ability to gain access can improve if you do your homework, act professionally, and are willing to give something back. Gaining access must be done in an ethical manner to ensure that relationships are not abused.
- Surveying involves gathering information from individuals using a questionnaire. Surveys can be descriptive or explanatory, involve populations or samples of populations, capture a moment or map trends, and can be administered in a number of ways.
- A good survey has the potential to reach a large number of respondents, generate standardized, quantifiable, empirical data (as well as some qualitative data), and offers confidentiality/anonymity. Credible data, however, can be difficult to generate.

- Conducting a survey capable of generating credible data requires thorough planning, meticulous instrument construction, comprehensive piloting, reflexive redevelopment, deliberate execution, and appropriate analysis.
- Interviewing involves asking respondents basically open-ended questions. Interviews can range from structured to unstructured, formal to informal, and can be one-on-one, or involve groups.
- Interviews are capable of generating both standardized quantifiable data and more in-depth qualitative data. However, the complexities of people and the complexities of communication can create many opportunities for miscommunication and misinterpretation.
- Conducting an interview that can generate relevant and credible data requires thorough planning, considered preparation of an interview schedule and recording system, sufficient piloting, reflexive modification, the actual interview, and appropriate analysis.
- Observation is a systematic method of data collection that relies on the researchers' ability to gather data through their senses. Observation can range from non-participant to participant, candid to covert, and from structured to unstructured.
- Observation provides the opportunity for researchers to document actual behaviour rather than responses related to behaviour. However, the observed can act differently when surveilled, and researchers's observations will be biased by their own worldviews.
- The collection of credible data through observation requires thorough planning, careful observation, thoughtful recording, reflexive review, considered refinements, and appropriate analysis.
- Document analysis refers to the collection, review, interrogation, and analysis of various forms of text as a primary source of research data. Documents suitable for analysis might be authoritative, agenda-based, personal, multimedia-based, or historical.
- Document analysis sees researchers working with pre-produced, rather than generated, texts. This requires researchers to consider two potential sources of bias: both the original author's and their own.
- The process of document analysis includes thorough planning, broad resource gathering, comprehensive review, deliberate interrogation, considered reflection and refinement, and appropriate analysis.

12 | Data Management and Analysis

'What in the world am I going to do with all this data?'

Chapter Preview

- Thinking Your Way Through Analysis
- Crunching the Numbers
- Working with Words
- Drawing Conclusions

THINKING YOUR WAY THROUGH ANALYSIS

'No delusion is greater than the notion that method … can make up for lack of mother-wit, either in science or in practical life.'

–Thomas Henry Huxley

So you've got your data, maybe a stack of completed questionnaires, a pile of interview transcripts, a mound of relevant documents, as well as your own research journal – some of which is even legible! The question now is what are you going to do with it? Well when it comes to dealing with data, I think one of the biggest challenges is resisting the temptation to relinquish control of the data to the methods and tools of the trade. No doubt, there are tremendously powerful and ever more user-friendly computer programs that can help you manage and analyze both quantitative and qualitative data. But there is NO substitute for the insight, acumen, and common sense – or the 'mother-wit' you will need to manage the process. Computer programs might be able to do the 'tasks' and will surely facilitate analysis, but it is the researcher who needs to work strategically, creatively, and intuitively to get a 'feel' for the data, to cycle between that data and existing theory, and to follow the hunches that can lead to unexpected yet significant findings. In short, researchers need to keep a keen sense of their overall project and think their way through analysis.

As highlighted in Figure 12.1, thinking your way through analysis is a process more comprehensive and complex than simply plugging numbers or words into a computer. Reflexive analysis involves staying as close to the data as possible – from initial collection right through to the drawing of final conclusions. It is a process that requires you to: manage and organize your raw data; systematically

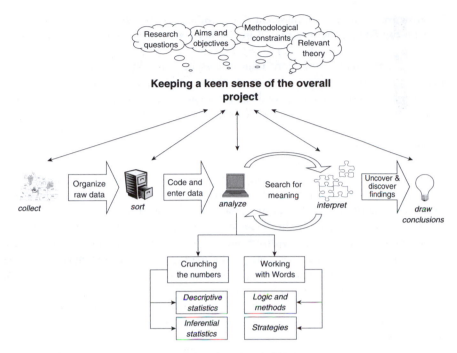

FIGURE 12.1   THE PROCESS OF REFLECTIVE ANALYSIS

code and enter your data; engage in reflective analysis appropriate for the data type; interpret meaning, uncover and discover findings; and, finally, draw relevant conclusions, all the while being sure to keep an overall sense of the project that has you consistently moving between your data and your research questions, aims and objectives, theoretical underpinnings, and methodological constraints.

Keeping a sense of the overall project

Keeping a sense of the overall project refers to the need to conduct your analysis in a critical, reflexive, and iterative fashion that cycles between your data and your overarching frameworks. Rather than hand your thinking over to a computer program, the process of analysis should see you persistently interrogating the data, and the findings that emerge from that data. Throughout the process of analysis you should find yourself asking the following types of question:

- ☑ How should I treat my data in order to best address my research questions?
- ☑ What do I expect to find?
- ☑ What don't I expect to find, and how can I look for it?
- ☑ How do my findings relate to my research questions?
- ☑ Are my findings confirming my theories? How? Why? Why not?
- ☑ Does my theory inform/help to explain my findings? In what ways?
- ☑ Can my unexpected findings link with alternate theories?

185

☑ **How might my methodological shortcomings be affecting my findings?**
☑ **Can my findings be interpreted in alternate ways? What are the implications?**

Stay engaged. I have seen more than one student produce an amazing array of 'findings', without knowing what it all meant. It is worth remembering that the most sophisticated analysis is worthless if you are struggling to grasp the implications of your findings to your overall project.

Managing the data

Once you put it all together you might be surprised by the amount of data you've collected. For the well organized, this might mean coded notebooks, labelled folders, sorted questionnaires, fastidiously transcribed interviews, etc. But for the less structured among us, it might mean digging through various scraps of paper, jotted notes, an assortment of cuttings, and bulging files. In either case, the task will be to build or create a 'data set' that can be managed and utilized throughout the process of analysis – and this is essential for both 'quantitative' and 'qualitative' data.

Now while dichotomizing 'quantitative' and 'qualitative' data might be quite standard in methods literature (see Chapter 7), it is rarely that neatly partitioned in practice. In fact, unless you specifically collect numerical data, i.e. age, height, income, years on the job, etc., most quantitative data starts out as words. These words then get coded numerically, i.e. religious affiliation, gender, level of satisfaction, etc. Now you may want to code all your data numerically and solely conduct statistical analysis, or you may want to capture words (or images for that matter) and be able to draw out themes in a manner that allows you to stay in touch with those words or images. Of course another logical possibility is that you will want to combine the power of words with the authority of numbers.

Regardless of approach, the goal is the same – a rigorous and systematic approach to data analysis that can lead to credible findings. In order to accomplish this goal, analysis often begins by:

- *Familiarizing yourself with appropriate software* – this involves accessing the packages and arranging any necessary training. Most universities have licences that allow students certain software access, and many provide relevant short courses. Programs themselves generally contain comprehensive tutorials complete with mock data sets. Some of the more common quantitative programs include SPSS – sophisticated and user friendly; SAS – often an institutional standard; and Minitab – more introductory (accessible at the websites www.spss.com, www.sas.com, and www.minitab.com, respectively). Excellent qualitative data analysis software such as NVIVO (used for thematic indexing, searching, and theorizing), ATLAS.ti (can be used for images as well as words), and DICTION (popular for content analysis) are also available and can be accessed through the website www.textanalysis.info
- *Logging your data* – data can come from a number of sources at various stages throughout the research process, so it's well worth keeping a record of your data as it is collected. Keep in mind that original data should be kept for a

reasonable period of time; researchers need to be able to trace results back to original sources.

- *Systematically organizing your data* – this involves grouping like sources, making any necessary copies, doing any preliminary coding, and conducting an initial cull of any notes, observations, etc. that are not relevant to the analysis.

- *Screening the data for any potential problems* – this includes checking to see if your data is legible and complete. If done early, you can uncover potential problems not picked up in your pilot, and make improvements to your data collection protocols.

- *Entering the data* – this involves systematically entering your data into a database or analysis program, as well as creating codebooks that describe your data and keep track of how it can be accessed. For quantitative analysis, codebooks often include: the respondent or group; the variable name and description; unit of measurement; date collected; and any relevant notes. Qualitative data can be managed by keeping records of: constructs; respondents; data collection procedures; collection dates; and any other notes relevant to the study.

CRUNCHING THE NUMBERS

It was not long ago that 'doing' statistics meant working formulae. But now 'doing' statistics is more about your ability to use statistical software packages. A colleague of mine recently asked me if students undertaking quantitative analysis should take an introductory statistics class. Well, unfortunately, many statistics classes lag behind the times and still have students manually calculating means, modes, medians, and standard deviations – and looking up p–values in a table in the back of a textbook.

What students really need is to get their hands dirty by working with relevant statistical programs. Now certainly, working these programs demands a basic understanding of the language and logic of statistics. But focusing on formulae is like trying to learn to ride a bike by being taught how to build one. Sure, being able to perform the mechanics can help you understand the logic of application (and there are many excellent resources that can help you build that knowledge), but if, like most students, your primary goal is to be able to undertake statistical analysis, your needs will include: (1) understanding the nature of variables; (2) understanding the role and function of both descriptive and inferential statistics; and (3) knowing what statistical tests are suitable for particular questions and data types.

While this chapter will familiarize you with the basic language and logic of statistics, it should be used in conjunction with hands-on data exploration (even if this is simply playing with the mock data sets provided in the software programs) so that the knowledge can be applied. Very few students can get their heads around statistics without getting into some data.

Variables

Understanding the nature of variables is essential to statistical analysis. Different data types demand discrete treatment. Using the appropriate statistical measures to both describe your data and to infer meaning from your data requires that you clearly understand distinguishing characteristics.

Cause and effect

Central to any statistical analysis is being able to clearly identify and distinguish your dependent and independent variables. While understanding the difference is not too tough, being able to readily identify each type comes with practice.

Dependent variables: The things you are trying to study or what you are trying to measure. For example, you might be interested in knowing what factors are related to good grades, high income, or chronic headaches – grades, income, and headaches would all be dependent variables.

Independent variables: What might be causing an effect on the things you are trying to understand. For example, IQ might affect grades, gender might affect income, while reading might cause headaches. The independent variables here are IQ, gender, and reading.

One way of identifying the dependent and independent variables is to simply ask what depends on what. Grades *depend* on IQ, or income *depends* on gender. It doesn't make sense to say gender depends on income (unless, of course, you are saving for a sex–change operation).

Measurement scales

Measurement scales refer to how we attempt to capture the ways in which units of analysis differ from one another in relation to a particular variable. As summed up in Table 12.1, there are four basic measurement scales that become respectively more precise: nominal, ordinal, interval, and ratio. The precision of each type is directly related to the types of statistical test that can be performed on them. The more precise the measurement scale, the more sophisticated the statistical analysis can be.

Nominal: Numbers are arbitrarily assigned to represent categories. The numbers are simply a coding scheme and have no numerical significance (and there-fore cannot be used to perform mathematical calculations). For example, in the case of gender you would use one number for female, say 1, and another for male, 2. Another common use might be religion, for example, Protestant = 1, Catholic = 2, Jewish = 3, etc. Each code should not overlap (be mutually exclusive) and together should cover all possibilities (be collectively exhaustive). The main function of nominal data is to allow researchers to tally respondents in order to understand population distributions.

Ordinal: This scale rank orders the categories in some meaningful way – there is an order to the coding. One example is socio-economic status (lower, middle, or upper class). Lower class may denote less status than the other two classes but the amount of the difference is not defined. Other examples include air travel (economy, business, first class), or items where respondents are asked to rank order selected choices (favourite beverages). Choices are ordered, but there is no indication of any magnitude of difference. Likert-type scales, in which respondents are asked to select a response on a point scale, i.e. 'I like to work independently' 1 = strongly disagree, 2 = disagree, 3 = neutral, 4 = agree, 5 = strongly agree, are ordinal since the precise difference in magnitude cannot be determined. Many researchers, however, treat Likert scales as interval because it allows them to perform more precise statistical tests.

Interval: In addition to ordering the data, this scale uses equidistant units to measure the difference between scores. This scale does not, however, have an absolute zero. For example, date – the year 2004 occurs 39 years after the year 1965, but time did not begin in AD 1. IQ is also considered an interval scale even though there is some debate over the equidistant nature between points.

Ratio: Not only is each point on a ratio scale equidistant, there is also an absolute zero. Examples of ratio data include age, height, distance, and income. Because ratio data are 'real' numbers, all basic mathematical operations can be performed.

TABLE 12.1 MEASUREMENT SCALES

	Nominal	Ordinal	Interval	Ratio
Classifies	✓	✓	✓	✓
Orders		✓	✓	✓
Equidistant units			✓	✓
Absolute zero				✓

Descriptive statistics

Descriptive statistics are used to describe and summarize the basic features of the data in a study, and are used to present quantitative descriptions in a manageable and intelligible form. The main function of descriptive statistics is to provide measures of central tendency, dispersion, and distribution shape. Such measures vary by data type, and are standard calculations in statistical programs.

Measuring central tendency

One of the most basic questions you can ask of your data centres on the 'average' or central tendency. For example, What was the average score on a test?, What is the average price of a house in a particular region?, or What do most people think about the amount of money spent on national defence? In statistics, there are three ways to measure central tendency: mode, median, and mean.

Mode: The most common value or values noted for a variable. Since nominal data is categorical and cannot be manipulated mathematically, it relies on mode as its measure of central tendency.

Median: The mid-point of a range. To find the median you simply arrange the values in ascending (or descending) order and find the middle value. This measure is generally used in ordinal data, and has the advantage of negating the impact of extreme values. Of course this can also be a limitation given that extreme values can be significant to a study.

Mean: The mathematical average. To calculate the mean, you add the values for each case, then divide by the number of cases. Because the mean is a mathematical calculation, it is used to measure central tendency for interval and ratio data, and cannot be used for nominal or ordinal data where numbers are used as 'codes'. For example, it makes no sense to average the 1s and 2s assigned to males and females.

Measuring dispersion
While measures of central tendency are a standard and highly useful form of data description and simplification, they need to be complimented with information on response variability. For example, say you had a group of students with IQs of 100, 100, 95, and 105, and another group of students with IQs of 60, 140, 65, and 135, the central tendency of both would be 100, but dispersion around the mean will require you to work with each group of students quite differently. There are several ways to calculate dispersion that vary in levels of precision.

Range: This is the simplest way to calculate dispersion, and is simply the highest minus the lowest value. For example, if your respondent ranged in age from 16 to 47, the range would be 31 years. While this measure is easy to calculate, it is dependent on extreme values alone, and ignores intermediate values.

Quartiles: This involves subdividing the range into four equal parts or 'quartiles' that include exactly ¼ of the cases. It is a commonly used measure of dispersion for ordinal data, or data whose central tendency is measured by a median. It allows researchers to compare the various quarters or present the inner 50% as a dispersion measure. This is known as the *inner-quartile range*.

Variance: This measure uses all values to calculate the spread around the mean, and is actually the 'average squared deviation from the mean'. It needs to be calculated from interval and ratio data and gives a good indication of dispersion. It is much more common, however, for researchers to use and present the square root of the variance, which is known as the standard deviation.

Standard deviation: This is the square root of the variance, and is the basis of many commonly used statistical tests for interval and ratio data. As explained below, its power comes into the fore with data that sits under a normal curve.

Measuring the shape of the data
To fully understand a data set, central tendency and dispersion need to be considered in light of the shape of the data, or how the data is distributed. As shown

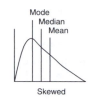

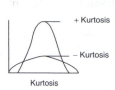

Normal   Skewed   Kurtosis

FIGURE 12.2   SHAPE OF THE DATA

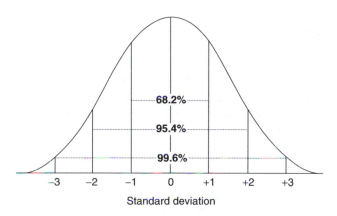

Standard deviation

FIGURE 12.3   AREAS UNDER THE NORMAL CURVE

in Figure 12.2, a normal curve is 'bell shaped'; the distribution of the data is symmetrical with the mode, median, and mean all converged at the highest point in the curve. If the distribution of the data is not symmetrical, it is considered skewed. In skewed data the mode, median, and mean fall at different points.

Kurtosis characterizes how peaked or flat a distribution is compared to a 'normal' distribution. Positive kurtosis indicates a relatively peaked distribution, while negative kurtosis indicates a flatter distribution.

The significance in understanding the shape of a distribution is in the statistical inferences that can be drawn. As shown in Figure 12.3, a normal distribution is subject to a particular set of rules regarding the significance of the standard deviation. Namely that:

- 68.2% of cases will fall within one standard deviation of the mean
- 95.4% of cases will fall within two standard deviations of the mean
- 99.6% of cases will fall within three standard deviations of the mean

These rules of the normal curve allow for the use of quite powerful 'parametric' statistical tests that are generally used with interval/ratio data. For data that does not follow the assumptions of a normal curve (nominal and ordinal data), the researcher needs to call on non-parametric statistical tests in making inferences.

Inferential statistics

While the goal of descriptive statistics is to describe and summarize, the goal of inferential statistics is to draw conclusions that extend beyond the immediate data. For example, inferential statistics can be used to estimate characteristics of the population from sample data, or to test various hypotheses about the relationship between different variables. Inferential statistics allow you to assess the probability that an observed difference is not just a fluke or chance finding. Inferential statistics is about conducting statistical tests that can show statistical significance.

Statistical significance
Statistical significance refers to a measure, or 'p-value', that assesses the actual probability that your findings are more than coincidental. Conventional p-values are .05, .01, and .001, which basically tells you that the probability your findings have occurred by chance is 5/100, 1/100, or 1/1000 respectively. Basically, the lower the p-value, the more confident researchers can be that findings are genuine. Keep in mind that researchers do not usually accept findings that have a p-value greater than .05 because the probability that findings are coincidental or caused by sampling error is too great.

Questions suitable to inferential statistics
It's easy to tell students to interrogate their data, but it doesn't tell them what they should be asking. Below are some common questions that, while not exhaustive, should give you some ideas for interrogating your data.

- ☑ **How does my sample compare to the general population?** These types of question explore a particular variable in relation to a population. For example, say you are conducting a study of university students. You might ask if the percentage of males/females in your sample, or their average age, or even their opinions, approximate that of the broader student population. Of course to answer these questions you will need population data for the greater student body.

- ☑ **Are there differences between two or more groups of respondents?** These types of question are very common and can be referred to as 'between subject'. For example, you might ask if male and female university students are likely to be different majors; or whether students of different ethnic backgrounds are likely to rank subjects differently; or whether students graduating with different majors have different starting salaries.

- ☑ **Have my respondents changed over time?** These types of question involve before and after data with either the same group of respondents or respondents who are matched by similar characteristics. They are often referred to as 'within subject'. An example of this type of question might be whether students' perceptions of the importance of university changes after their first semester.

- ☑ **Is there a relationship between two or more variables?** These types of question can look for either correlations (simply an association) or cause and effect. Examples of correlation question might be, 'Is there an association between hours of study and perceived value of study?' or, 'Is there a correlation between how much you enjoy university and the type of job you are likely to get upon graduation?' Questions looking for cause and effect differentiate dependent and independent variables. For example, 'Does starting salary *depend* on major?' Or, 'Does course satisfaction *depend* on hours of study?' Cause-and-effect relationships can also look to more than one independent variable to explain variation in the dependent variable. For example, 'Does starting salary *depend* on a combination of major, age, and socio-economic status?'

Selecting the right statistical test

There is a baffling array of statistical tests available to help you in your quest for statistical significance, and programs such as SPSS and SAS are capable of running such tests without researchers needing to know the technicalities of their mathematical operations. The difficulty, however, arises in knowing what statistical tests are appropriate. Now while you should keep in mind that choosing the right test can be highly context sensitive, the job has been made easier by test selectors now available on the internet and through programs such as MODSTAT and SPSS. Nevertheless, if you don't have a pretty good handle on the terms and concepts discussed above, i.e. the nature of your variables (independent/dependent), scales of measurement (nominal, ordinal, interval, ratio), distribution shape (normal or skewed), the types of question you want to ask, and the types of conclusions you are trying to draw, even the use of a statistics selector can become an exercise in confusion.

While there are literally hundreds of statistical tests available to researchers, Table 12.2 covers the most common tests for univariate (one variable), bivariate (two variable), and multivariate (three or more variable) data. The table can be read down the first column for univariate data, or as a grid for exploring the relationship between two or more variables. Once you know what tests to conduct, your statistical software should be able to run the analyses and assess statistical significance.

WORKING WITH WORDS

> 'Not everything that can be counted counts,
> and not everything that counts can be counted.'
>
> –Albert Einstein

While statistical tests allow researchers to assess the 'significance' of their findings, statistics relies on the reduction of meaning to numbers. This opens the door for two considerable concerns: (1) there are many social meanings that cannot be reduced to numbers; and (2) even if this reduction were possible, there would be a loss of 'richness' associated with the process.

These two concerns have led to the development of a plethora of various paradigm- and discipline-based approaches to qualitative data analysis over the past decades. For students strongly encamped within a particular paradigm/discipline this may not be too problematic, but for those students working – as this book advocates – from questions up, wading through the literature to find an appropriate and effective analysis strategy can be a real challenge. Many students end up: (1) spending a huge amount of time attempting to work through the vast array of approaches/literature; (2) haphazardly selecting one method that may or may not

TABLE 12.2 SELECTING STATISTICAL TESTS

Univariate	Bi/multivariate		
	NOMINAL	ORDINAL	INTERVAL/RATIO (Assumption of normality – if not normal use ordinal tests)
NOMINAL 2-point scale: gender – 1 = female, 2 = male	Compare 2 or more Groups: **Chi Squared**	Compare 2 groups: **Mann–Whitney** 3 or more groups: **Kruskal–Wallis**	Compare 2 or more groups: **ANOVA followed by t-test**
3-point scale: religion – 1 = Catholic, 2 = Protestant and 3 = Jewish Central tendency: **Mode** Dispersion: **N/A** Compare sample to population: **Chi squared**	Compare within same group over times: 2 pts: **McNemar test** 3+ pts: **Cochran's Q**	Compare within same group over 2 times: 2 pts: **Wilcoxon signed rank test** 3+ pts: **Cochran's Q** 3 or more times (2+ pts): **Freidman's test**	Compare within same group over times (2+ pts): **ANOVA followed by t-test**
	Relationship with other variables: Yes/no: **Chi squared** Strength 2 pts:**Phi** Strength 3+ pts: **Lambda**	Relationship with other variables: Yes/no: **Chi squared** Strength 2+ pts: **Lambda**	Relationship with other variables: Yes/no: **Pearson's product moment correlation** Strength: **f-test**
			With 2 or more independent and 1 dependent variable: **MANOVA**
			2+ dependent variable and 3+ groups: **Multiple regression** or **Path analysis**
ORDINAL TV viewing – order of preference, 1 = sitcoms, 2 = dramas, 3 = movies, 4 = news, 5 = reality TV OR Likert scale 1 = strongly disagree, 2 = disagree, 3 = neutral, etc.		Relationship with other variables: Small sample <10: **Kendall's Tau** Larger Sample: **Spearman's Rho** With 1 variable as dependent: **Somer's d**	Relationship with other variables:
Central tendency: **Median**		Small sample <10: **Kendall's Tau**	**Jaspen's coefficient of multiserial correlation**
Dispersion: **Interquartile range**		Larger sample: **Spearman's Rho**	With the interval/ratio variable as dependent: **ANOVA**
Compare sample to population: **Kolmogrov Smirnov**		With 1 variable as dependent: **Somer's d**	
INTERVAL/RATIO Interval – IQ score Ratio – real numbers, age, height, weight Central tendency: **Mean**			Relationship with other variables – no dependent/independent distinction: **Pearson's product moment correlation**
Dispersion: **Standard deviation**			With 1 independent and 1 dependent variable: **Pearson's linear correlation**
Compare sample to population: **t-test**			With 2 or more independent and 1 dependent variable: **Multiple regression**
			With 2 or more independent and 2 or more dependent variables: **Canonical correlation**

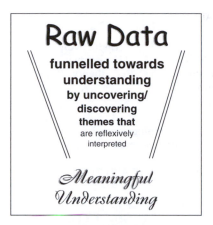

FIGURE 12.4   FUNNELLING DOWN TOWARDS MEANING

be appropriate to their project; (3) conducting their analysis without any well-defined methodological protocols; or (4) doing a combination of the above.

The goal of this section is two-fold. This first is to work you through the logic and methods that underpin most qualitative data analysis strategies. The second is to overview some of the more commonly used strategies complete with links for further exploration.

Logic and methods

Whether it be qualitative or quantitative data, the main game of any form of analysis is to move from raw data to meaningful understanding. In quantitative methods, this is done through statistical tests of coded data that assess the significance of findings; coding the data is preliminary to any analyses and interpretation. In qualitative analysis, understandings are built by a process of uncovering and discovering themes that run through the raw data, and by interpreting the implication of those themes for the research questions. In qualitative analysis, coding such themes is not preliminary to any analysis, but is part and parcel of interpretative practice itself.

As shown in Figure 12.4, the process of qualitative data analysis involves the use of inductive (discovering) and/or deductive (uncovering) reasoning to generate and interpret relevant themes in order to achieve meaningful understanding.

Moving between induction and deduction

While deductive reasoning (hypothesis verification/theory testing) is strongly associated with positivist/quantitative research, and inductive reasoning (to derive theory from specific instances) is seen as central to post-positivist/qualitative research, in practice the distinction is not so clear-cut. In fact, as shown in Figure 12.5, analysis is often dependent on inductive and deductive cycles of reasoning. For example, you may design your study so that theory can emerge through inductive processes, but as those theories begin to emerge from the data, it is likely

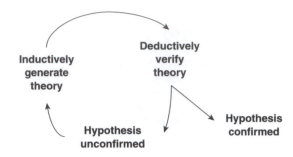

FIGURE 12.5   CYCLES OF INDUCTIVE AND DEDUCTIVE REASONING

that you will move towards a process of confirmation. In this case, theory generation depends on progressive verification. On the other hand, the credibility of those testing hypotheses through deductive verification can depend on their willingness to acknowledge the unexpected. Researchers need to be able to inductively generate alternate explanations.

Thematic analysis

As highlighted in Figure 12.4, to move from raw data to meaningful understanding is a process reliant on the generation/exploration of relevant themes. While many of these themes are likely to be discovered though inductive analysis, themes can also be identified through engagement with the literature, prior experiences of the researcher, and the nature of the research question. Themes can also emerge from insights garnered through the process of data collection. Now whether themes are inductively generated or deductively verified, there is a need for rich engagement with the documents, transcripts, and texts that make up a researcher's raw data.

This process of 'textual' engagement often occurs as the data is collected and involves reading, overviewing, and annotating the text prior to systematic thematic coding. Textual engagement can then happen at a number of levels. Qualitative data can be explored for the words that are used, the concepts that are discussed, the linguistic devices that are called upon, and the non-verbal cues noted by the researcher.

- *Exploring words* – words can lead to themes through exploration of their repetition, or through exploration of their context and usage (sometimes called key words in context). Specific cultural connotations of particular words can also lead to relevant themes. Patton (2001) refers to this as 'indigenous categories', while Strauss and Corbin (1998) refer to it as 'in vivo' coding.

  To explore word-related themes researchers systematically search a text to find all instances of a particular word (or phrase), making note of its context/meaning. Several software packages such as DICTION or CONCORDANCE can quickly and efficiently identify and tally the use of particular words and even present such findings in a quantitative manner.

- *Exploring concepts* – concepts can be deductively uncovered by searching for themes generated from: the literature; the hypothesis/research question; intuitions; or prior experiences. Concepts/themes may also be derived from 'standard' social science categories of exploration, i.e. power, race, class, gender, etc. On the other hand, many researchers will look for concepts to emerge inductively from their data without any preconceived notions. With predetermined categories, researchers need to be wary of 'fitting' their data to their expectations, and not being able to see alternative explanations. However, purely inductive methods are also subject to bias since unacknowledged subjectivities can direct thematic emergence. As discussed above, working towards meaningful understanding often involves both inductive and deductive processes.

  For search for both inductively and deductively derived concepts is generally done through a line-by-line or paragraph-by-paragraph reading, wherein the researcher can engage in what grounded theory proponents refer to as 'constant comparison' (Glaser and Strauss 1967). In constant comparison, concepts and meaning are explored in each text and then compared with previously analysed texts to draw out both similarities and disparities.

- *Exploring linguistic devices* – metaphors, analogies, and even proverbs are often explored because of their ability to bring richness, imagery, and empathetic understanding to words. These devices often organize thoughts and facilitate understanding by building connections between speakers and an audience. Once you start searching for such linguistic devices, you will find they abound in both the spoken and written word. Qualitative data analysts often use these rich metaphorical descriptions to categorize divergent meanings of particular concepts.

- *Exploring non-verbal cues* – one of the difficulties in moving from raw data to rich meaning is what is lost in the process. And certainly the tendency in qualitative data collection and analysis is to concentrate on words, rather than the tone and emotive feeling behind the words, the body language that accompanies the words, or even words not spoken. Yet this world of the non-verbal can be central to thematic exploration. If your raw data, notes, or transcripts contain non-verbal cues, it can lend significant meaning to content and themes. Exploration of tone, volume, pitch, and pace of speech; the tendency for hearty or nervous laughter; the range of facial expressions and body language; and shifts in any or all of these can be central in a bid for meaningful understanding.

Looking for interconnections

Once the texts have been explored for relevant themes, the quest for meaningful understanding generally moves to an exploration of the relationship between and among various themes. For example, you may look to see if the use of certain words and/or concepts is correlated with the use of other words and/or concepts. Or you may explore whether certain words/concepts are associated with a particular range of non-verbal cues or emotive states. You may also look to see if there is a connection between the use of particular metaphors and non-verbal cues. And of course, you may want to explore how individuals with particular characteristics vary on any of these dimensions.

Interconnectivities are assumed to be both diverse and complex, and can point to the relationship between conditions and consequences, or how the experiences of the individual relate to more global themes. Conceptualization and abstraction can become quite sophisticated and can be linked to both model-building and theory-building.

Becoming familiar with the strategies

As stated, the array of qualitative data analysis strategies can be intimidating. But if you have a handle on their basic logic and methods, their exploration can be less daunting. The goals of each strategy and the data they explore may vary, but methods are generally consistent.

While Table 12.3 may not be comprehensive enough to get you started in any particular branch of qualitative data analysis, it does provide a comparative summary of some of the more commonly used strategies. The table's first row summarizes recent attempts to define and create methods for overarching qualitative data analysis, while subsequent rows outline the goals and procedures of more common paradigmatic- or discipline-based approaches. In constructing this summary, I have tried to refer you to the most recent literature that provides clear articulation of 'methods', as well as refer you to software that is appropriate to the task. It is worth keeping in mind that rather than pure adoption of any one approach, you can draw insights from the various strategies in a bid to evolve an approach that best cycles between your data and your own research agenda.

A note on grounded theory

According to Strauss and Corbin, grounded theory is 'theory that was derived from data systematically gathered and analysed through the research process' (1998: 12). In order to generate grounded theory, researchers engage in a rigorous and iterative process of data collection and 'constant comparative' analysis that finds raw data brought to increasingly higher levels of abstraction until theory is generated. This method of theory generation (which shares the same name as its product – grounded theory) has embedded within it very well-defined and clearly articulated techniques for data analysis. And it is precisely this clear articulation of grounded theory techniques that have seen them become central to many qualitative data analysis strategies. It's therefore well worth delving into the literature.

The tendency for research methods texts (and thus student researchers) to unreflexively refer to grounded theory techniques as standard methods for qualitative data analysis, however, often leads to the false assumption that all qualitative data analysis must be inductive and free from any theoretical presuppositions. This need not be the case. While the techniques of grounded theory are often instrumental to

TABLE 12.3 QUALITATIVE DATA ANALYSIS STRATEGIES

Overarching qualitative data analysis strategies:

	Goals	Procedures	Software
Boyatzis (1998) Miles and Huberman (1994) Wolcott (1994)	*To interpret non-numerical data (verbal and non-verbal communication, stories, texts, images, signs, symbols, etc.)*	***Varied but generally include:*** *Generation of themes through the process of coding, annotating, and searching for interconnections.* ***May involve:*** • *quantification of words used* • *development of typologies, taxonomies, and matrices* • *use of metaphor* • *both inductive and deductive logic*	*Qualitative software now abounds. A comprehensive list is available at* www.textanalysis.info

Specialized qualitative data analysis strategies:

	Goals	Procedures	Software
Content analysis Neuendorf (2001) Weber (1990)	To interpret meaning in speech and text	Can involve linguistic 'quantification' where words are units of analysis that are tallied. Can also refer to thematic analysis through coding.	DICTION HAMLET CONCORDANCE NUD*IST/NVIVO MAXqda
Discourse analysis Hoey (2000) Wood and Kroger (2000)	To interpret language as it is situated in a socio-historic context	Rather than focus on simply what is said, discourse analysis explores language as it constitutes and embodies a socio-historic context tied to power and knowledge. Analysis necessarily involves 'critical' data exploration.	NUD*IST/NVIVO MAXqda The Ethnograph ATLAS.TI
Narrative analysis Clandinin and Connelly (1999) Riessman (1993)	To interpret the 'stories' of individuals	Data collection and interpretation is often iterative with focus on story building. Metaphors seen as important.	NUD*IST/NVIVO MAXqda The Ethnograph ATLAS.TI
Conversation analysis Psathas (1994) Ten Have (1999)	To understand the structure and construction of conversation	Painstakingly transcribed conversations are explored for structural organization of talk including turn-taking and sequential ordering.	CLAN-CA Available at: http://childes.psy.cmu.edu

(Continued)

TABLE 12.3   CONTINUED

	Goals	Procedures	Software
Semiotics Chandler (2001) Gottdiener et al. (2003)	To interpret the meanings behind signs and symbols	Involves identification of 'cognitive domains' and attempts to deconstruct specific meanings in order to reconstruct understanding.	NUD*IST/NVIVO MAXqda The Ethnograph ATLAS.TI (good for images)
Hermeneutics Herda (1999) Van Manen (1990)	To interpret text in a dialogic fashion	Involves moving in and out of text using a 'hermeneutic spiral' centred on alternate perspectives – global vs detailed/ conventional vs critical, etc.	NUD*IST/NVIVO MAXqda The Ethnograph ATLAS.TI
Grounded theory Glaser and Strauss (1967) Strauss and Corbin (1998)	To generate theory directly from data	Highly inductive (analytic induction). Use of 'constant comparative method' to explore each data source in relation to those previously analysed. Involves coding, memoing, and concept mapping.	NUD*IST/NVIVO MAXqda The Ethnograph ATLAS.TI

qualitative data analysis, the need to generate theory directly from data will not be appropriate for all researchers, particularly those wishing to test 'hypotheses' or mine their data for predetermined categories of exploration.

DRAWING CONCLUSIONS

In many ways, this chapter ends in the same way it began, by reminding you how important it is to 'think your way through analysis' and 'keep a strong sense of the overall project'. Your findings and conclusions need to: (1) flow from analysis; and (2) show clear relevance to your project's overall research questions, aims, and objectives. In short, drawing appropriate, relevant, and significant conclusions is about:

- searching for answers, but not forcing fitting your findings to portray a world without ambiguity and complexity
- pulling together all the significant/important findings of your study and considering why and how they are significant/important
- considering your findings in light of the current research 'literature'
- considering your findings in light of the limitations and methodological constraints of your study. Consider whether subjectivities were managed; methods were approached with consistency; 'true essence' was captured; findings are applicable outside the immediate frame of reference; and whether the research processes can be verified (see Chapter 5)
- and, finally, clearly linking your findings to your research question, aims and objectives, and relevant theory

Further Reading

I have tried to put together a diverse range of readings that are fairly recent (unless seminal), practical, and applied. Keep in mind that you really can't go past www.amazon.com when tyring to find the latest books on virtually any topic. Not only is the search facility pretty good, but the information (especially for newer titles) generally includes an overall description, the table of contents, and editorial and customer reviews.

Quantitative analysis

Bryman, A. and Cramer, D. (1996) *Quantitative Data Analysis with Minitab: A Guide for Social Scientists.* London: Routledge.

Bryman, A. and Cramer, D. (2001) *Quantitative Data Analysis with SPSS Release 10 for Windows.* London: Routledge.

Bryman, A. and Hardy, M. A. (eds) (2004) *Handbook of Data Analysis.* London: Sage.

Der, G. and Everitt, B. S. (2001) *Handbook of Statistical Analyses Using SAS.* Boca Raton, FL: CRC Press.

Jefferies, J. and Diamond, I. (2001) *Beginning Statistics: An Introduction for Social Scientists.* London: Sage.

Salkind, N. J. (2000) *Statistics for People Who (Think They) Hate Statistics.* London: Sage.

Qualitative analysis

Boyatzis, R. E. (1998) *Transforming Qualitative Information: Thematic Analysis and Code Development.* London: Sage.

Miles, M. and Huberman, A. (1994) *Qualitative Data Analysis: An Expanded Source Book.* Thousand Oaks, CA: Sage.

Silverman, D. (2001) *Interpreting Qualitative Data: Methods for Analysing Talk, Text and Interaction.* London: Sage.

Wolcott, H. F. (1994) *Transforming Qualitative Data: Description, Analysis, and Interpretation.* London: Sage.

Content analysis

Neuendorf, K. A. (2001) *The Content Analysis Guidebook.* London: Sage.

Weber, R. P. (1990) *Basic Content Analysis.* London: Sage.

Discourse analysis

Hoey, M. (2000) *Textual Interaction: An Introduction to Written Discourse Analysis.* London: Routledge.

Wood, L. A. and Kroger, R. O. (2000) *Doing Discourse Analysis: Methods for Studying Action in Talk and Text.* Thousand Oaks, CA: Sage.

Narrative analysis

Clandinin, D. J. and Connelly, F. M. (1999) *Narrative Inquiry: Experience and Story in Qualitative Research.* San Francisco: Jossey-Bass.

Riessman, C. K. (1993) *Narrative Analysis.* London: Sage.

Conversation analysis

Psathas, G. (1994) *Conversation Analysis: The Study of Talk-in-Interaction.* London: Sage.

Ten Have, P. (1999) *Doing Conversation Analysis: A Practical Guide.* Thousand Oaks, CA: Corwin Press.

Semiotics

Chandler, D. (2001) *Semiotics: The Basics.* London: Routledge.

Gottdiener, M., Lagopoulos, A. and Boklund-Lagopoulos, K. (eds) (2003) *Semiotics.* London: Sage.

Hermeneutics

Herda, E. (1999) *Research Conversations and Narrative: A Critical Hermeneutic Orientation in Participatory Inquiry.* New York: Praeger.

Van Manen, M. (1990) *Researching Lived Experience: Human Science for an Action Sensitive Pedagogy.* New York: State University of New York Press.

Grounded theory

Glaser, B. and Strauss, A. (1967) *Discovery of Grounded Theory.* Chicago: Aldine.

Strauss, A. and Corbin, J. (1998) *Basics of Qualitative Research: Techniques and Procedures for Developing Grounded Theory.* London: Sage.

CHAPTER SUMMARY

- While computer programs can facilitate analysis, it is the researcher who needs to strategically, creatively, and intuitively analyze the data. It is crucial for researchers to keep a keen sense of the overall project and think their way through analysis.
- Analysis should be approached as a critical, reflexive, and iterative process that cycles between data and an overarching research framework.
- Managing data involves familiarizing yourself with appropriate software; developing a data management system; systematically organizing the data; conducting a preliminary screening; and entering the data into a computer program.
- Being able to do statistics no longer means being able to work with formulae. It is much more important for student researchers to be familiar with the language and logic of statistics, and be competent in the use of statistical software.
- Different data types demand discrete treatment, so it's important to be able to distinguish variables by both cause and effect (dependent or independent), and their measurement scales (nominal, ordinal, interval, and ratio).
- Descriptive statistics are used to summarize the basic feature of a data set through measures of central tendency (mode, median, and mean), dispersion (range, quartiles, variance, and standard deviation), and distribution (skewness and kurtosis).
- Inferential statistics allow researchers to assess their ability to draw conclusions that extend beyond the immediate data. For example, if a sample represents the population; if there are differences between two or more groups; if there are changes over time; or if there is a relationship between two or more variables.
- Selecting the right statistical test relies on knowing the nature of your variables, their scale of measurement, their distribution shape, and the types of question you want to ask.
- In qualitative data analysis, there is a common reliance on words and images to draw out rich meaning, but there is an amazing array of perspectives on the precise focus of, and techniques for conducting, analysis.

- The methods and logic of qualitative data analysis involve uncovering and discovering themes that run through the raw data, and interpreting the implication of those themes for research questions.
- Qualitative data analysis often involves: moving through cycles of inductive and deductive reasoning; thematic exploration (based on word, concepts, literary devices, and non-verbal cues); and exploration of the interconnections among themes.
- There are a number of paradigm/discipline-based strategies for qualitative data analysis including: overarching methodologies; content, discourse, narrative, and conversation analysis; semiotics; hermeneutics; and grounded theory.
- Your findings and conclusions need to flow from analysis and show clear relevance to your overall project. Findings should be considered in light of significance, current research literature, limitations of the study, and, finally, your questions, aims, objectives, and theory.

13 | The Challenge of Writing-Up

'How will I ever manage to put this together on paper?'

Chapter Preview

- **The Writing Challenge**
- **Writing as 'Conversation'**
- **Preparing for Submission**
- **The Importance of Dissemination**

THE WRITING CHALLENGE

> 'Composition is, for the most part,
> an effort of slow diligence and steady perseverance...'
>
> –Samuel Jackson

I have not come across many students who consider writing-up an easy or hassle-free process. Regardless of the dimension or scope of the project (your current project is likely to be your first or your biggest), writing-up is usually approached with a sense of apprehension and wariness. Well, it's no wonder when you consider that writing-up is likely to be a relatively unpractised form of writing that has major consequences attached to its quality. In fact, research is often judged not by what you did, but by your ability to report on what you did.

This chapter attempts to offer students some practical strategies for negotiating the writing process in a way that improves the overall quality of the project, and makes the task less daunting. It covers: the need to see writing as part and parcel of the research journey rather than just an account of that journey; the need to draft strong storylines that engage others in your research 'conversation'; the nitty gritty of preparing your document for submission and assessment; and, finally, the importance of disseminating your work.

Process or product

1. Write and submit a research proposal; 2. conduct the research; 3. write up the report. It was not long ago that this three-step process was seen as standard for conducting research and producing a report. And while less and less academics

advocate this process, it is a process whose legacy seems to linger in the practice of many supervisors and their students. This, however, can be perilous for those inexperienced in research. For many, 'writing' can be a huge obstacle. If you leave it until the end you risk writer's block, which can lead to inevitable delays in completion (Chapter 2 offers a fuller discussion of managing some of the difficulties associated with the research/writing process).

More commonly accepted (if not entirely practised), is writing as a process central to each stage of the research journey. It should be considered an activity that progresses as your research progresses. For example, if you formulate even your most initial ideas in written form, you will have begun to produce notes for the first draft of your 'introduction' and 'methods', and annotating your sources can lead to preliminary drafts of your 'literature review'. These sections can then be redrafted as you go through the process of data collection. Similarly, preliminary analysis and writing throughout data collection will provide you with a good start on 'findings'.

Keep in mind that even if you're a procrastinator and you're not that keen on writing as you go, it is a highly attractive option compared to facing the daunting prospect of having to start your writing from scratch when you complete your data collection and analysis.

Writing as analysis

Very few people can formulate all their ideas in their heads before they commit them to paper. Ideas almost always evolve as you write, and in this way each draft of your writing will drive the evolution of your ideas. 'Writing as you go' thereby provides much more than a head start to the report production process. Writing itself can be a form of analysis or even a method of inquiry.

Writing can be central to the construction and interpretation of meaning, and can move you from the production of specific descriptive understandings, through to broader synthesis, and on to crafting significant, relevant, logical, and coherent storylines. In fact, many find writing and rewriting the key to bringing storylines into focus. Now while this is true for all types of research (it is virtually impossible to evolve ideas if they stay planted in the realm of the mind), it is particularly relevant to research that sits under post-positivist (subjectivist, interpretivist, or constructivist) paradigms that demand iterative engagement with narrative, discourse and/or text.

WRITING AS 'CONVERSATION'

When I write or give a lecture, even though it's only my words on the page or my voice speaking, I try to remember that my goal is to engage my audience in a 'conversation'; and I try to keep the unspoken side of that conversation firmly in my mind.

For an audience to appreciate what you have to say, you need to engage their thinking, predict their questions, and respond to their inquiries. Very few people have the ability to sit through a monotonous monologue or stay engaged in dry and turgid writing – they need to be mentally, intellectually, and/or emotionally involved.

When it comes to your research report, the ultimate goal is not just writing up what you did and what you found; the real goal is to explain, illuminate, and share your research with others. Writing-up is thus a communication process that demands consideration of your readers. They may not be able to iteratively respond, but it is their response that gauges your success. In writing up, it is therefore particularly important to consider how the frameworks you decide on and the storylines you construct will best engage your readers in an account of your research journey.

Deciding on a structure

When it comes to a framework or structure for writing up, there is certainly a 'standard' approach that is recognized, accepted, expected, and strongly advocated. This is the introduction, literature review, methods, findings, and conclusion format that dominates the literature. But there are also a host of alternative structural possibilities based on, for example: chronology – how events unfolded over time; or theory-building – how theory was inductively generated; or the findings-first model – where you give readers your conclusion up-front, then say how you got there. While these alternative frameworks are sometimes considered more appropriate for research sitting under the post-positive umbrella, deciding on the most appropriate framework depends on the 'conversation' you believe is best suited to both your story and your audience.

The standard conversation

If you consider writing up an interactive communication process, it's easy to see why so many researchers, regardless of paradigm, adopt the standard format. It is a format that: (a) is expected; and (b) answers a reader's questions in a sequence quite natural to the flow of a normal conversation. In fact, the 'standard conversation' is one you may have already had on several occasions as people ask you about your research. As shown in Table 13.1, the questions and their respective answers can easily structure a report or thesis.

While the standard format may not suit all approaches to research, it is a format that undeniably limits the work that readers need to do to make sense of your write-up, and therefore your research. This is something that should never be underestimated whether your goal is examination, publication, or broad dissemination.

Alternative conversations

In considering 'alternative conversations', it is essential that readers do not get 'lost' as you attempt to take them through your research project. While you may feel that an alternative framework best suits your research, it is absolutely crucial that readers do not end up scratching their heads and questioning the credibility of your entire research project just because they are unfamiliar or uncomfortable with the way you have chosen to write it up. Two cases where the 'risks' of alternative conversations are minimized, and perhaps even rewarded, are:

TABLE 13.1 THE 'STANDARD' CONVERSATION

The questions	The answers that structure the chapters/sections of the conventional report
So tell me what your research is about?	Title Abstract Introduction • research question(s) • hypothesis (as appropriate)
And why did you choose this particular topic/question?	Introduction • rationale
What do you hope to achieve?	Introduction • aims and objectives
I really don't know much about this, can you fill me in?	Background • recent literature and prior research (literature review – this is covered quite extensively in Chapter 6) • theory (current and seminal as appropriate) • context (social, cultural, historic, and geographic)
How exactly did go about doing your research?	Research design/Approach • methodological approach (framework) • methods (techniques/procedures) • limitations
And what did you find out?	Findings/results/emergent story • text, tables, graphs, charts, themes, quotes, etc. Discussion • analysis, interpretation, and meaning of findings
How would you explain the relevance/importance of what you've done?	Conclusion • implications • significance • recommendations (particularly important in applied research)

1. When you are using a format that is widely accepted as appropriate for your particular paradigmatic, disciplinary, or methodological approach. For example, the use of a 'theory-building structure' for studies that have adopted a grounded theory approach, or perhaps a 'chronological structure' for a case study exploring change.
2. When you know (or can confidently assume) that your audience is likely to be open to a more creative structure. If your write-up is to be assessed, consider whether your examiner(s) is likely to be open to the alternative, i.e. they have

written, or have students who have written, in alternative ways. If they are firmly planted in the positivist tradition, you may want to reconsider your approach or, if possible, your examiner. If your goal is to have your research published, the key will be to find a journal for which the alternative is quite standard.

You may, however, be determined to 'buck the system' and go down the creative and alternative route even without wider acceptance or any assurance of reader openness. If this is the case, it's essential that you argue the logic of your structure up front, and that this structure takes your reader through a clear and coherent storyline, such that the logic of the structure becomes self-evident.

Crafting the story

Good conversationalists not only know how to listen and interact, they also know how to tell a damn good story. Yes your write-up needs to report on your research, but it should do more … it should unfold, it should engage, and it should tell an interesting story. As the author of that story you will need to:

- *Become familiar with the craft* – very few authors are not avid readers. As you read through your literature, take note of not just content, but structure and style. Also have a look at theses or reports that have been well received. They may not be prototypes, but they can certainly give you some sense of the shape of your end product.
- *Find a voice* – this is quite tricky in academic writing. Under the positivist paradigm, the convention is to avoid the first person (this is so your research does not appear to be tainted with personal bias and subjectivities). But even within the positivist paradigm, this convention is relaxing since objectivity is no longer seen as reliant upon masking a researcher's role. While the conventional style may still be formal, it does allow for some use of an active first-person voice. Under post-positivist paradigms, recognition of researcher role is paramount. Consequently, there are no moratoriums against the use of first person. This, however, can leave students struggling to negotiate formality, as they move between a relaxed conversation and a logical/comprehensive research account. The key is a consistent style that will be deemed appropriate to your project.
- *Craft the story line* – whether you opt for a standard or alternative structure, your report will need to have a beginning, a middle, and an end, and incorporate the answers to the questions (or similar questions) in Table 13.1 in some logical fashion. The goal is to engage your readers, peak their interest, and take them through your research journey in a way that unfolds the story and logically leads to your conclusion. Writing a creative working title, constructing one or more draft outlines, and writing a one-page abstract (a task many researchers find exceptionally difficult but extremely focusing) can help you organize the story you wish to tell.
- *Make convincing arguments* – the quality and credibility of your final document, as well as its individual sections/chapters, is largely dependent on your ability

to construct logical and convincing arguments. Whether it be a study's rationale, a review of the literature, or the presentation of methods, findings, and conclusions, the process of research demands more than simple summary and reporting. It is a process reliant on the ability of the author to convince, reason, and argue a case.

• *Write/construct your first draft* – you can think about it, and you can keep thinking about it, but it won't happen unless you do it. If you've constructed writing as part of the research process rather than its product, the bones of your first draft will be there for you to put together and flesh out. If, however, you follow the 'write up after' approach, you will need to gather the notes, and put it all down on paper. Regardless of approach, students generally find they need more time than they initially thought to write up that first draft.

PREPARING FOR SUBMISSION

There is no doubt that the journey from first draft to submission can be long and challenging. In fact, contrary to the desire of just about every fibre in your body, you may find that your final document does not retain much from that first draft. The irony of course, is that you couldn't get to that final draft without that first draft and all the drafts in between. Once you have written your first draft, getting to the submission stage relies on getting appropriate feedback and being prepared to draft and redraft your document.

Seeking feedback

Getting relevant feedback is essential in your ability to move from a first to a final draft. Now you might think that getting feedback would be a straightforward process, but that isn't always the case. You need to be specific in your requests, prepared for criticality, and able to process and respond to – at times – conflicting advice.

Asking for feedback

I once had a PhD candidate hand in a **first** draft of a chapter to a co-supervisor for comment. Well he got comments alright, but it was all to do with spelling, grammar, and even proper margins for quotes. While that might be really helpful for a final draft, it was completely useless at the first-draft stage. Even worse, this student had waited over two months for that ever so enlightening advice.

What this experience brings home is the need to ask the right people for advice, and to be specific in your requests. It's important to know where you are in the process and ask for comments related to your current needs. A good strategy is to ask your readers to comment on the same questions you need to ask yourself as you work through various drafts of your document (see questions in the next section). If it's a first draft, you'll probably want advice on overall ideas, arguments, logic, and structure, while later stages will see you seeking suggestions for consistency, coherence, readability, and, finally, copy editing.

These various types of feedback may see you asking a variety of people for their opinions. Keep in mind that while the advice of your supervisor(s) can be invaluable, so too can be the advice of colleagues, peers, and family. In fact, at some stage, it is worth asking a non-specialist to read your work to see if the logic makes sense to them – because it should. And don't forget to try to get a sense of time-frame. It can take some readers months to get back to you.

Now knowing who to ask and what to ask is one thing, but being willing to hand over what you have written is another. What if your fears of being 'incompetent' are validated? Handing over is always exposing, but keep in mind that fears of incompetence are often a crisis of confidence – not a lack of ability. And besides, it's better to find out if you are off-track early than wait until you have invested a huge amount of time in an iffy direction.

Receiving feedback

You get back your draft. If you're lucky, it's full of constructive, relevant, and thought-provoking comments. You should be happy – not only has someone put in a lot of time and effort, but they have provided you with a road map for moving forward. But instead of being happy you're devastated. In fact, you feel insulted, frustrated, and even incompetent. Now personally, I would prefer it if feedback on my own work was limited to validation of just how clever I am. But what I really need – like it or not – is criticality. You need more than validation to move forward, and you need to be ready to hear it. It's important that you don't take criticism personally, or take suggestions as insults. If you do, writing-up will become an emotional minefield.

Okay, so you've processed the feedback and are trying not to take it personally – so now what do you do? Well unreflexive incorporation is just as bad as ignoring the advice. You need to mentally take the feedback onboard, consider it in light of the source, and work through the implications the advice has for what you're trying to say. And of course this is particularly important if you find yourself getting conflicting advice. Talk to your supervisor/lecturer, but remember it's your work and you're the one who needs to make the final call.

Drafting, redrafting, and redrafting some more

Every year students come across a particularly eloquent piece of writing and tell me, 'But I just can't write like that. I'm not a natural writer.' The likelihood is that neither is the author of that particularly eloquent work. Yes, it may sing in its final form, but that final form may have taken draft upon draft to be realized. I have yet to read, assess, or write a first (or even second) draft that could not be significantly improved. From ideas and structure, to spelling and layout, the road to final submission takes all writers through a process of working and reworking their writing.

Reworking the first draft

There is no doubt that it's tempting to finish that last sentence of your conclusion and say 'I am done!', and certainly finishing a complete first draft is worth celebrating.

But don't get too carried away. When you step back, take stock, and rigorously assess your writing, you are likely to find that the process of writing itself has evolved your ideas, and that your conceptualizations have moved beyond what you initially managed to capture on paper. As you work through your first draft ask yourself:

- ☑ **Is this making sense? Does the logic flow? Do I need to alter the structure?**
- ☑ **Do I need to incorporate more material/ideas, or are sections really repetitive?**
- ☑ **Am I happy with my overall argument, and is it coming through?**
- ☑ **Does each chapter or section have a clear and obvious point or argument?**
- ☑ **Have I sought and responded to feedback?**

Reworking the second draft

Once you're happy with the overall ideas, arguments, logic, and structure, it's time to fine tune your arguments and strive for coherence and consistency. In doing this ask yourself:

- ☑ **How can I make my arguments/points clearer? Do I 'waffle on' at any point? Am I using lots of jargon and acronyms? Should I incorporate some/more examples?**
- ☑ **Do I want to include some/more diagrams, photos, maps, etc.?**
- ☑ **Is the structure coherent? Are there clear and logical links between chapters and sections?**
- ☑ **Is there consistency within and between chapters and sections? Do I appear to contradict myself at any point?**
- ☑ **Is the length on target?**
- ☑ **Have I sought and responded to feedback?**

Moving towards the penultimate draft

Being ready to move towards a penultimate draft implies that you are reasonably happy with the construction and logic of the arguments running throughout and within your document. Attention can now be turned to fluency, clarity, and over-all readability. Ask yourself:

- ☑ **Are there ways I can further increase clarity? Are my terms used consistently? Have I gotten rid of unnecessary jargon?**
- ☑ **Are there ways I can make this read more fluently? Can I break up my longer sentences? Can I rework my one-sentence paragraphs?**
- ☑ **Are there ways I can make this more engaging? Can I limit the use of passive voice? Do I come across as apologetic? Are my arguments strong and convincing?**
- ☑ **Am I sure I have protected the confidentiality of my respondents?**
- ☑ **Have I guarded against any potential accusations of plagiarism? Have I checked and double-checked my sources, both in the text and in the references or bibliography?**
- ☑ **Have I written and edited my preliminary and end pages, i.e. title page, table of contents, list of figures, acknowledgments, abstract, preface, appendices, and references?**

- ☑ Have I thoroughly checked my spelling and grammar?
- ☑ Have I done a word count?
- ☑ Have I sought and responded to feedback?

Producing the final draft

You'd think that if you did all the above, you'd surely be ready to hand in the final document. Not quite, you now need to do a final edit. If it's a large work and you can swing it, you might want to consider using a copy editor (particularly if English is your second language). It's amazing what editorial slip-ups someone with specialist skills can find, even after you've combed through your own work a dozen times. Some things you may want to ask prior to submission are:

- ☑ Have I looked for typos of all sorts?
- ☑ Have I triple checked spelling (especially those things spell checkers cannot pick up like typing form instead of from).
- ☑ Have I checked my line spacing, fonts, margins, etc.?
- ☑ Have I numbered all pages, including preliminary and end pages sequentially? Have I made sure they are all in the proper order?
- ☑ Have I checked through the final document to make sure there were no printing glitches?

Box 13.1 Saying Goodbye – Scout's Story

I took the final draft of my thesis to the book binder in the same week I took my first born to kindergarten, so needless to say it was a week of high anxiety. Off went my baby; the baby I had conceived, nurtured, and cried over. The baby that left me sleepless and made me feel incompetent – but also the baby that saw me grow and cope in ways I would have never thought possible. When it was time to say goodbye, I was both proud and nervous, and it was only with great trepidation that I handed over that now somewhat matured baby to those in charge of the next phase.

Oh yeah, I almost forgot to tell you – I dropped my daughter off at school the next day and we were both fine.

THE IMPORTANCE OF DISSEMINATION

Before finishing off, I just want to quickly mention the importance of dissemination. Okay, as a student researcher your immediate goal may be a grade or even a degree, but don't forget that the ultimate goal of research is to contribute to a body of knowledge; and your findings cannot add to a body of knowledge if they are not disseminated.

If you've undertaken a major project, you might want to consider publication. In fact, if you're pursuing a PhD, it's well worth trying to publish some of your work as you go. Not only can it focus your thesis, it can also be invaluable for your career. Now the ultimate in publication is a single-authored work in an international refereed journal, and this is a worthy goal. But it is one that can be quite difficult for the inexperienced researcher to achieve. Another option is co–authorship. Quite often, your supervisor will be willing to co–author a work, which will give you expert advice and put more weight behind your submission. Just be sure to openly discuss issues of primary authorship.

You can also consider presenting your work at conferences. Not only does this allow you to disseminate your work, it also gives you experience and confidence in this type of forum; can help you generate new research ideas; and of course allows you to network. Finally, you can disseminate your work (in either verbal or written form) to interested stakeholders. If your study is relevant to a community group, local government authority, or particular workplace, it's well worth sharing your findings. If your research has added something of significance to a body of knowledge, you might as well get it out there.

Further Reading

I think the best place to start your search for further readings is within your institution. Subject/course outlines, style guides, and manuals produced by and for your institution/programme will not only provide you with hard-and-fast criteria, they are also likely to steer you in directions that meet with more general expectations. You can then turn to readings such as the following for more detailed information on managing the writing process.

Arnold, J., Poston, C. and Witek, K. (1999) *Research Writing in the Information Age*. Boston, MA: Allyn and Bacon.

Evans, D. and Gruba, P. (2002) *How to Write a Better Thesis*. Melbourne: Melbourne University Press.

Strunk, W. Jr. and White, E. B. (1999) *Elements of Style*. Boston, MA: Allyn and Bacon.

CHAPTER SUMMARY

- Research write-ups are often a relatively unpractised form of writing that can challenge and intimidate students. Once considered an activity that commenced once research was complete, it is now commonly recommended as a practice that should be incorporated throughout the research process.
- Writing itself can be a form of analysis and can be central to the construction and interpretation of meaning. It can also be instrumental in the development of significant, relevant, logical, and coherent storylines.

- The goal of your write-up is to share your research with others. It should be thought of as a communication process or a 'conversation' that demands consideration of your readers.
- Your write-up can follow a standard structure that follows the introduction, literature review, methods, findings, then conclusion format, or it can follow an alternative structure that may better suit a particular project's aims and objectives. While alternative structures can allow for more creative expression, the standard format gives readers what they tend to expect.
- Your research write-up should unfold as an interesting story. As the author of that story you need to become familiar with the craft, find a voice, create a storyline, make convincing arguments, and get down to the business of writing.
- Preparing your document for submission involves getting appropriate feedback and being prepared to draft and redraft your document.
- Incorporation of relevant feedback requires both specific and appropriate requests and a willingness to, if not welcome, then at least accept criticality.
- Moving from first to final draft is a multi-stage process that sees you working systematically through the development of, logic and argument, coherence and consistency, fluency and readability, and; finally, copy editing.
- The ultimate goal of any research project is to add to a body of knowledge. Once your project is complete, it's worth thinking about broader dissemination.

Bibliography

Angrosino, M. V. and Mays de Perez, K. A. (2000) 'Rethinking Observation: From Method to Context', in N. K. Denzin and Y. S. Lincoln (eds), *Handbook of Qualitative Research*. Thousand Oaks, CA: Sage. pp. 673–702.

Arnold, J., Poston, C. and Witek, K. (1999) *Research Writing in the Information Age.* Boston, MA: Allyn and Bacon.

Babbie, E. (2000) *Practice of Social Research.* Belmont, CA: Wadsworth.

Bakeman, R. and Gottman, J. M. (1997) *Observing Interaction: An Introduction to Sequential Analysis.* Cambridge: Cambridge University Press.

Bell, J. (ed.) (2000) *Doing Your Research Project: A Guide for First-time Researchers in Education and Social Science.* Buckingham: Open University Press.

Berg, B. L. (2000) *Qualitative Research Methods for the Social Sciences.* Boston, MA: Allyn and Bacon.

Berger, P. and Luckmann, T. (1967) *The Social Construction of Reality: A Treatise in the Sociology of Knowledge.* New York: Anchor.

Berk, R. A. and Rossi, P. H. (1999) *Thinking about Program Evaluation.* Thousand Oaks, CA: Sage.

Bickman, L. and Rog, D. J. (1998) *Handbook of Applied Social Research Methods.* Thousand Oaks, CA: Sage.

Blaxter, L., Hughes, C. and Tight, M. (2001) *How to Research.* Buckingham: Open University Press.

Boyatzis, R. E. (1998) *Transforming Qualitative Information: Thematic Analysis and Code Development.* London: Sage.

Bryman, A. and Cramer, D. (1996) *Quantitative Data Analysis with Minitab: A Guide for Social Scientists.* London: Routledge.

Bryman, A. and Cramer, D. (2001) *Quantitative Data Analysis with SPSS Release 10 for Windows.* London: Routledge.

Bryman, A. and Hardy, M. A. (eds) (2004) *Handbook of Data Analysis.* London: Sage.

Burns, R. (2000) *Introduction to Research Methods.* Frenchs Forest, NSW: Longman.

Button, G. (ed.) (1991) *Ethnomethodology and the Human Sciences.* New York: Cambridge University Press.

Cavana, R. L., Delahaye, B. L. and Sekaran, U. (2000) *Applied Business Research: Qualitative and Quantitative Methods.* New York: John Wiley and Sons.

Chandler, D. (2001) *Semiotics: The Basics.* London: Routledge.

Chen, H. (1999) *Theory Driven Evaluations.* Thousand Oaks, CA: Sage.

Cherry, C., Godwin, D. and Staples, J. (1993) *Is the Left Brain Always Right?* Melbourne: Hawker Brownlow Education.

Clandinin, D. J. and Connelly, F. M. (1999) *Narrative Inquiry: Experience and Story in Qualitative Research.* San Francisco: Jossey-Bass.

Converse, J. and Presser, S. (1986) *Survey Questions: Handcrafting the Standardized Questionnaire*. Newbury Park, CA: Sage.

Coulon, A. (2000) *Ethnomethodology*. London: Sage.

Creswell, J. W. (1994) *Qualitative and Quantitative Approaches*. London: Sage.

Creswell, J. W. (1998) *Qualitative Inquiry and Research Design: Choosing Among Five Traditions*. London: Sage.

Crotty, M. (1998) *The Foundations of Social Research: Meaning and Perspective in the Research Process*. St Leonards: Allen and Unwin.

Cryer, P. (1996) *The Research Student Guide to Success*. Buckingham: Open University Press.

Denscombe, M. (1998) *The Good Research Guide: For Small-scale Social Research*. Buckingham: Open University Press.

Denzin, N. K. (2003) *Performance Ethnography: Critical Pedagogy and the Politics of Culture*. London: Sage.

Denzin, N. K. and Lincoln, Y. S. (eds) (1998) *Strategies of Qualitative Inquiry*. Thousand Oaks, CA: Sage.

Denzin, N. K. and Lincoln, Y. S. (eds) (2000) *Handbook of Qualitative Research*. Thousand Oaks, CA: Sage.

Der, G. and Everitt, B. S. (2001) *Handbook of Statistical Analyses Using SAS*. Boca Raton, FL: CRC Press.

Duffy, B. (2000) 'The Analysis of Documentary Evidence', in J. Bell (ed.), *Doing Your Research Project: A Guide for First-time Researchers in Education and Social Science*. Buckingham: Open University Press. pp. 106–17.

Egan, G. (1994) *The Skilled Helper: A Problem Management Approach to Helping* (5th edn). Pacific Grove, CA: Brooks/Cole.

Elliston, F. and McCormick, P. (eds) (1977) *Husserl: Exposition and Appraisals*. Notre Dame, IN: Notre Dame University Press.

Ely, M., Anzul, M., Friedman, T., Garner, D. and Steinmetz, A. C. (1991) *Doing Qualitative Research: Circles within Circles*. New York: Falmer.

Emerson, R. M. (ed.) (1983) *Contemporary Field Research: A Collection of Readings*. Prospect Heights, IL: Waveland Press.

Evans, D. and Gruba, P. (2002) *How to Write a Better Thesis*. Melbourne: Melbourne University Press.

Fals Borda, O. and Rahman, M. A. (1991) *Action and Knowledge: Breaking the Monopoly with Participatory Action Research*. New York: Intermediate Technology/Apex Press.

Fielding, N. (2002) 'Qualitative Interviewing', in N. Gilbert (ed.), *Researching Social Life*. London: Sage. pp. 135–53.

Findlay, A. (1965) *A Hundred Years of Chemistry*. London: Duckworth.

Finnegan, R. (1996) 'Using Documents', in R. Sapsford and V. Jupp (eds), *Data Collection and Analysis*. London: Sage. pp. 138–51.

Fontana, A. and Frey, J. H. (2000) 'The Interview: From Structured Questions to Negotiated Text', in N. K. Denzin and Y. S. Lincoln (eds), *Handbook of Qualitative Research*. Thousand Oaks, CA: Sage. pp. 645–72.

Freire, P. (1970) *Pedagogy of the Oppressed*. New York: Herder & Herder.

Garfinkel, H. (1967) *Studies in Ethnomethodology*. Englewood Cliffs, NJ: Prentice-Hall.

Geertz, C. (2000) *The Interpretation of Cultures*. New York: Basic Books.

Glaser, B. (1992) *Basics of Grounded Theory Analysis: Emergence versus Focus.* Mill Valley, CA: Sociology Press.

Glaser, B. and Strauss, A. (1967) *Discovery of Grounded Theory.* Chicago: Aldine.

Goode, W. J. and Hatt, P. K. (eds) (1952) *Methods of Social Research.* New York: McGraw-Hill.

Gottdiener, M., Lagopoulos, A. and Boklund-Lagopoulos, K. (eds) (2003) *Semiotics.* London: Sage.

Greenwood, D. and Levin, M. (1998) *Introduction to Action Research: Social Research for Social Change.* Thousand Oaks, CA: Sage.

Grills, S. (ed.) (1998) *Doing Ethnographic Research.* London: Sage.

Hamersley, M. and Atkinson, P. (1995) *Ethnography: Principles in Practice.* London: Routledge.

Hart, C. (2000) *Doing a Literature Review.* London: Sage.

Hart, C. (2001) *Doing a Literature Search.* London: Sage.

Heidegger, M. (1996) *Being and Time: A Translation of Sein and Zeit.* Trans. J. Stambaugh. New York: State University of New York Press.

Herda, E. (1999) *Research Conversations and Narrative: A Critical Hermeneutic Orientation in Participatory Inquiry.* New York: Praeger.

Hoey, M. (2000) *Textual Interaction: An Introduction to Written Discourse Analysis.* London: Routledge.

Holder, I. (2000) 'The Interpretation of Documents and Material Culture', in N. K. Denzin and Y. S. Lincoln (eds), *Handbook of Qualitative Research.* Thousand Oaks, CA: Sage. pp. 703–16.

Hood, S., Mayall, B. and Oliver, S. (eds) (1999) *Critical Issues in Social Research: Power and Prejudice.* Buckingham: Open University Press.

Janesick, V. (1998) 'The Dance of Qualitative Research Design: Metaphor, Methodolatry, and Meaning', in N. K. Denzin and Y. S. Lincoln (eds), *Strategies of Qualitative Inquiry.* Thousand Oaks, CA: Sage. pp. 35–55.

Janesick, V. (2000) 'The Choreography of Qualitative Research Design: Minuets, Improvisations, and Crystallizations', in N. K. Denzin and Y. S. Lincoln (eds), *Handbook of Qualitative Research.* Thousand Oaks, CA: Sage. pp. 379–99.

Jefferies, J. and Diamond, I. (2001) *Beginning Statistics: An Introduction for Social Scientists.* London: Sage.

Kemmis, S. and McTaggart, R. (2000) 'Participatory Action Research', in N. K. Denzin and Y. S. Lincoln (eds), *Handbook of Qualitative Research.* Thousand Oaks, CA: Sage. pp. 567–605.

Kolb, D. A. (1984) *Experiential Learning: Experience as the Source of Learning and Development.* Englewood Cliffs, NJ: Prentice-Hall.

Kvale, S. (1996) *InterViews: An Introduction to Qualitative Research Interviewing.* Thousand Oaks, CA: Sage.

Layder, D. (1998) *Sociological Practice: Linking Theory and Social Research.* London: Sage.

Lee, R. M. (2000) *Unobtrusive Methods in Social Research.* Buckingham: Open University Press.

Lèvi-Strauss, C. (1966) *The Savage Mind.* Chicago: University of Chicago Press.

Levy, P. S. and Lemeshow, S. (1999) *Sampling of Populations: Methods and Applications.* New York: Wiley-Interscience.

Lewin, K. (1946) 'Action Research and the Minority Problems', *Journal of Social Issues* 2: 34–6.

Lincoln, Y. S. and Guba, E. G. (1985) *Naturalistic Inquiry.* Beverly Hills, CA: Sage.

Lofland, J. and Lofland, L. H. (1995) *Analyzing Social Settings: A Guide to Qualitative Observation and Analysis.* Belmont, CA: Wadsworth.

Lohr, S. L. (1998) *Sampling: Design and Analysis.* Pacific Grove, CA: Brooks/Cole.

Marton, F. and Säljö, R. (1976) 'On Qualitative Differences in Learning: Outcome and Process', *British Journal of Educational Psychology* 46: 4–11.

McNiff, J. and Whitehead, J. (2002) *Action Research: Principles and Practice.* London: Routledge.

Miles, M. and Huberman, A. (1994) *Qualitative Data Analysis: An Expanded Source Book.* Thousand Oaks, CA: Sage.

Miller, G. and Dingwall, R. (eds) (1997) *Context and Method in Qualitative Research.* London: Sage.

Moran, D. (2000) *Introduction to Phenomenology.* London: Routledge.

Morse, J. M. (1998) 'Designing Funded Qualitative Research', in N. K. Denzin and Y. S. Lincoln (eds), *Strategies of Qualitative Inquiry.* Thousand Oaks, CA: Sage. pp. 56–85.

Moustakas, C. (2000) *Phenomenological Research Methods.* London: Sage.

Neuendorf, K. A. (2001) *The Content Analysis Guidebook.* London: Sage.

Neuman, W. L. (1997) *Social Research Methods: Qualitative and Quantitative Approaches,* Boston, MA: Allyn and Bacon.

O'Leary, Z. (1999) *Reaction, Introspection and Exploration: Diversity in Journeys out of Faith.* Kew, Victoria: CRA.

O'Leary, Z. (2001) 'Conversations in the Kitchen', in A. Bartlett and G. Mercer (eds), *Postgraduate Research Supervision: Transforming (R)elations.* New York: Peter Lang. pp. 195–8.

Oppenheim, A. N. (1992) *Questionnaire Design, Interviewing and Attitude Measurement.* London: Pinter.

Orna, L. (1995) *Managing Information for Research.* Buckingham: Open University Press.

Patton, M. Q. (2001) *Qualitative Research and Evaluation Methods.* Thousand Oaks, CA: Sage.

Peavey, F. (2003) *Strategic Questioning.* San Francisco: Crabgrass. Available at: http://www.crabgrass.org

Phillips, E. M. and Pugh, D. S. (2000) *How To Get a PhD: A Handbook for Students and their Supervisors.* Buckinghamshire: Open University Press.

Potter, S. (2002) *Doing Postgraduate Research.* London: Sage.

Prior, L. (2003) *Using Documents in Social Research.* London: Sage.

Psathas, G. (1994) *Conversation Analysis: The Study of Talk-in-Interaction.* London: Sage.

Punch, K. (1998) *Introduction to Social Research.* London: Sage.

Quantz, R. A. (1992) 'On Critical Ethnography (with some postmodern considerations)', in W. L. Millroy, J. Preissle and M. D. LeCompte (eds), *The Handbook of Qualitative Research in Education.* New York: Academic Press. pp. 470–505.

Ragin, C. C. and Becker, H. S. (1992) *What is a Case? Exploring the Foundations of Social Inquiry.* New York: Cambridge University Press.

Rahman, A. (ed.) (1994) *People's Self-Development: Perspectives on Participatory Action Research: A Journey Through Experience.* London: Zed Books.

Rao, P. S. R. S., Rao, Poduri, S. R. S. and Miller, W. (2000) *Sampling Methodologies with Applications.* New York: Lewis Publishers.

Reason, P. and Bradbury, H. (2001) *Handbook of Action Research: Participative Inquiry and Practice.* London: Sage.

Richardson, L. (2000) 'Writing: A Method of Inquiry', in N. K. Denzin and Y. S. Lincoln (eds), *Handbook of Qualitative Inquiry.* Thousand Oaks, CA: Sage. pp. 936–48.

Riessman, C. K. (1993) *Narrative Analysis.* London: Sage.

Robson, C. (2000) *Real World Research.* Oxford: Blackwell.

Root, M. (1993) *Philosophy of Social Science: The Methods, Ideals and Politics of Social Inquiry.* Oxford: Blackwell.

Rossi, P. H., Freeman, H. E. and Lipsey, M. W. (1999) *Evaluation: A Systematic Approach.* Thousand Oaks, CA: Sage.

Rossman, G. and Rallis, S. (1998) *Learning in the Field: An Introduction to Qualitative Research.* Thousand Oaks, CA: Sage.

Rubin, H. J. and Rubin, I. S. (1995) *Qualitative Interviewing.* Thousand Oaks, CA: Sage.

Rudestam, K. E. and Newton, R. R. (2001) *Surviving Your Dissertation: A Comprehensive Guide to Content and Process.* London: Sage.

Sacks, H. (1992) *Lectures on Conversation.* Oxford: Basil Blackwell.

Salkind, N. J. (2000) *Statistics for People Who (Think They) Hate Statistics.* London: Sage.

Schensul, J. and LeCompte, D. (eds) (1999) *The Ethnographer's Toolkit* (7 vols). London: Sage.

Schuman, H. and Presser, S. (1996) *Question and Answers in Attitude Surveys: Experiments on Question Form, Wording, and Context.* San Diego: Academic Press.

Schutz, A. (1967) *The Phenomenology of the Social World.* Trans. G. Walsh and F. Lehnert. Evanston, IL: North Western University Press.

Shulman, J. and Asimov, I. (eds) (1988) *Isaac Asimov's Book of Science and Nature Quotation.* New York: Weidenfeld & Nicolson.

Silverman, D. (ed.) (1997) *Qualitative Research: Theory, Methods and Practice.* London: Sage.

Silverman, D. (2001) *Interpreting Qualitative Data: Methods for Analysing Talk, Text and Interaction.* London: Sage.

Singleton, R. and Straits, B. C. (1999) *Approaches to Social Research.* New York: Oxford University Press.

Smith, S., Willm, D. G. and Johnson, N. A. (eds) (1997) *Nurtured by Knowledge: Learning To Do Participatory Action Research.* New York: Apex Press.

Sokolowski, R. (2000) *Introduction to Phenomenology.* New York: Cambridge University Press.

Spielberg, H. (1982) *The Phenomenological Movement.* Dordrecht: Kluwer Academic Press.

Stake, R. E. (1995) *The Art of Case Study Research.* Thousand Oaks, CA: Sage.

Stake, R. E. (2000) 'Case Studies', in N. K. Denzin and Y. S. Lincoln (eds), *Handbook of Qualitative Research.* Thousand Oaks, CA: Sage. pp. 435–54.

Strauss, A. (1987) *Qualitative Analysis for Social Scientists.* Cambridge: Cambridge University Press.

Strauss, A. and Corbin, J. (1998) *Basics of Qualitative Research: Techniques and Procedures for Developing Grounded Theory.* London: Sage.

Stringer, E. (1999) *Action Research.* Thousand Oaks, CA: Corwin Press.

Strunk, W. Jr. and White, E. B. (1999) *Elements of Style.* Boston, MA: Allyn and Bacon.

Ten Have, P. (1999) *Doing Conversation Analysis: A Practical Guide.* Thousand Oaks, CA: Corwin Press.

Thomas, J. (1993) *Doing Critical Ethnography.* Newbury Park, CA: Sage.

Thompson, S. K. (2002) *Sampling.* New York: John Wiley and Sons.

Thompson, S. K. and Seber, G. A. (1996) *Adaptive Sampling.* New York: John Wiley and Sons.

Tortu, S., Goldsamt, L. A. and Hamid, R. (eds) (2001) *A Practical Guide to Research and Services with Hidden Populations.* Boston, MA: Allyn and Bacon.

Van Manen, M. (1990) *Researching Lived Experience: Human Science for an Action Sensitive Pedagogy.* New York: State University of New York Press.

Wainer, H. (2000) *Drawing Inferences from Self-selected Samples.* Mahwah, NJ: Lawrence Erlbaum Associates.

Weber, M. ([1904] 1949) 'Objectivity in Social Science and Social Policy', in M. Weber, *The Methodology of the Social Science.* New York: Free Press.

Weber, R. P. (1990) *Basic Content Analysis.* London: Sage.

Whyte, W. F. (ed.) (1991) *Participatory Action Research.* Newbury Park, CA: Sage.

Wisker, G. (2001) *The Postgraduate Research Handbook: Succeed with Your MA, MPhil, EdD and PhD.* Basingstoke: Palgrave.

Wolcott, H. F. (1994) *Transforming Qualitative Data: Description, Analysis, and Interpretation.* London: Sage.

Wood, L. A. and Kroger, R. O. (2000) *Doing Discourse Analysis: Methods for Studying Action in Talk and Text.* Thousand Oaks, CA: Sage.

Yin, R. K. (2002) *Case Study Research: Design and Methods.* Thousand Oaks, CA: Sage.

Zuber-Skerritt, O. (ed.) (1996) *New Directions in Action Research.* London: Falmer Press.

Index